Honeymoons :
journeys from
the altar /
392.
5
1861330

Honeymoons: Journeys from the Altar

Honeymoons

Journeys from the Altar

edited by Roger Hudson
and Rose Baring

ELAND
London

First published by Eland Publishing Ltd
61 Exmouth Market, London EC1R 4QL in 2009

Editorial content © Roger Hudson & Rose Baring
All extracts © of the authors, as attributed in the
text and acknowledgements

ISBN 978 0 907871 59 0

Cover design and typesetting by Emily Gibson
Cover image: Just Married © H. Armstrong
Roberts/CORBIS
Printed in the UK by CPI William Clowes Beccles NR34 7TL

Contents

VII A Sense of Foreboding

VIII Marrying for Money or Convenience

IX Honeymoon Disasters

Acknowledgements

These acknowledgements constitute a continuation of the copyright page. For permission to reprint copyright material grateful acknowledgement is due to:

The Provost and Fellows of Eton College for permission to quote from the *Letters of Elizabeth Barrett Browning to Mary Mitford*; Gerald Duckworth & Co Ltd. for permission to use an extract from *Iris* by John Bayley and 'Here We Are' from *The Collected Dorothy Parker* by Dorothy Parker; Sutton Publishing Ltd. for permission to reproduce an extract from *Wedding Tour* by Emily Birchall; Rachel Campbell and Caroline Blakiston for permission to include 'Honeymoon' by Noel Blakiston; the Estate of Paul Bowles and the Wylie Agency (UK) Ltd for permission to use 'Call at Corazón' by Paul Bowles; the Random House Group Ltd., for permissions to include an extract from *Thy Hand Great Anarch* by Nirad Chaudhuri, published by Chatto & Windus, from *Earthly Paradise* by Colette, published by Secker & Warburg and from *The Snows of Kilimanjaro* by Ernest Hemingway; Aitken Alexander Associates, for permission to use an extract from *Scenes from Married Life* by William Cooper, and from *Tolstoy: A Biography* by A. N. Wilson; Alan Brodie Representation Ltd. on behalf of the estate of Noel Coward for permission to use an extract from *Private Lives* by Noel Coward; the Penguin Group (UK) Ltd for permission to use Isak Dinesen's 'The Pearls' from *Winter's Tales*; Grove/Atlantic, Inc. for permission to use 'A Change of Plan' from *The Collected Short Fiction of Bruce Jay Friedman* by Bruce Jay Friedman; David

Higham Associates, for permission to use an extract from *May We Borrow Your Husband?* by Graham Greene and an extract from *Busman's Honeymoon* by Dorothy L Sayers, published by Hodder; Faber & Faber for permission to reproduce 'You Hated Spain' from *Birthday Letters* by Ted Hughes and 'Wedding Wind' from *Whitsun Weddings* by Philip Larkin; Lucas Alexander Whitley Ltd for permission to use an extract from *Shopaholic and Sister* by Sophie Kinsella; Oxford University Press for permission to use extracts from *The Mendelssohns on Honeymoon*, edited by Peter Ward Jones and from *Grasmere Journal* by Dorothy Wordsworth, edited by Pamela Woolf; Sheil Land Associates and the Penguin Group (UK) Ltd for permission to use an extract from *Wide Sargasso Sea* by Jean Rhys; Pushkin Press for permission to quote an extract from *Journey by Moonlight* by Antal Szerb; The Hanbury Agency and the Estate of Gamel Woolsey for permission to reproduce an extract from *One Way of Love* by Gamel Woolsey; The Blake Friedmann Agency on behalf of the Estate of Carol Shields for permission to use extracts from *The Stone Diaries* and *Larry's Party*; John Julius Norwich for permission to use an extract from Diana Cooper's *The Rainbow Comes and Goes* and Adrian and Philip Goodman for permission to use an extract from *Ottoline: The Early Memoirs* by Lady Ottoline Morrell.

Every effort has been made to trace copyright holders, but in a few cases this has proved impossible. The publishers apologize for any errors or omissions in the preceding list, and would be grateful to be notified of any corrections that should appear in any reprint.

The editors would also like to thank the following for their suggestions and advice: Jill Hughes, John Julius Norwich, Matthew Sturgis, William Dalrymple, Jon Cook, Katri Skala, Jeremy Lewis, Lucy Lethbridge, A. N. Wilson and Rosey and Antony Gray.

Introduction

Feel the pulse of a Jamaican beach on a Saturday evening – the sun goes down through a blood-orange sky and there's a throbbing background bass of reggae. Local couples, their skin hot and fragrant from a day of sunshine, stand waist-deep in the purple water, swaying, kissing, laughing and gyrating. There's a lazy, sensual feel, product of the heat, the ganja, the music and the weekend.

I'm marvelling at the scene, sitting under a tree with a can of Red Stripe. In the foreground my husband of a few days is busy with a group of children, constructing an imaginary universe from palm fronds and sand. Smoke and the smell of frying fish issue from a beached wooden boat nearby, and suddenly I can see the future: the delicious fresh meal we will eat with our fingers in the next hour or so, the night of dancing and velvet darkness, and beyond it the children we will have and the fun they will have on the beaches of our life. It's a moment of intense certainty and pleasure, a moment that could only happen at that turning point in my life, my honeymoon.

A honeymoon these days is rarely the first holiday a couple takes together but it is still a significant way-post on the journey that is their life together. You've shed the build-up to the day itself, made a public declaration of your love, said goodbye to the mother-in-law in her preposterous hat and you are finally alone again, with the future laid out before you. It is yours to decide, yours to mould into shape. And that is why writers have been so drawn to the subject. As two paths converge to make one, how will the new, shared future be negotiated? For many of the people in this book, the honeymoon is the first holiday they have ever been on together, and the first time they have shared a bed. Here, before us, are their early, tremulous attempts to define that future.

Over the years, writers have explored the dramatic possibilities from every angle. There are bawdy 17th-century ballads, gleefully exploiting the difference between the naivety of the wife and the experience of her husband. There are the innocently erotic possibilities of the first 'legal' coupling, the out-and-out bliss of a long-anticipated physical union. There are explorations of Italy focussing on the pleasures of wine and food after life in post-war, austerity Britain, and unusual honeymoons where bride and groom speak for the first time on their wedding night, or where the union is a secret and life goes on as before with only stolen moments of passion. The range of writing, from John Donne to Ernest Hemingway, from Leo Tolstoy to Ted Hughes, from Dorothy Parker to Sophie Kinsella, all speak of the enduring fascination of this pivotal moment.

Just as my own honeymoon dipped from that sandy high to moments of uncertainty and bewilderment, within these covers all is not a bed of roses. There are moments of heartbreaking disappointment, even cruelty, and skeletons which swing out unbeckoned from cupboards. But there are also misunderstandings overcome and tender moments when the new couple marvels at the possibilities ahead of them. Last word goes to Elizabeth Barrett Browning, honeymooning in Pisa with her poet husband, Robert:

> We have been married two months, and every hour has bound me to him more and more; if the beginning was well, still better it is now—that is what he says to me, and I say back again day by day.

Rose Baring

I Bliss

A Tutor's Letter

Windham Family

A letter, written in the late 1680s, by the Revd William Nevar, to his former pupils Ashe and William Windham of Felbrigg Hall in Norfolk.

I DATE THIS LETTER from the happiest day of my life, a Levitical Conjurer[1] transformed me this morning from an Insipid, Unrelishing Batchelour into a Loving Passionate Husband, but in the midst of all the raptures of approaching Joys, some of my thoughts must fly to Felbrigg, and tho I am calld away 17 times in a minute to new exquisite dainties, yet I cannot resist the inticing temptation of conversing with you, and acquainting you, with tears in my Eyes, that I am going to lose my Maidenhead, but you'll think perhaps of the old Saying, that some for Joy do cry, and some for Sorrow sing. Colonel Finch, who honours us with his merry company, tells me of dismall dangers I am to run before the next Sun shines upon me, but the Spouse of my bosom being of a meek, forgiving temper, I hope she will be mercifull, and not suffer a young beginner to dye in the Experiment. I commend myself to your best prayers in this dreadfull Juncture, and wishing you speedily such a happy night, as I have now in prospect...

1. A pedantic and whimsical name for a vicar

From *Scenes from Married Life*

William Cooper

William Cooper's (real name, Harry Huff) novel Scenes from
Provincial Life, *published in 1950 can be seen now as something of a
trend-setter for the 'Angry Young Men' like John Braine, John Wain,
Kingsley Amis and Alan Sillitoe who got into print later that decade.
In 1961 he published the first of three sequels,* Scenes from Married
Life, *which continue the story of his hero Joe Lunn. Like the author, he
is a civil servant. The girl he marries, Elspeth, is a teacher, the friend
of his best friend Robert's wife.*

I NEEDED SOME CASH with which to take Harry and Barbara out to
dinner. We had invited them earlier in the week, without telling
them that by then we should be married. Our reasons were
sentiment. We could never forget that it was under their roof that
we had met for the first time—tenderest recollections moved us, of
dancing at their New Year's Eve Party, of 'The Dark Town Strutters'
Ball' in which I hauled Elspeth up from the floor and first looked
into her eyes—'This is the one for me!' And then later, supreme
cause for our gratitude, Harry's crucial question, asked out of
selfless, uninquisitive affection for us: 'When are you two going to
get married?' There was no argument between Elspeth and me
about whom we should take out to dinner on our first day married.
Thank goodness for Harry and Barbara! was how we expressed our
feelings towards them in anticipation of seeing them.

It happened that before they arrived, Elspeth and I expressed
our feelings towards each other. We mixed ourselves some martinis
and then set about bathing and changing—a procedure fraught
with the likelihood of expressing marital feeling. I was standing in
my vest and shorts, getting a clean shirt out of a drawer, when
Elspeth came from the bathroom, holding a towel in front of her.
The towel gave her a delightful air of modesty and unconcern.

'That looks nice,' I said as she went past.

She pretended not to hear.

'It would be wonderful just to see a bit more,' I said, and kissed her on the shoulder.

She turned to look at me. Without make-up her complexion had a glossy sheen: there were damp curls of hair on her temples.

'Darling!' I put my arms round her.

'The towel's damp.'

I took it away.

Her cheeks went pink. 'Darling, you know what time it is?'

'Indeed I do.'

I pushed her quietly backwards to the bed. 'You're wonderful!' I whispered, leaning over her.

'Harry and Barbara'll be at the door at any moment.'

'I'm practically at it, now.'

'Darling!'

We had to be quick. At any moment the doorbell might ring and we could not pretend we were out. I began to sweat. A race against time. A race against time.

We won it.

'Oh!' I said.

Elspeth was quiet.

'Well . . .' I murmured. For a few moments we were both quiet. I glanced at Elspeth—just at the moment to catch her yawning. We burst into laughter.

'Good Heavens! Just look at the time!' On the chest of drawers I saw the remainder of the drink I had been carrying round with me while I got dressed. I drank it. I handed Elspeth hers and she sat up and drank it. We kissed each other; and then we began to rush into our clothes.

'They'll be here any minute.'

We saw each other in a mirror, looking pink in the face. I was knotting my tie.

The doorbell rang.

'There they are.' I put on my jacket, kissed Elspeth's bare arm, and ran to let in Barbara and Harry.

Harry and Barbara stared at me briefly: I suppose I stared briefly at them—after all, there was no reason why I should not.

'Come in!' I cried. 'You wonderful pair. . . .' I was still thinking Thank goodness for Harry and Barbara! I kissed Barbara on the cheek and shook Harry's hand. They followed me into the living-room. They congratulated me again on my new status.

I was just pouring some drinks for them when Elspeth came in. All three of us now stared briefly at her. She looked sparkling—in my eyes her whole outline seemed to shimmer—and the moment I caught her glance I knew that our expression of marital feeling, in combination with a couple of martinis, had produced one of those bursts of hilarity-cum-elation that are impossible to hide.

'I'm afraid we've had a drink already,' I said, as I handed glasses to Harry and Barbara.

'So I see,' said Barbara with a smile.

...

We awoke next morning before the alarm went off, and I stretched out to find the catch on top of the clock which prevented the bell from ringing. There was scarcely any light coming through the gap in the curtains. The air in the room seemed close and scented. I rolled quietly back into my place.

Elspeth was stirring. As it were in sleep, her hand came on to my waist and her breasts brushed across my chest. I kissed her on the eyelids.

'Darling,' she murmured.

'My wife.'

She stretched a little, away from me, and then came back. 'I feel so sleepy. . . .'

I whispered 'So do I', more not to disturb the warm drowsy atmosphere than to express the whole truth. In one way I felt sleepy: in another I was obviously not. Our first morning married. My thoughts drifted round the idea for a few moments, and then began to circle round another idea. I put my hand on the small of her back and pressed.

Everything was so quiet that I could hear the clock ticking.

We stayed for a while, just touching each other. I kissed her again.

'I feel so sleepy,' she murmured in a different way.

I whispered: 'I'll go very, very gently. So that it won't wake you up.'

I felt her kiss my shoulder.

With Elspeth lying drowsily, I acted according to my stated intention; but of course the fallacy in it began to assert itself, and soon she could no longer seem to be asleep. As I did not suppose either of us had ever thought she could, I was not specially conscience-stricken—after all, what nicer way was there, I asked myself on her behalf, of coming awake.

In due course we both came fully awake. Our first morning married. . . . I had time now to consider it at leisure. When I thought I must be getting a bit heavy, I raised myself on my elbows and looked at Elspeth. She smiled at me. Her dark hair was strewn across her forehead and I caught a glimmer of light from her eyes. I thought of a quotation, something about on such a morning it being bliss to be alive, and kissed her enthusiastically under the chin from one ear to the other. Having read physics at Oxford and not English Literature, I was never able to lay my hands quickly and accurately on quotations; yet I never felt it held me back.

'Goodness, it's warm in here,' I said, pushing off the bed-clothes. I switched the light on.

Elspeth said: 'We forgot to take the flowers out of the room last night.'

This explained why the air smelt so scented to me when I woke up. I smelt it now. 'A good job, too,' I said.

Elspeth laughed and put her arm round my neck. 'I don't mind, darling,' she said. 'You can't be having baths all the time.'

All the time. I made no comment on the implications of that. 'Just think!' I said, looking into her eyes, 'you're here to stay. . . .'

Although I was looking into her eyes, I noticed she was yawning. I exclaimed.

Elspeth blushed. 'It wasn't a yawn, really.'

'I'd like to know what else it was.'

She glanced away with an expression so melting, as if I had touched some secret she was keeping, that I kissed her again.

After that I said: 'Now I really must get up and have a bath. Do you realise what time it is?'

Though it was our first morning married, we had both got to go to work as usual. The alarm clock, with its bell put out of action, had given a frustrated click a quarter of an hour ago. I jumped out of bed, gave Elspeth a parting slap, and went to the bathroom. We were already late.

I was late getting to the office. I sent for Froggatt, in order to put the news of my changed status into the official grapevine. To my mind it was worthy of an office notice, being much more piquant than the records of transfer and promotion which formed the typical content of Froggatt's communications. Anyway, I was transferred, I was promoted. Transferred to respectability, promoted to the ranks of decent ordinary men. Married!

Froggatt looked at me with his drooping, bloodhound eyes and permitted his long face a momentary gleam of amusement.

'May I be the first person here to congratulate you?' he said, in the musical lugubrious tone wherein he combined to perfection that mixture of superficial deference and underlying opposite which characterises the Executive Class.

'You may,' I said. I was delighted to see his feeling for his status 'the first person here' peeping through his genuine congratulation. 'Thank you.'

'I take it you'll inform Accounts.'

'Accounts,' I said.

'You'll have a different code number for tax purposes now,' he said. 'As I'm sure you know.'

I tried to look as if I did know.

'In fact you'll get a rebate for the whole of the present tax-year, won't you? As from last April.'

I had often been irritated by Froggatt's getting at logger-heads with the inhabitants of the snake-pit, but at moments such as this I forgave him. This kind of support was just what an S.E.O. was for.

'If you like,' he said, 'I'll notify Accounts. Then they can get in touch with you.'

'Excellent.' In the past Accounts' getting into touch with me had usually meant they were going to try and disallow the taxi-fares on my claims for travel expenses...

From *Cousin Rosamund*

Rebecca West

Rebecca West's novel Cousin Rosamund *was published posthumously in 1985, the last instalment of the story that began in* The Fountain Overflows *(1957). Rose is a concert pianist, but still a virgin in her thirties, who has convinced herself she 'could never have a lover, faithful or faithless. I cannot love anyone except the people I have loved since I was a child,' like her sister Mary and her cousin Rosamund. But the composer Oliver, whose wife was seduced away from him and then died, proves her wrong. They honeymoon by the Mediterranean, but whether in France or Italy is unclear.*

IN OUR BED in the villa by the Mediterranean my husband slid from my body and said, 'How I hate all Wagner. Tristan and Isolde is nothing like it, is it? It is so sharp and clear, and the Tristan music is like two fat people eating thick soup. Drinking thick soup,' he corrected himself pedantically, and yawned and nuzzled his face against my shoulder, and was asleep. I ran my arm down his straight back. When I had thought of his face in the train to Reading, it had seemed to me more right than nature could make it, it was as if a master craftsman had worked on it. His body was like that too. I enjoyed everything about being married, though I could not have endured it with any other husband but Oliver. I was amazed at lovemaking. It was so strange to come, when I was nearly middle-aged, on the knowledge that there was another state of being than any I had known, and that it was the state normal for humanity, that I was a minority who did not know it. It was as if I had learned that there was a sixth continent, which nearly everybody but me and a few others had visited and in which, now I had come to it, I felt like a native, or as if there was another art as well as music and painting and literature, which was not only preached, but actually practised, by nearly everybody, though they were silent about their accomplishment. It was fantastic that nobody should speak of what pervaded life and determined it, yet it was inevitable, for language could not describe it. I looked across Oliver at the window, which we had opened after we had put out the light and there was no fear of attracting mosquitoes. There was the sea, glittering with moonlight, the dark mountains above it, then the sky dusted with other earths, which looking at us might not know that our globe was swathed in this secret web of nakedness that kept it from being naked of people, chilly with lack of love and life, a barren top spinning to no purpose. Their architecture would be as fantastic but would not be the same, because there were not two of anything alike, every person was different, every work of art was different, every act of love was different, every world was different. It was a pity we did not know the end to which this wealth was to be put, but surely if this plenitude existed, and not the nothingness which somehow seemed to be more natural, more what one would have expected (though it is the one state of which the universe had and could have no experience), we might conclude that all would be well. I could believe that this precious intricate creature I held in my arms, who made love and wrote music, would never be destroyed

. . .

. . . it was long before I felt in need of [Cousin Rosamund]; not, certainly, during the two months of our honeymoon, when all time, all space, was crowded by our love. The earth, the sea, the sun, the sky, and light itself were all our accomplices. We walked on the hill and the hot air tingled with sharp scents of the pines and the herbs underfoot; at noon we sat on the gritty heights of the ruined fortress and looked down on the wide sea, white under the noon, and the horizon was tense as a stretched bow; in the market, cool under a sanctuary tent, walled in by the honey-coloured stone houses, the fish lay silver and rose and dappled on the slabs, the meat was crimson, the vegetables were green and purple and red, the flowers were white and scarlet and blue and gold, the women sat by smirking like the midwives of creation; on the beaches brown bodies were supple, and at last their primary purpose was known to me, but was still a secret. At any hour of the day we swam, our skins encrusted with salt; if I ran my lips along his arm or mine I could taste the sea; there was no hour when it was not good to make love, but when the night fell there was a special harmony between creation and our state. It was so strange that this new ecstatic life ran parallel with the life I knew. There was a piano in the villa, of course we could not have gone there had there not been one, and I practised for my autumn season in a dream, yet competently, perhaps more aware of error than I was before, more confident that in my body I possessed an extraordinary machine.

From *The Rainbow*

D. H. Lawrence

In D. H. Lawrence's novel, The Rainbow *(1915), Anna, step-daughter of Tom Brangwen, has married Will Brangwen, his nephew, at Christmas. They have left the wedding party to spend their first married night in a nearby cottage where the male Brangwens decide to serenade them.*

THE PARTY TALKED on slowly. Brangwen looked at his watch. 'Let's go an' give 'em a carol,' he said. 'We s'll find th' fiddles the 'Cock an' Robin."

'Ay, come on,' said Frank.

Alfred rose in silence. The brother-in-law and one of Will's brothers rose also.

The five men went out. The night was flashing with stars. Sirius blazed like a signal at the side of the hill, Orion, stately and magnificent, was sloping along.

Tom walked with his brother Alfred. The men's heels rang on the ground. . .

They went over the field, where a thin, keen wind blew round the ball of the hill; in the starlight. They came to the stile, and to the side of Anna's house. The lights were out, only on the blinds of the rooms downstairs, and of a bedroom upstairs, firelight flickered.

'We'd better leave 'em alone,' said Alfred Brangwen.

'Nay nay,' said Tom. 'We'll carol 'em, for th' last time.'

And in a quarter of an hour's time, eleven silent, rather tipsy men scrambled over the wall, and into the garden by the yew-trees, outside the windows where faint firelight glowed on the blinds. There came a shrill sound, two violins and a piccolo shrilling on the frosty air.

'In the fields with their flocks abiding.' A commotion of men's voices broke out singing in ragged unison.

Anna Brangwen had started up, listening, when the music began. She was afraid.

'It's the wake,' he whispered.

She remained tense, her heart beating heavily, possessed with strange, strong fear. Then there came the burst of men's singing, rather uneven. She strained still, listening.

'It's Dad,' she said, in a low voice.

They were silent, listening.

'And my father,' he said.

She listened still. But she was sure. She sank down again into bed, into his arms. He held her very close, kissing her. The hymn rambled on outside, all the men singing their best, having forgotten everything else under the spell of the fiddles and the tune. The firelight glowed against the darkness in the room. Anna could hear her father singing with gusto.

'Aren't they silly?' she whispered.

And they crept closer, closer together, hearts beating to one another. And even as the hymn rolled on, they ceased to hear it.

And the honeymoon continues:

Will Brangwen had some weeks of holiday after his marriage, so the two took their honeymoon in full hands, alone in their cottage together.

And to him, as the days went by, it was as if the heavens had fallen, and he were sitting with her among the ruins, in a new world, everybody else buried, themselves two blissful survivors, with everything to squander as they would. At first, he could not get rid of a culpable sense of licence on his part. Wasn't there some duty outside, calling him and he did not come?

It was all very well at night, when the doors were locked and the darkness drawn round the two of them. Then they were the only inhabitants of the visible earth, the rest were under the flood. And being alone in the world, they were a law unto themselves, they could enjoy and squander and waste like conscienceless gods.

But in the morning, as the carts clanked by, and children shouted down the lane: as the hucksters came calling their wares, and the church clock struck eleven, and he and she had not got up yet, even to breakfast: he could not help feeling guilty, as if he were committing a breach of the law—ashamed that he was not up and doing.

'Doing what?' she asked. 'What is there to do? You will only lounge about.'

Still, even lounging about was respectable. One was at least in connection with the world, then. Whereas now, lying so still and peacefully while the daylight came obscurely through the drawn blind, one was severed from the world, one shut oneself off in tacit denial of the world. And he was troubled.

But it was so sweet and satisfying lying there talking desultorily with her. It was sweeter than sunshine, and not so evanescent. It was even irritating the way the church clock kept on chiming: there seemed no space between the hours, just a moment, golden and still, whilst she traced his features with her finger-tips, utterly careless and happy, and he loved her to do it.

But he was strange and unused. So suddenly, everything that had been before was shed away and gone. One day, he was a bachelor, living with the world. The next day, he was with her, as remote from the world as if the two of them were buried like a seed in darkness. Suddenly, like a chestnut falling out of a burr, he was shed naked and glistening on to a soft, fecund earth, leaving behind him the hard rind of worldly knowledge and experience. There it lay, cast off, the worldly experience. He heard it in the hucksters' cries, the noise of carts, the calling of children. And it was like the hard shed rind, discarded. Inside, in the softness and stillness of the room, was the naked kernel, that palpitated in silent activity, absorbed in reality.

Inside the room was a great steadiness, a core of living eternity. Only far outside, at the rim, went on the noise and the distraction. Here at the centre the great wheel was motionless, centred upon itself. Here was a poised, unflawed stillness that was beyond time, because it remained the same, inexhaustible, unchanging, unexhausted.

As they lay close together, complete and beyond the touch of time or change, it was as if they were at the very centre of all the slow wheeling of space and the rapid agitation of life, deep, deep inside them all, at the centre where there is utter radiance, and eternal being, and the silence absorbed in praise: the steady core of all movements, the unawakened sleep of all wakefulness. They found themselves there, and they lay still, in each other's arms; for their moment they were at the heart of eternity, whilst time roared far off, forever far off, towards the rim.

Then gradually they were passed away from the supreme centre, down the circles of praise and joy and gladness, further and further out, towards the noise and the friction. But their hearts had burned and were tempered by the inner reality, they were unalterably glad.

Gradually they began to wake up, the noises outside became more real. They understood and answered the call outside. They counted the strokes of the bell. And when they counted midday, they understood that it was midday, in the world, and for themselves also.

It dawned upon her that she was hungry. She had been getting hungrier for a lifetime. But even yet it was not sufficiently real to rouse her. A long way off she could hear the words 'I am dying of hunger.' Yet she lay still, separate, at peace, and the words were unuttered. There was still another lapse.

And then, quite calmly, even a little surprised, she was in the present, and was saying:

'I am dying with hunger.'

'So am I,' he said calmly, as if it were of not the slightest significance. And they relapsed into the warm, golden stillness. And the minutes flowed unheeded past the window outside.

Then suddenly she stirred against him.

'My dear, I am dying of hunger,' she said.

It was a slight pain to him to be brought to.

'We'll get up,' he said, unmoving.

And she sank her head on to him again, and they lay still, lapsing. Half consciously, he heard the clock chime the hour. She did not hear.

'Do get up,' she murmured at length, 'and give me something to eat.'

'Yes,' he said, and he put his arms round her, and she lay with her face on him. They were faintly astonished that they did not move. The minutes rustled louder at the window.

'Let me go then,' he said.

She lifted her head from him, relinquishingly. With a little breaking away, he moved out of bed, and was taking his clothes. She stretched out her hand to him.

'You are so nice,' she said, and he went back for a moment or two.

Then actually he did slip into some clothes, and, looking round quickly at her, was gone out of the room. She lay translated again into a pale, clearer peace. As if she were a spirit, she listened to the noise of him downstairs, as if she were no longer of the material world.

It was half past one. He looked at the silent kitchen, untouched from last night, dim with the drawn blind. And he hastened to draw up the blind, so people should know they were not in bed any later. Well, it was his own house, it did not matter. Hastily he put wood in the grate and made a fire. He exulted in himself, like an adventurer on an undiscovered island. The fire blazed up, he put on the kettle. How happy he felt! How still and secluded the house was! There were only he and she in the world.

But when he unbolted the door, and, half dressed, looked out, he felt furtive and guilty. The world was there, after all. And he had felt so secure, as though this house were the Ark in the flood, and all the rest was drowned. The world was there: and it was afternoon. The morning had vanished and gone by, the day was growing old. Where was the bright, fresh morning? He was accused. Was the morning gone, and he had lain with blinds drawn, let it pass by unnoticed?

He looked again round the chill, grey afternoon. And he himself so soft and warm and glowing! There were two sprigs of yellow jasmine in the saucer that covered the milk-jug. He wondered who had been and left the sign. Taking the jug, he hastily shut the door. Let the day and the daylight drop out, let it go by unseen. He did not care. What did one day more or less matter to him. It could fall into oblivion unspent, if it liked, this one course of daylight.

'Somebody has been and found the door locked,' he said when he went upstairs with the tray. He gave her the two sprigs of jasmine. She laughed as she sat up in bed, childishly threading the flowers in the breast of her nightdress. Her brown hair stuck out like a nimbus, all fierce, round her softly glowing face. Her dark eyes watched the tray eagerly.

'How good!' she cried, sniffing the cold air. 'I'm glad you did a lot.' And she held out her hands eagerly for her plate. 'Come back to bed, quick—it's cold.' She rubbed her hands together sharply.

He put off what little clothing he had on, and sat beside her in the bed.

'You look like a lion, with your mane sticking out, and your nose pushed over your food,' he said.

She tinkled with laughter, and gladly ate her breakfast.

The morning was sunk away unseen, the afternoon was steadily going too, and he was letting it go. One bright transit of daylight gone by unacknowledged! There was something unmanly, recusant in it. He could not quite reconcile himself to the fact. He felt he ought to get up, go out quickly into the daylight, and work or spend himself energetically in the open air of the afternoon, retrieving what was left to him of the day.

But he did not go. Well, one might as well be hung for a sheep as for a lamb. If he had lost this day of his life, he had lost it. He gave it up. He was not going to count his losses. She didn't care. She didn't care in the least. Then why should he? Should he be behind her in recklessness and independence? She was superb in her indifference. He wanted to be like her.

She took her responsibilities lightly. When she spilled her tea on the pillow, she rubbed it carelessly with a handkerchief, and turned over the pillow. He would have felt guilty. She did not. And it pleased him. It pleased him very much to see how these things did not matter to her.

When the meal was over, she wiped her mouth on her handkerchief quickly, satisfied and happy, and settled down on the pillows again, with her fingers in his close, strange, fur-like hair.

The evening began to fall, the light was half alive, livid. He hid his face against her.

'I don't like the twilight,' he said.

'I love it,' she answered.

He hid his face against her, who was warm and like sunlight. She seemed to have sunlight inside her. Her heart beating seemed like sunlight upon him. In her was a more real day than the day could give: so warm and steady and restoring. He hid his face against her whilst the twilight fell, whilst she lay staring out with her unseeing dark eyes, as if she wandered forth untrammelled in the vagueness. The vagueness gave her scope and set her free.

To him, turned towards her heart-pulse, all was very still and very warm and very close, like noon-tide. He was glad to know this warm, full noon. It ripened him and took away his responsibility, some of his conscience.

They got up when it was quite dark. She hastily twisted her hair into a knot, and was dressed in a twinkling. Then they went downstairs, drew to the fire, and sat in silence, saying a few words now and then.

Her father was coming. She bundled the dishes away, flew round and tidied the room, assumed another character, and again seated herself. He sat thinking of his carving of Eve. He loved to go over his carving in his mind, dwelling on every stroke, every line. How he loved it now! When he went back to his Creation-panel again, he would finish his Eve, tender and sparkling. It did not satisfy him yet. The Lord should labour over her in a silent passion of Creation, and Adam should be tense as if in a dream of immortality, and Eve should take form glimmeringly, shadowily, as if the Lord must wrestle with His own soul for her, yet she was a radiance.

'What are you thinking about?' she asked.

He found it difficult to say. His soul became shy when he tried to communicate it.

'I was thinking my Eve was too hard and lively.'

'Why?'

'I don't know. She should be more—,' he made a gesture of infinite tenderness.

There was a stillness with a little joy. He could not tell her any more. Why could he not tell her any more? She felt a pang of disconsolate sadness. But it was nothing. She went to him.

Her father came, and found them both very glowing, like an open flower. He loved to sit with them. Where there was a perfume of love, anyone who came must breathe it. They were both very quick and alive, lit up from the other-world, so that it was quite an experience for them, that anyone else could exist.

But still it troubled Will Brangwen a little, in his orderly, conventional mind, that the established rule of things had gone so utterly. One ought to get up in the morning and wash oneself and be a decent social being. Instead, the two of them stayed in bed till nightfall, then got up; she never washed her face, but sat there talking to her father as bright and shameless as a daisy opened out of the dew. Or she got up at ten o'clock, and quite blithely went to bed again at three, or at half past four, stripping him naked in the daylight, and all so gladly and perfectly, oblivious quite of his qualms. He let her do as she liked with him, and shone with strange pleasure. She was to dispose of him as she would. He was translated with gladness to be in her hands. And down went his qualms, his maxims, his rules, his smaller beliefs, she scattered them like an expert skittle-player. He was very much astonished and delighted to see them scatter.

He stood and gazed and grinned with wonder whilst his Tablets of Stone went bounding and bumping and splintering down the hill, dislodged for ever. Indeed, it was true as they said, that a man wasn't born before he was married. What a change indeed!

Wedding Wind

Philip Larkin

The wind blew all my wedding-day,
And my wedding-night was the night of the high wind;
And a stable door was banging, again and again,
That he must go and shut it, leaving me
Stupid in candlelight, hearing rain,
Seeing my face in the twisted candlestick,
Yet seeing nothing. When he came back
He said the horses were restless, and I was sad
That any man or beast that night should lack
The happiness I had.

    Now in the day
All's ravelled under the sun by the wind's blowing.
He has gone to look at the floods, and I
Carry a chipped pail to the chicken-run,
Set it down, and stare. All is the wind
Hunting through clouds and forests, thrashing
My apron and the hanging cloths on the line.
Can it be borne, this bodying-forth by wind
Of joy my actions turn on, like a thread
Carrying beads? Shall I be let to sleep
Now this perpetual morning shares my bed?
Can even death dry up
These new delighted lakes, conclude
Our kneeling as cattle by all-generous waters?

II Getting to Know You

Elegy XX

John Donne

This elegy, one of Donne's most famous, is also simply entitled 'Going to Bed'. Let us allow ourselves to assume that 'madam' is his very new wife . . .

Come, madam, come, all rest my powers defy;
Until I labour, I in labour lie.
The foe ofttimes, having the foe in sight,
Is tired with standing, though he never fight.
Off with that girdle, like heaven's zone glittering,
But a far fairer world encompassing.
Unpin that spangled breast-plate, which you wear,
That th'eyes of busy fools may be stopp'd there.
Unlace yourself, for that harmonious chime
Tells me from you that now it is bed-time.
Off with that happy busk, which I envy,
That still can be, and still can stand so nigh.
Your gown going off such beauteous state reveals,
As when from flowery meads th'hill's shadow steals.
Off with your wiry coronet, and show
The hairy diadems which on you do grow.
Off with your hose and shoes; then softly tread
In this love's hallow'd temple, this soft bed.
In such white robes heaven's angels used to be
Revealed to men; thou, angel, bring'st with thee
A heaven-like Mahomet's paradise; and though
Ill spirits walk in white, we easily know
By this these angels from an evil sprite;

Those set our hairs, but these our flesh upright.
        Licence my roving hands, and let them go
Before, behind, between, above, below.
Oh, my America, my Newfoundland,
My kingdom, safest when with one man mann'd,
My mine of precious stones, my empery;
How am I blest in thus discovering thee!
To enter in these bonds, is to be free;
Then, where my hand is set, my seal shall be.
        Full nakedness! All joys are due to thee;
As souls unbodied, bodies unclothed must be
To taste whole joys. Gems which you women use
Are like Atlanta's ball cast in men's views;
That, when a fool's eye lighteth on a gem,
His earthly soul might court that, not them.
Like pictures, or like books' gay coverings made
For laymen, are all women thus array'd.
Themselves are only mystic books, which we
—Whom their imputed grace will dignify—
Must see reveal'd. Then, since that I may know,
As liberally as to thy midwife show
Thyself; cast all, yea, this white linen hence;
There is no penance due to innocence:
        To teach thee, I am naked first; why then,
What needst thou have more covering than a man?

From *Bel-Ami*

Guy de Maupassant

Georges Duroy, more than a bit of a bounder, is the 'bel-ami' of Guy de Maupassant's novel, published in 1885. His old army friend Forestier puts Duroy's feet on the first rungs of the ladder to becoming a successful journalist, though it is Mme Forestier who teaches him how to write. When Forestier dies, Duroy marries his widow.

THE YOUNG MAN, who now signed his articles D. de Cantel, his News Column, Duroy, and the political commentary that he began to write from time to time, du Roy, spent half of every day with his fiancée, who treated him with a sisterly familiarity which was however touched by genuine though disguised affection, a sort of amorous impulse dissimulated as a weakness. She had decided that the marriage should take place in complete secrecy, in the presence of witnesses alone, and that they would leave the same evening for Rouen. Next day they would visit the journalist's aged parents, and stay with them for a few days.

Duroy had done his best to make her give up this project, but not having succeeded, he finally gave in.

Accordingly, when May 10th arrived, the newly married pair, considering the religious ceremony superfluous, as they had invited no guests, went home to finish their packing after a brief appearance at the Town Hall; then they drove to the Gare Saint Lazare and took the six o'clock train for Normandy. They had scarcely exchanged a dozen words up to the moment when they found themselves alone in the compartment. As soon as they were off, they looked at each other and burst out laughing, to conceal a certain embarrassment they both felt.

The train passed slowly through the Batignolles station, into the shabby outskirts between the fortifications and the Seine.

Duroy and his wife from time to time made a common-place remark or two, and then turned once more to look out of the window.

As they passed over the Asnières bridge, an impulse of gaiety came over them at the sight of the river covered with boats and fishermen and rowers. The sun, a powerful sun of May, shed its slanting rays on to all the craft, and on to the calm river, that seemed motionless, without a ripple on its surface, fixed beneath the heat and radiance of the dying day. A sailing barge, in the middle of the stream, its two huge triangles of white canvas stretched to each gunwale to catch the faintest breath of wind, looked like an enormous bird about to fly away.

'I love the Paris suburbs,' murmured Duroy. 'I have recollections of certain dishes of fried fish which were some of the best I have ever eaten.'

'And the boats,' she answered. 'It's so delightful to glide over the water at sunset.'

They said no more, as though not venturing to continue these nostaligic reminiscences of their past lives, perhaps already silently indulging in the lyricism of regret.

Duroy, who was sitting opposite his wife, took her hand, and kissed it slowly.

'When we get back,' he said, 'we will go and dine sometimes at Chatou.'

'But we shall have so many things to do,' she murmured, in a tone that seemed to imply: 'we must sacrifice our inclination to our advantage.'

He was still holding her hand, wondering with some anxiety how he should effect the transition to caresses. He would not have been perturbed in the same way by a young girl's ignorance; but the alert and wary intelligence that he sensed in Madeleine made him feel awkward. He was afraid she might think him silly—too timid or too rough, too slow or too enterprising.

He squeezed the hand spasmodically, without receiving any response to his appeal.

'It seems to me very odd that you should be my wife.'

She seemed surprised. 'Why?'

'I don't know, it seems odd. I want to kiss you, and I'm surprised to find I have the right to do so.'

She calmly offered him her cheek, which he kissed as he might have kissed a sister's.

'The first time I saw you,' he went on, '(you remember—at that dinner to which Forestier invited me) I thought: By Jove, if I could find a woman like that. Well, it's done. I have found her.'

'That's very nice of you,' she murmured.

And she looked at him squarely, with a slightly quizzical look in her ever-smiling eyes.

He thought to himself: 'I'm too cold. I'm stupid. I ought to go quicker than this.' And he said:

'How did you first get to know Forestier?'

She answered, with sly malice: 'Are we going to Rouen to talk about my late husband?'

He blushed.

'I'm a fool. You make me nervous.'

She was delighted.

'Do I? Is it possible? How can that be?'

He was now sitting close beside her, when she exclaimed:

'Look!—a stag.'

The train was running through the Forest of Saint-Germain, and she had seen a startled deer leap across an avenue at one bound.

Duroy, leaning over her as she was looking through the open window, imprinted a long kiss, a lover's kiss, on the back of her neck.

She remained for a few moments motionless; then, raising her head, she said:

'You're tickling me—do stop.'

But he did not move, and gently skimmed his curled moustache, in a prolonged and provocative caress, over the white neck.

She shook herself. 'Do stop.'

He had slipped his right hand behind her, clasped her head and turned it towards him. Then he dashed at her mouth like a hawk upon its prey.

She struggled, thrust him away, and tried to free herself. At last she succeeded, and again said:

'Please do stop.'

He did not listen, he clutched her in his arms, kissing her with avid trembling lips, and tried to push her backwards on to the carriage seat.

She freed herself with a great effort, and getting up briskly, she exclaimed:

'Look here, Georges, you must stop this sort of thing. We are not children, after all, we can quite well wait until Rouen.'

He remained seated, very flushed, and frozen by her sage remonstrance; then, having partly recovered his composure, he said gaily:

'All right, I'll wait; but I shan't say another word until we get there. And remember that we are now going through Poissy.'

'I will do the talking,' said she.

She sat down again quietly beside him.

And she talked very practically about what they would do on their return. They had better keep on the flat where she lived with her first husband, and Duroy would also inherit Forestier's duties and salary on the *Vie Française*. In point of fact, she had, before their marriage, settled all the financial details of the establishment with the precision of a man of business. They had joined forces under the system of separate estates, and every possible eventuality had been provided for; death, divorce, the birth of one or more children. The young man brought in four thousand francs, so he said, but of this sum he had already borrowed fifteen hundred. The rest came from savings effected in the course of the year, in anticipation of the event. The lady brought in forty thousand francs left her by Forestier, so she said.

She mentioned him once more, as an excellent example. 'He was a very economical fellow, very orderly and industrious. He would have made a fortune in a very short time.'

Duroy was not listening, being intent upon his own thoughts.

She paused from time to time, to pursue an idea in her own mind, and then went on:

'In three or four years' time you may well be earning from thirty to forty thousand francs a year. That is what Charles would have had, if he had lived.'

Georges, who was beginning to find these injunctions rather tedious, replied:

'I thought we were not going to Rouen to talk about your late husband.'

She gave him a little tap on the cheek.

'True,' she laughed. 'I apologise.'

He was sitting with his hands laid rather affectedly on his knees, in the attitude of a good little boy.

'You look silly like that,' she said.

'This is how I am to behave, as you pointed out to me just now, and I shall continue to do so.'

'Why?' she asked.

'Because it is you who have taken over the management of the establishment, and even of my person. It concerns you, indeed, as a widow.'

She was rather taken aback. 'What exactly do you mean?'

'You have experience that should dispel my ignorance, and a practical knowledge of marriage which ought to enlighten my bachelor innocence—there?'

'Really!' she exclaimed.

'That is how it stands,' he went on. 'I don't know women; you do know men, being a widow; you will have to undertake my education, this evening; and you may as well begin it at once; so there!'

'Well!' she exclaimed with amusement. 'If you are relying on me for that! ...'

He went on, in the voice of a schoolboy mumbling out his lesson: 'Certainly I do ... I rely on you to give me proper instruction ... in twenty lessons ... ten for the rudiments, reading and grammar ... ten for more advanced matters—the rhetoric of the subject, so to speak. I am an ignoramus.'

She laughed in high good humour.

'You silly fellow!'

'That's better,' said he; 'and now that you are becoming a little more familiar, I shall do so too, and tell you that I adore you, darling, more and more, every second, and that Rouen seems a very long way away!'

He was now speaking with the intonations of an actor, and with a pleasant play of feature which amused a lady accustomed to the jovialities of the great bohemia of the literary world.

She threw a sidelong glance at him, and thought him really

29

charming; at that moment she was torn between the desire one has to pick and eat the apple, and the hesitations of common sense, which suggests that one had better wait for dinner and eat it at due time.

Then she said, blushing faintly at the thoughts that assailed her mind. 'As you are to be my little pupil, give heed to my experience, my wide experience. Kisses in a railway carriage are no good. They ruin the stomach.'

Then she blushed more deeply as she murmured:

'Never spend money before it is earned.'

He grinned, in animation at the sly suggestions that he felt had slipped into that lovely mouth; he made the sign of the cross, and his lips moved as though he were muttering a prayer. 'I have just put myself under the protection of St. Anthony, patron saint of Temptation. Henceforward, I am made of bronze.'

The night came softly down, enveloping in transparent shadow, like an insubstantial veil of crepe, the expanse of country on their right. The train was running alongside the Seine; and the pair looked down into the river, winding like a broad ribbon of polished metal beside the line, dotted with red reflections, patches of colour fallen from the sky which the departing sun had dipped in purple and in fire. These splashes of light dimmed and darkened and then gradually vanished. And the countryside sank into gloom, with that ominous shudder, that shudder of death, that passes over the earth in every dusk.

The melancholy of evening came through the open window, and entered into the souls, lately so gay, of the married pair, who now fell into silence.

They had drawn closer to each other to look at that agony of the day, of that lovely, clear May day.

At Nantes a man had come in to light the small oil lamp that shed its yellow, flickering radiance on to the grey cloth of the upholstery.

Duroy put an arm round his wife's waist and clasped her to him. The sharp desire of a little while before had been transformed into affection, a rather languid affection, a tepid longing for little comforting caresses—the caresses with which a child is lulled to sleep.

And he murmured softly: 'I am going to love you very much, my little Made.'

The soft voice aroused the woman, a quick tremor thrilled over her flesh, and she offered him her mouth as she leaned over him, for he had laid his cheek against the warm pillow of her breasts. There followed a long kiss, a dumb deep kiss, then a quiver, an abrupt and wild embrace, a brief breathless struggle and a violent and clumsy act of sex. After which they lay in each other's arms, both a little disillusioned, tired but still affectionate, until the whistle of the train announced an approaching station.

And she said, as she smoothed the hair over her temples with the tips of her fingers:

'Really!—we behave like a couple of silly children.'

But he kissed her hands, one after the other with feverish speed, and answered:

'I adore you, my little Made.'

Until Rouen they sat almost motionless, cheek to cheek, their eyes staring at the darkness through the window, where they could now and again see the lights of houses passing by; and they dreamed, glad to feel so near together, in the growing expectation of a freer and more intimate embrace.

They drove to an hotel looking on to the quay, and went to bed after a very light supper.

The chambermaid awakened them next morning, just after eight o'clock.

From *The Memoirs of Ottoline Morrell*

Lady Ottoline Morrell (1873–1938), hostess of the Bloomsbury Group and of many other artists and writers at Garsington Manor, went to Ravello near Amalfi on her honeymoon in 1902. She and her husband Philip later had what amounted to an 'open marriage', with both taking frequent lovers. Perhaps the most famous of her affairs was with Bertrand Russell. This did not prevent her from recalling the early days of her marriage in her memoirs.

I S A HONEYMOON ever an ideally blissful time, as the name seems to denote? I doubt if it is for anyone over twenty-five. Old habits that have been formed by living alone have to be broken, adaptation begins, and to anyone serious and nervous these first days of joint life assume an exaggerated importance, mutual likes and dislikes are watched with microscopic eyes, and if in all things they do not correspond, the whole of the future seems at stake. The small fact even of new clothes and shoes tends to make these days uncomfortable and odd. However, we found nothing to despair of, and our days were very interesting and happy, sightseeing in Florence, Naples and Rome, reading aloud Carlyle, Past and Present, poetry, Gibbon, Milton . . . I think the old convention that a honeymoon is to be spent 'à deux' is with many other of the old-established conventions regarding manners and personal life, very wise. There is so much to learn about one's new companion, and indeed about oneself in these new circumstances, for one sees oneself with his eyes, and this is accomplished more happily alone and when not interrupted by casual friends.

From *Busman's Honeymoon*

Dorothy Sayers

In Busman's Honeymoon *(1937) Dorothy Sayers at last gets her hero, the amateur sleuth Lord Peter Wimsey, to the altar with Harriet Vane, whom he had saved from a wrongful conviction for murder in an earlier novel. Lord Peter has indulged his bride by buying an old farmhouse called Talboys, which she had known well in her childhood, and it is there that they arrive for their wedding night in Mrs Merdle, his Lordship's Daimler (the literary references flow unrelentingly throughout the book). Bunter, his manservant, accompanies them, nursing two-and-a-half dozen of vintage port wrapped in an eiderdown on the back seat. They find the house locked and nothing ready for their arrival. Attempts to light fires are thwarted by blocked chimneys and oil stoves won't function because of defective wicks. But after dining on emergency supplies (paté de foie, quails-in-aspic, hock), matters can proceed. It is the next morning before Bunter finds the body, essential in any self-respecting detective story, of the previous owner in the cellar.*

'A T ANY RATE,' said Peter, lighting the cigarettes, 'the matches still seem to strike on the box; all the laws of Nature have not been suspended for our confusion. We will muffle ourselves in overcoats and proceed to keep each other warm in the accepted manner of benighted travellers in a snow-bound country. "If I was on Greenland's coast," and all that. Not that I see any prospect of a six-months' night; I wish I did; it is already past midnight.'

Bunter vanished upstairs, kettle in hand.

'If', said her ladyship, a few minutes later, 'you would remove that contraption from your eye, I could clean the bridge of your nose. Are you sorry we didn't go to Paris or Mentone after all?'

'No, definitely not. There is a solid reality about this. It's convincing, somehow.'

'It's beginning to convince me, Peter. Such a series of domestic accidents could only happen to married people. There's none of that artificial honeymoon glitter that prevents people from discovering each other's real characters. You stand the test of tribulation remarkably well. It's very encouraging.'

'Thank you – but I really don't know that there's a great deal to complain of. I've got you, that's the chief thing, and food and fire of sorts, and a roof over my head . . . I might, perhaps, have preferred rather more hot water and less oil about my person. Not that there is anything essentially effeminate about paraffin – but I disapprove on principle of perfumes for men.'

'It's a nice, clean smell,' said his wife, soothingly, 'much more original than all the powders of the merchant. And I expect Bunter will manage to get it off you.'

'I hope so,' said Peter. He remembered that it had once been said of '*ce blond cadet de famille ducale anglaise*' – said, too, by a lady who had every opportunity of judging – that '*il tenait son lit en Grand Monarque et s'y démenait en Grand Turc.*' The Fates, it seemed, had determined to strip him of every vanity save one. Let them. He could fight this battle naked. He laughed suddenly.

'*Enfin du courage! Embrasse-moi, chérie. Je trouverai quandmême le moyen de te faire plaisir. Hein? tu veux? dis donc!*'

'*Je veux bien.*'

'Dearest!'

'Oh, Peter!'

'I'm sorry – did I hurt you?'

'No. Yes. Kiss me again.'

It was at some point during the next five minutes that Peter was heard to murmur: 'Not faint Canaries but ambrosial'; and it is symptomatic of Harriet's state of mind that at the time she vaguely connected the faint canaries with the shabby tigers – only tracing the quotation to its source some ten days later.

Bunter came downstairs. In one hand he had a small and steaming jug, and in the other a case of razors and a sponge-bag. A bath-towel and a pair of pyjamas hung from his arm, together with a silk dressing-gown.

'The fire in the bedroom is drawing satisfactorily. I have contrived to heat a small quantity of water for your ladyship's use.'

His master looked apprehensively.

'But what to me, my love, but what to me?'

Bunter made no verbal reply, but his glance in the direction of the kitchen was eloquent. Peter looked thoughtfully at his own fingernails and shuddered.

'Lady,' said he, 'get you to bed and leave me to my destiny.'

The wood upon the hearth was flaring cheerfully, and the water, what there was of it, was boiling. The two brass candle-sticks bore their flaming ministers bravely, one on either side of the mirror. The big fourposter, with its patchwork quilt of faded blues and scarlets and its chintz hangings dimmed by age and laundering, had, against the pale, plastered walls, a dignified air as though of exiled royalty. Harriet, warm and powdered and free at last from the smell of soot, paused with the hair-brush in her hand to wonder what was happening to Peter. She slipped across the chill dark of the dressing-room, opened the farther door, and listened. From somewhere far below came an ominous clank of iron, followed by a loud yelp and a burst of half-suffocating laughter.

'Poor darling!' said Harriet . . .

, She put out the bedroom candles. The sheets, worn thin by age, were of fine linen, and somewhere in the room there was a scent of lavender. . . Jordan river. . . A branch broke and fell upon the hearth in a shower of sparks, and the tall shadows danced across the ceiling.

The door-latch clicked, and her husband sidled apologetically through. His air of chastened triumph made her chuckle, though her blood was thumping erratically and something seemed to have happened to her breath. He dropped on his knees beside her.

'Sweetheart,' he said, his voice shaken between passion and laughter, 'take your bridegroom. Quite clean and not the least paraffiny, but dreadfully damp and cold. Scrubbed like a puppy under the scullery pump!'

'Dear Peter!'

('. . . en Grand Monarque . . .')

'I think,' he went on, rapidly and almost indistinguishably, 'I think Bunter was enjoying himself. I have set him to clean the blackbeetles out of the copper. What does it matter? What does anything matter? We are here. Laugh, lover, laugh. This is the end of the journey and the beginning of all delight.'

Mr Mervyn Bunter, having chased away the beetles, filled the copper, and laid the fire ready for lighting, wrapped himself up in two greatcoats and a rug and disposed himself comfortably in a couple of arm-chairs. But he did not sleep at once. Though not precisely anxious, he was filled with a kindly concern. He had (with what exertions!) brought his favourite up to the tape and must leave him now to make the running, but no respect for the proprieties could prevent his sympathetic imagination from following the cherished creature every step of the way. With a slight sigh he drew the candle towards him, took out a fountain-pen and a writing-pad, and began a letter to his mother. The performance of this filial duty might, he thought, serve to calm his mind.

'Dear Mother, – I write from an "unknown destination" –

'What was that you called me?'
'Oh, Peter – how absurd! I wasn't thinking.'
'What did you call me?'
'My lord!'
'The last two words in the language I ever expected to get a kick out of. One never values a thing till one's earned it, does one? Listen, heart's lady – before I've done I mean to be king and emperor.'

It is no part of the historian's duty to indulge in what a critic has called 'interesting revelations of the marriage-bed'. It is enough that the dutiful Mervyn Bunter at length set aside his writing materials, blew out the candle, and composed his limbs to rest; and that, of the sleepers beneath that ancient roof, he that had the hardest and coldest couch enjoyed the quietest slumbers.

Lady Peter Wimsey propped herself cautiously on one elbow and contemplated her sleeping lord. With the mocking eyes hidden and the confident mouth relaxed, his big, bony nose and tumbled hair gave him a gawky, fledgling look, like a schoolboy. And the hair itself was almost as light as tow – it was ridiculous that anything male should be as fair as that. No doubt when it was damped and sleeked down for the day his head would go back to its normal barley-corn colour. Last night, after Bunter's ruthless pumping, it had affected her much as the murdered Lorenzo's glove affected Isabella, and she had had to rub it dry with a towel before cradling it where, in the country phrase, it 'belonged to be'.

Bunter? She spared him a stray thought from a mind drugged with sleep and the pleasure that comes with sleep. Bunter was up and about; she could faintly hear doors opening and shutting and furniture being moved down below. What an amazing muddle it had all been! But he would miraculously put everything right – wonderful Bunter – and leave one free to live and not bother one's head. One vaguely hoped Bunter had not spent the whole night chasing black beetles, but for the moment what was left of one's mind was concentrated on Peter – being anxious not to wake him, rather hoping he would soon wake up of his own accord and wondering what he would say when he did. If his first words were French one would at least feel certain that he retained an agreeable impression of the night's proceedings; on the whole, however, English would be preferable, as showing that he remembered quite distinctly who one was.

As though this disturbing thought had broken his sleep, he stirred at that moment, and, without opening his eyes, felt for her with his hand and pulled her down against him. And his first word was neither French nor English, but a long interrogative 'M'mmm?'

'M'm!' said Harriet, abandoning herself. 'Mais quel tact, mon dieu! Sais-tu enfin qui je suis?'

'Yes, my Shulamite, I do, so you needn't lay traps for my tongue. In the course of a mis-spent life I have learnt that it is a gentleman's first duty to remember in the morning who it was he took to bed with him. You are Harriet, and you are black but comely. Incidentally, you are my wife, and if you have forgotten it you will have to learn it all over again' . . .

'Peter!'
'Heart's desire?'
'Somebody's frying bacon.'
'Nonsense. People don't fry bacon at dawn.'
'That was eight by the church clock and the sun's simply blazing in.'

'Busy old fool, unruly sun – but you're right about the bacon. The smell's coming up quite distinctly. Through the window, I think. This calls for investigation. . . . I say, it's a gorgeous morning. . . . Are you hungry?'

'Ravenous.'

'Unromantic but reassuring. As a matter of fact, I could do with a large breakfast myself. After all, I work hard for all living. I'll give Bunter a hail.'

'For God's sake put some clothes on – if Mrs Ruddle sees you hanging out of the window like that she'll have a thousand fits.'

'It'll be a treat for her. Nothing so desirable as novelty. I expect old man Ruddle went to bed in his boots. Bunter! Bun-ter! . . . Damn it, here is the Ruddle woman. Stop laughing and chuck me my dressing-gown. . . . Er – good morning Mrs Ruddle. Tell Bunter we're ready for breakfast, would you?'

'Right you are, my lord,' replied Mrs Ruddle (for after all he was a lord). But she expressed herself later in the day to her friend Mrs Hodges.

'Mother-naked, Mrs 'Odges, if you'll believe me. I declare I was that ashamed I didn't know w'ere to look. And no more 'air on 'is chest than wot I 'as meself.'

'That's gentry,' said Mrs Hodges, referring to the first part of the indictment. 'You've only to look at the pictures of them there sun-bathers as they call them on the Ly-doh. Now, my Susan's first were a wunnerful 'airy man, just like a kerridge-rug if you take my meaning. But', she added cryptically, 'it don't foller, for they never 'ad no family, not till 'e died and she married young Tyler over at Pigott's.'

When Mr Bunter tapped discreetly at the door and entered with a wooden bucket full of kindling, her ladyship had vanished and his lordship was sitting on the window-ledge smoking a cigarette.

'Good morning, Bunter. Fine morning.'

'Beautiful autumn weather, my lord, very seasonable. I trust your lordship found everything satisfactory.'

'H'm. Bunter, do you know the meaning of the expression arrière-pensée?'

'No, my lord.'

'I'm glad to hear it.'

From *One Way of Love*
Gamel Woolsey

WHEN SHE WENT upstairs Alan was waiting for her. He had stayed in her rooms quietly reading all evening. She had never slept with him before, never gone to bed with him and she felt shy. Alan was in bed first and put out the light. Mariana had undressed in the bathroom. At the edge of the bed she dropped her dressing-gown and, groping in the dark, felt for the edge of the covers, but Alan was expecting her and she was received in his arms. She was tired—she wanted to lie still and sleep. But she was enfolded by Alan's desirous body. And she tried to kiss him back as he kissed her, to meet his limbs with hers and share his passion—for was this not her wedding night?

But it was charming to wake the next morning just at dawn, and see her own dark, curling hair mixed with Alan's short, bronze curls. She laughed secretly at his face because it was crinkled in sleepy protest against the brightness of the day. Her head lay still on Alan's shoulder. They had slept all night in one another's arms. The early sun and the chilly spring air came in through the open windows.

Alan stirred, murmured inarticulately and pulled her closer to him. He lay without speaking while tides of love and desire for her seemed to pour through his blood. Then he raised himself on one elbow and looked down at Mariana. She smiled back at him and saw that his eyes were heavy with desire.

The hour when dreams are deeper and winds are colder.
The hour when young love wakes on a white shoulder.

—he whispered to her. Half asleep, she felt no desire. The morning air, clear and fresh like spring water, chilled her face and her bare arms and neck. But her body lay warm and softly sunk in Alan's arms: relaxed and still drowsy, she yielded to his body. His passion was perfectly meaningless to her in this hour, but she did not dislike it. It neither hurt her nor troubled her, and when it was over she stretched out her arms in the chilly morning air with the careless, indifferent happiness of a young animal waking at dawn.

39

From *The Mendelssohns on Honeymoon*

On 28 March 1837 the 27-year-old Felix Mendelssohn, the leading German composer of his day, married Cecile Jeanrenaud, whose family, though in origin Huguenot, moved in patrician circles in Frankfurt. On their honeymoon, wending their way up the Rhine towards Freiburg in the southern Black Forest, Cecile kept a diary, with the occasional interjection (in italics) from Felix.

29 March

WE LEFT MAINZ in the excellent carriage and, with warm rain falling, drove through lovely country along the Rhine past the famous wine-growing villages to Worms. Found a dreadful inn there, with a cold room and no trace of any comforts. There was, however, one agreeable thing which I will refrain from mentioning!

31 March

Departure from Worms after the table d'hote dinner, and arrival in Speyer at a nice family inn with obliging hosts. Brief hour by the stove and organization of our room. (*Roast beef with prunes! Genius of a waiter!*)

5 April

In the afternoon Felix played the organ of an atrociously decorated church – a wretched box of whistles.

7 April

Blinded by snow on the roofs as soon as we woke up. Two decisions – one difficult, not to travel – the other easy, 'To stay in bed'.

8 April

Felix parted with reluctance from the waiter, the inn, and from everything in Speyer . . . Arrival at the Hotel de Paris in Strasbourg. Torrent of waiters.

9 April

Felix went off to the Minster in the morning and returned quite enchanted, and dragged me away from *the dirty laundry in which I was deeply immersed* (many thanks for the fine compliment)! I walked with him through the old narrow streets until all of a sudden we stood before this miracle. Mutual astonishment. (*Note: i.e. the Minster was astonished, and we were astonished.*)

13 April

Departure from Strasbourg at nine ... Midday meal at Kenzingen. Blunt conversation with the doctor, who wanted to alarm us on account of the influenza epidemic. In the afternoon the scenery became ever more beautiful as we approached the mountains. Funny little postilion. *Yes!!!*

24 April

Freiburg im Breisgau. In order to add to yet more newly gathered violets, Felix bought me a beautiful bunch of hyancinths, roses, and other spring flowers, which continued to smell sweetly in our room all day and often all night too. In the afternoon we went for a long drive to the Suggental (a valley north of Freiburg). On the way we met a very pretty peasant girl. Felix immediately took notice of her and cast a backward glance at her a couple of times. After that it only needed a few casual facial expressions and words to make me quite stubbornly melancholic and jealous by the time we arrived at the inn at the entrance of the valley. We climbed up the hill behind the inn, where Felix complained about pains. I, however, behaved very badly. After some time I began to blink, without Felix being able to discover why; he pressed me about it, but my thoughts became more and more gloomy, and he more and more exasperated. Meanwhile it had started to rain, and we sat by the inn doors as mute as two fish. We walked up the hill, but nothing helped – Felix's asking and his irritation made me ever more silent and obtuse. I did nothing but weep, tormenting him and myself. The carriage was harnessed in the meantime, and we drove home, at first accompanied by a fine sunset, then by pelting rain, and only when back home did we completely become our old selves again. I told Felix my absurd thoughts, and he was once more kind and affectionate towards me. A firm resolution never to be sulky again without being able to give a man a reason. Felix spent the whole evening playing all my favourite pieces to me so beautifully. Thus was the matrimonial quarrel settled. *Don't be angry with me, dear Cecile.*

Treaclemoon, Yorkshire 1815

Lord Byron

Lord Byron reports to his confidante Lady Melbourne (mother of the future Prime Minister) on what he called his 'treaclemoon'. She was also the aunt of his wife Annabella (Bell) Milbanke whose family home was at Seaham in County Durham.

Halnaby, near Darlington, January 3d. 1815

M Y DEAREST Aunt—We were married yesterday at ten upon ye. Clock—so there's an end of that matter and the beginning of many others.—Bell has gone through all the ceremonies with great fortitude—and I am much as usual and your dutiful nephew. All those who are disposed to make presents may as well send them forthwith and pray let them be handsome—and we wait your congrats. besides—as I am sure your benediction is very essential to all our undertakings.——Lady Mil[bank]e was a little hysterical and fine-feeling—and the kneeling was rather tedious—and the cushions hard—but upon the whole it did vastly well.—The drawing-room at Seaham was the scene of our conjunction—and thus we set off according to approved custom to be shut up by ourselves.——You would think we had been married these 50 years—Bell is fast asleep on a corner of the Sopha, and I am keeping myself awake with this epistle—she desires her love—and mine you have had ever since we were acquainted.

Halnaby, January 7th

Bell & I go on extremely well so far without any other company than our own selves as yet—I got a wife and a cold on the same day—but have got rid of the last pretty speedily—I don't dislike this place—it is just the spot for a Moon—there is my only want a library—and thus I can always amuse myself—even if alone—I have great hopes this match will turn out well—I have found nothing as yet that I could wish changed for the better—but Time does wonders—so I won't be too hasty in my happiness.——I will tell you all about the ceremony when we meet,—it went off very pleasantly—all but the cushions—which were stuffed with Peach-stones I believe—and made me make a face that passed for piety.— My love to all my relatives—by the way what do they mean to give me? I will compromise provided they let me choose what I will have instead of their presents—nothing but what they could very well spare.—

Seaham—January 22d.

Mine Aunt—This day completes my 27th. year of existence and (save a day) my '3 weeks after marriage'—I am 4 years and 3 months older than Bell who will be twenty three on May 17th.—I suppose this is a fair disproportion.——Yesterday I came here— somewhat anent my imperial will—but never mind—you know I am a very good natured fellow—and the more easily governed because not ashamed of being so—and so Bell has her own way— and no doubt means to keep it—for which reason I prodigiously applaud your having written 2 letters to her—and—only 3 to me— and one of them full of Lady Blarney (by way of emetic) &c. &c. which I presume you meant me to show—by the way—I cannot sufficiently admire your cautious style since I became chicken-pecked—but I love thee—ma Tante—and therefore forgive your doubts—implied but not expressed—which will last—till the next scrape I get into—and then we shall wax confidential again—and I shall have good advice—I look upon you as my Good Genius.—I am scribbling in my dressing room—and Bell is in bed—so you ought to think the length of this epistle a large effort of complaisance.

Seaham-February 2nd

The Moon is over—but Bell & I are as lunatic as heretofore—she does as she likes—and don't bore me—and we may win the Dunmow flitch of bacon for anything I know—Mamma and Sir Ralph [Milbanke] are also very good—but I wish the last would not speak his speech at the Durham meeting above once a week after it's first delivery.———I won't betray you if you will only write me something worth betraying.—I suppose your 'C—noir' is + but if + were a Raven or a Griffin I must still take my omens from her flight—I can't help loving her though—I have quite enough at home to prevent me from loving any one essentially for some time to come.—We have two visitors here—a Mrs. & Miss Somebody— the latter plain—and both hum-drum—they have made me so sleepy that I must [say] Goodnight

ever yours most nepotically

B

The Dunmow flitch was awarded each year in that Essex village to what was adjudged to be the most loving couple there. The plus sign stands for Augusta Leigh, Byron's half-sister and recent lover. His love for her, combined with his homosexual inclinations are presumed to be the reasons why his wife left the marital home and demanded a separation at the start of 1816, very shortly after the Byrons' daughter Ada was born.

Samuel Rogers, the banker, poet and gossip, recalled in his Table Talk *a passage from Byron's manuscript* Memoirs, *destroyed after his death.*

On his marriage-night, Byron suddenly started out of his first sleep; a taper, which burned in the room, was casting a ruddy glare through the crimson curtains of the bed; and he could not help exclaiming, in a voice so loud that he wakened Lady B. 'Good God, I am surely in hell!'

When Byron was living in Pisa in 1822, and Shelley was also there with his entourage, a second cousin of Shelley's, an ex-Indian Army officer called Thomas Medwin, joined them and decided he would try to Boswellise Byron. He set about recording his after-dinner conversation, also prompting him with well-placed questions like any modern journalist recording a celebrity interview. The results were published in 1824 under the title Conversations with Lord Byron. *This adds some detail to what Bryon says of his honeymoon in his letters.*

I shall never forget the 2d of January! Lady Byron (Byrn, he pronounced it) was the only unconcerned person present; Lady Noel, her mother, cried; I trembled like a leaf, made the wrong responses, and after the ceremony called her Miss Milbanke.

After the ordeal was over, we set off for a country-seat of Sir Ralph's [Milbanke's]; and I was surprised at the arrangements for the journey, and somewhat out of humour to find a lady's maid stuck between me and my bride. It was rather too early to assume the husband; so I was forced to submit, but it was not with a very good grace. Put yourself in a similar situation, and tell me if I had not some reason to be in the sulks. I have been accused of saying, on getting into the carriage, that I had married Lady Byron out of spite, and because she had refused me twice. Though I was for a moment vexed at her prudery, or whatever you may choose to call it, if I had made so uncavalier, not to say brutal a speech, I am convinced Lady Byron would instantly have left the carriage to me and the maid (I mean the lady's). She had spirit enough to have done so, and would properly have resented the affront.

Our honeymoon was not all sunshine; it had its clouds: and Hobhouse has some letters which would serve to explain the rise and fall in the barometer – but it was never down to zero.

Seventeenth-Century Wedding Nights

*In 1604 the young diplomat Dudley Carleton described what went on
at the bedding of the bride and groom at a court wedding that year.
'There was none of our accustomed forms omitted, of bride cakes, sops
in wine, giving of gloves, laces and points [strings that attached one
piece of clothing to another] . . . and at night there was sewing into the
sheet, casting of the bride's left hose, and twenty other pretty sorceries.'
In the 1680s the traveller Henri Musson went into much greater detail:*

WHEN BED-TIME is come the bride-men pull off the bride's
garters, which she had before untied that they might hang
down and so prevent a curious hand coming too near her knee. This
done, and the garters being fastened to the hats of the gallants, the
bride-maids carry the bride into the bed chamber, where they
undress her and lay her in bed. The bridegroom, who by the help of
his friends is undressed in some other room, comes in his night-
gown as soon as possible to his spouse, who is surrounded by
mother, aunt, sisters, and friends, and without any further
ceremony gets into bed. Some of the women run away, others
remain, and the moment after-wards they are all got together again.
The bride-men take the bride's stockings, and the bride-maids the
bridegroom's; both sit down at the bed's feet and fling the stockings
over their heads, endeavouring to direct them so as that they may
fall upon the married couple. If the man's stockings, thrown by the
maids, fall upon the bride-groom's head, it is a sign she will quickly
be married herself; and the same prognostic holds good of the
woman's stockings thrown by the man. Oftentimes these young
people engage with one another upon the success of the stockings,
though they themselves look upon it to be nothing but sport. While
some amuse themselves agreeably with these little follies, others are
preparing a good posset, which is a kind of caudle, a potion made
up of milk, wine, yolks of eggs, sugar, cinnamon, nutmeg, etc. This
they present to the young couple, who swallow it down as fast as

they can to get rid of so troublesome company; the bridegroom prays, scolds, entreats them to be gone, and the bride says ne'er a word, but thinks the more. If they obstinately continue to retard the accomplishment of their wishes, the bridegroom jumps up in his shirt, which frightens the women and puts them to flight. The men follow them, and the bridegroom returns to the bride.

Musson's account allows us to grasp the references in the anonymous 'Ballad of Arthur Bradley' published in 1661:

> Then 'gan the sun decline,
> And everyone thought it time
> To go unto his home,
> And leave the bridegroom alone.
> To 't, to 't quoth lusty Ned,
> We'll see them both in bed;
> For I will jeopard a joint
> But I will get his codpiece point . . .
> And thus the day was spent
> And no man homeward went,
> That there was such crowding and thrusting
> That some were in danger of bursting,
> To see them go to bed.
> For all the skill they had,
> He was got to his bride,
> And laid him close by her side,
> They got his points and garters,
> And cut them in pieces like quarters . . .
> And then did they foot it and toss it
> Till the cook had brought up the posset,
> The bride-pie was brought forth,
> A thing of mickle worth,
> And so all at the bed side
> Took leave of Arthur and his bride.

But the best verses in this vein are from Robert Herrick's splendidly titled 'Nuptiall Joug, or Epithalamie, on Sir Clipseby Crew and his

47

Lady'. An Epithalamium (Latin) or Epithalamion (Greek) is a poem composed specifically to celebrate a wedding.

And to your more bewitching, see, the proud
Plumpe Bed beare up, and swelling like a cloud,
    Tempting the two too modest; can
    Yee see it brusle like a Swan,
        And you be cold
To meet it, when it woo's and seemes to fold
    The Armes to hugge it? throw, throw
Your selves into the mighty over-flow
        Of that white Pride, and Drowne
    The night, with you, in floods of Downe.

The bed is ready, and the maze of Love
Lookes for the treaders; every where is wove
    Wit and new misterie; read, and
    Put in practise, to understand
        And know each wile,
Each hieroglyphick of a kisse or smile;
    And do it to the full; reach
High in your own conceipt, and some way teach
        Nature and Art, one more
    Play, than they ever knew before.

If needs we must for Ceremonies-sake,
Blesse a *Sack-posset*; Luck go with it; take
    The Night-Charme quickly; you have spells,
    And magicks for to end, and hells,
        To passe; but such
And of such Torture as no one would grutch
    To live therein for ever: Frie
And consume, and grow again to die,
        And live, and in that case,
    Love the confusion of the place.

But since It must be done, dispatch, and sowe

Up in a sheet your Bride, and what if so
    It be with Rock, or walles of Brasse,
    Ye Towre her up, as *Danae* was;
        Thinke you that this,
Or hell it selfe a powerfull Bulwarke is?
    I tell yee no; but like a
Bold bolt of thunder he will make his way,
        And rend the cloud, and throw
    The sheet about, like flakes of snow.

All now is husht in silence; *Midwife-moone*,
With all her *Owle-ey'd* issue begs a boon
    Which you must grant; that's entrance;
    Which extract, all we can call pith
        And quintiscence
Of Planetary bodies; so commence
    All faire *Constellations*
Looking upon yee, that two Nations
        Springing from two such Fires,
    May blaze the vertue of their Sires.

From *Anna Karenina*

Leo Tolstoy

Tolstoy's fascination with the conundrum of marriage lies at the heart of Anna Karenina. *Here, we eavesdrop on the thoughts of Levin, Leo Tolstoy's alter-ego in the novel.*

LEVIN HAD BEEN married three months. He was happy, but not at all in the way he had expected to be. At every step he found his former dreams disappointed, and new, unexpected surprises of happiness. He was happy; but on entering upon family life he saw at every step that it was utterly different from what he had imagined. At every step he experienced what a man would experience who, after admiring the smooth, happy course of a little boat on a lake, should get himself into that little boat. He saw that it was not all sitting still, floating smoothly; that one had to think too, not for an instant to forget where one was floating; and that there was water under one, and that one must row; and that his unaccustomed hands would be sore; and that it was only to look at it that was easy; but that doing it, though very delightful, was very difficult.

As a bachelor, when he had watched other people's married life, seen the petty cares, the squabbles, the jealousy, he had only smiled contemptuously in his heart. In his future married life there could be, he was convinced, nothing of that sort; even the external forms, indeed, he fancied, must be utterly unlike the life of others in everything. And all of a sudden, instead of his life with his wife being made on an individual pattern, it was, on the contrary, entirely made up of the pettiest details, which he had so despised before, but which now, by no will of his own, had gained an extraordinary importance that it was useless to contend against. And Levin saw that the organization of all these details was by no means so easy as he had fancied before. Although Levin believed himself to have the most exact conceptions of domestic life, unconsciously, like all men, he pictured domestic life as the happiest enjoyment of love, with nothing to hinder and no petty cares to distract. He ought, as he conceived the position, to do his work, and to find repose from it in the happiness of love. She ought to be beloved, and nothing more. But, like all men, he forgot that she too would want work. And he was surprised that she, his poetic, exquisite Kitty, could, not merely in the first weeks, but even in the first days of their married life, think, remember, and busy herself about tablecloths, and furniture, about mattresses for visitors, about a tray, about the cook, and the dinner, and so on. While they were still engaged, he had been struck by the definiteness with which she had declined the tour abroad and decided to go into the country, as though she knew of something she wanted, and could still think of something outside her love. This had jarred upon him then, and now her trivial cares and anxieties jarred upon him several times. But he saw that this was essential for her. And, loving her as he did, though he did not understand the reason of them, and jeered at these domestic pursuits, he could not help admiring them. He jeered at the way in which she arranged the furniture they had brought from Moscow; rearranged their room; hung up curtains; prepared rooms for visitors; a room for Dolly; saw after an abode for her new maid; ordered dinner of the old cook; came into collision with Agafea Mihalovna, taking from her the charge of the stores. He saw how the old cook smiled, admiring her, and listening to her inexperienced, impossible orders, how mournfully and tenderly Agafea Mihalovna shook her head over the young mistress's new arrangements. He saw that Kitty was extraordinarily sweet when, laughing and crying, she came to tell him that her maid, Masha, was used to looking upon her as her young lady, and so no one obeyed her. It seemed to him sweet, but strange, and he thought it would have been better without this.

He did not know how great a sense of change she was experiencing; she, who at home had sometimes wanted some favourite dish, or sweets, without the possibility of getting either, now could order what she liked, buy pounds of sweets, spend as much money as she liked, and order any puddings she pleased.

She was dreaming with delight now of Dolly's coming to them with her children, especially because she would order for the children their favourite puddings and Dolly would appreciate all her new housekeeping. She did not know herself why and wherefore, but the arranging of her house had an irresistible attraction for her. Instinctively feeling the approach of spring, and knowing that there would be days of rough weather too, she built her nest as best she could, and was in haste at the same time to build it and to learn how to do it.

This care for domestic details in Kitty, so opposed to Levin's ideal of exalted happiness, was at first one of the disappointments; and this sweet care of her household, the aim of which he did not understand, but could not help loving, was one of the new happy surprises.

Another disappointment and happy surprise came in their

quarrels. Levin could never have conceived that between him and his wife any relations could arise other than tender, respectful and loving, and all at once in the very early days they quarrelled, so that she said he did not care for her, that he cared for no one but himself, burst into tears, and wrung her arms.

This first quarrel arose from Levin's having gone out to a new farmhouse and having been away half an hour too long, because he had tried to get home by a short cut and had lost his way. He drove home thinking of nothing but her, of her love, of his own happiness, and the nearer he drew to home, the warmer was his tenderness for her. He ran into the room with the same feeling, with an even stronger feeling than he had had when he reached the Shtcherbatskys' house to make his offer. And suddenly he was met by a lowering expression he had never seen in her. He would have kissed her; she pushed him away.

'What is it?'

'You've been enjoying yourself,' she began, trying to be calm and spiteful. But as soon as she opened her mouth, a stream of reproach, of senseless jealousy, of all that had been torturing her during that half hour which she had spent sitting motionless at the window, burst from her. It was only then, for the first time, that he clearly understood what he had not understood when he led her out of the church after the wedding. He felt now that he was not simply close to her, but that he did not know where he ended and she began. He felt this from the agonizing sensation of division that he experienced at that instant. He was offended for the first instant, but the very same second he felt that he could not be offended by her, that she was himself. He felt for the first moment as a man feels when, having suddenly received a violent blow from behind, he turns round, angry and eager to avenge himself, to look for his antagonist, and finds that it is he himself who has accidentally struck himself, that there is no one to be angry with, and that he must put up with and try to soothe the pain.

Never afterwards did he feel it with such intensity, but this first time he could not for a long while get over it. His natural feeling urged him to defend himself, to prove to her she was wrong; but to prove her wrong would mean irritating her still more and making the rupture greater that was the cause of all his suffering. One habitual feeling impelled him to get rid of the blame and to pass it on to her. Another feeling, even stronger, impelled him as quickly as possible to smooth over the rupture without letting it grow greater. To remain under such undeserved reproach was wretched, but to make her suffer by justifying himself was worse still. Like a man half-awake in an agony of pain, he wanted to tear out, to fling away the aching place, and coming to his senses, he felt that the aching place was himself. He could do nothing but try to help the aching place to bear it, and this he tried to do.

They made peace. She, recognizing that she was wrong, though she did not say so, became tenderer to him, and they experienced new, redoubled happiness in their love. But that did not prevent such quarrels from happening again, and exceedingly often too, on the most unexpected and trivial grounds. These quarrels frequently arose from the fact that they did not yet know what was of importance to each other and that all this early period they were both often in a bad temper. When one was in a good temper, and the other in a bad temper, the peace was not broken; but when both happened to be in an ill-humour, quarrels sprang up from such incomprehensibly trifling causes, that they could never remember afterwards what they had quarrelled about. It is true that when they were both in a good temper their enjoyment of life was redoubled. But still this first period of their married life was a difficult time for them.

During all this early time they had a peculiarly vivid sense of tension, as it were, a tugging in opposite directions of the chain by which they were bound. Altogether their honeymoon – that is to say, the month after their wedding – from which from tradition Levin expected so much, was not merely not a time of sweetness, but remained in the memories of both as the bitterest and most humiliating period in their lives. They both alike tried in later life to blot out from their memories all the monstrous, shameful incidents of that morbid period, when both were rarely in a normal frame of mind, both were rarely quite themselves.

It was only in the third month of their married life, after their return from Moscow, where they had been staying for a month, that their life began to go more smoothly.

Pisa, 1846

Elizabeth Barrett Browning

Robert Browning recorded his marriage to Elizabeth Barrett in the shortest possible form: 'Sat. Septr. 12, 1846, 1/4 11–11 1/4 a.m.' But there was much lying behind this abbreviation. For two years Browning had regularly visited the invalid Elizabeth at her family home in Wimpole Street before she reached the conclusion that there was no other remedy for her than to marry him clandestinely, without her father's permission (since he certainly would not have given it, if asked), and return to Wimpole Street. They escaped a few days later to the warmth of Italy, and came to rest in Pisa.

THE ONLY TIME I met R.B. clandestinely was in the parish church, where we were married before two witnesses—it was the first and only time. I looked, he says, more dead than alive, and can well believe it, for I all but fainted on the way, and had to stop for sal volatile at a chemist's shop. The support through it all was *my trust in him*, for no woman who ever committed a like act of trust has had stronger motives to hold by. Now may I not tell you that his genius, and all but miraculous attainments, are the least things in him, the moral nature being of the very noblest, as all who ever knew him admit? Then he has had that wide experience of men which ends by throwing the mind back on itself and God; there is nothing incomplete in him, except as all humanity is incompleteness. The only wonder is how such a man, whom any woman could have loved, should have loved *me*; but men of genius, you know, are apt to love with their imagination. Then there is something in the sympathy, the strange, straight sympathy which unites us on all subjects. If it were not that I look up to him, we should be too alike to be together perhaps, but I know my place better than he does, who is too humble. Oh, you cannot think how well we get on after six weeks of marriage! If I suffer again it will not be through *him*.

The change of air has done me wonderful good notwithstanding the fatigue, and I am renewed to the point of being able to throw off most of my invalid habits, and of walking quite like a woman. Mrs. Jameson said the other day, 'You are not *improved*, you are *transformed*.' We have most comfortable rooms here at Pisa, and have taken them for six months, in the best situation for health, and close to the Duomo and Leaning Tower. It is a beautiful, solemn city. . . .

We have been married two months, and every hour has bound me to him more and more; if the beginning was well, still better it is now—that is what he says to me, and I say back again day by day. Then it is an 'advantage' to have an inexhaustible companion who talks wisdom of all things in heaven and earth, and shows besides as perpetual a good humour and gaiety as if he were—a fool, shall I say? or a considerable quantity more, perhaps. As to our domestic affairs, it is not to *my* honour and glory that the 'bills' are made up every week and paid more regularly 'than hard beseems', while dear Mrs. Jameson laughs outright at our miraculous prudence and economy, and declares that it is past belief and precedent that we should not burn the candles at both ends, and the next moment will have it that we remind her of the children in a poem of Heine's who set up housekeeping in a tub, and inquired gravely the price of coffee. . . .

Oh, Pisa is so beautiful and so full of repose, yet not *desolate*; it is rather the repose of sleep than of death. Then after the first ten days of rain, which seemed to refer us fatally to Alfieri's '*piov e ripiove*', came as perpetual a divine sunshine, such cloudless, exquisite weather that we ask whether it may not be June instead of November. Every day I am out walking, while the golden oranges look at me over the walls, and when I am tired Robert and I sit down on a stone to watch the lizards. . . . We have driven up to the foot of mountains, and seen them reflected down in the little pure lake of Aseuno, and we have seen the pine woods, and met the camels laden with faggots all in a line. . . .

We are not in the warm orthodox position by the Arno, because we heard with our ears one of the best physicians of the place advise against it. 'Better,' he said, 'to have cool rooms to live in and warm walks to go out along.' The rooms we have are rather over-cool perhaps; we are obliged to have a little fire in the sitting-room, in the mornings and evenings that is; but I do not fear for the winter, there is too much difference to my feelings between this November and any English November I ever knew. We have our dinner from the Trattoria at two o'clock, and can dine our favourite way on thrushes and chianti with a miraculous cheapness, and no trouble, no cook, no kitchen; the prophet Elijah or the lilies of the field took as little thought for their dining, which exactly suits us. It is a continental fashion which we never cease commending. Then at six we have coffee, and rolls of milk, made of milk, I mean, and at nine our supper (call it supper, if you please) of roast chestnuts and grapes. So you see how primitive we are, and how I forget to praise the eggs at breakfast. The worst of Pisa is, or would be to some persons, that, socially speaking, it has its dullnesses; it is not lively like Florence, not in that way. But we do not want society, we shun it rather. We like the Duomo and the Campo Santo instead.

On December 19, 1846, Elizabeth wrote to Mary Russell Mitford:

Robert and I are deep in the fourth month of wedlock; there has not been a shadow between us, not a *word* (and I have observed that all married people confess to *words*), and that the only change I can lay my finger on in him is simply and clearly an increase of affection. Now, I need not say it if I did not please, and I should not please, you know, to tell a story. The truth is, that I who always did certainly believe in love, yet was as great a sceptic as you about the evidences thereof, and having held twenty times that Jacob's serving fourteen years for Rachel was not too long by fourteen days, I was not a likely person (with my loathing dread of marriage as a loveless state, and absolute contentment with single life as the alternative to the great majorities of marriages), I was not likely to accept a feeling not genuine, though from the hand of Apollo himself, crowned with his various godships. Especially too, in my position, I could not, would not, should not have done it. Then, genuine feelings are genuine feelings, and do not pass like a cloud. We are as happy as people can be, I do believe, yet are living in a way to *try* this new relationship of ours—in the utmost seclusion and perpetual *tête-à-tête*—no amusement nor distraction from without, except some of the very dullest Italian romances which throw us back on the memory of Balzac with reiterated groans. . .

The *padrone* in this house sent us in as a gift (in gracious recognition, perhaps, of our lawful paying of bills) an immense dish of oranges—two hanging on a stalk with the green leaves still moist with the morning's dew—every great orange of twelve or thirteen with its own stalk and leaves. Such a pretty sight! And better oranges, I beg to say, never were eaten, when we are barbarous enough to eat them day by day after our two-o'clock dinner, softening, with the vision of them, the winter which has just shown itself. Almost I have been as pleased with the oranges as I was at Avignon by the *pomegranate* given to me much in the same way. . . Yet, in shame and confusion of face, I confess to not being able to appreciate it properly. Olives and pomegranates I set on the same shelf, to be just looked at and called by their names, but by no means eaten bodily.

Shoreham, 1841

Cecilia Ridley

Cecilia Ridley was the daughter of the distinguished judge Sir James Parke, later Lord Wensleydale. She was born in 1819 and married Sir Matthew Ridley a Northumbrian baronet, at Ampthill in Bedfordshire on 21 September 1841. Next day Cecilia wrote to her mother from Burford Bridge in Surrey, where they spent the first night on their way to their honeymoon at Shoreham in Sussex.

I HAD NO TIME to write last night. We arrived here at half past seven having had a delightful journey, everything as comfortable as possible and myself as happy as you could wish me to be. They gave us two post-boys with red and yellow racing jackets at St. Alban's, but with these we went but slowly, the goodness of the turn-out being all centred in the said jackets. We changed in a *twink* by Vauxhall Bridge and got here it seemed to me very quickly. Heseltine [her maid] began forthwith to Mylady me and assumed an unbounded respect for me. She poured out 'your Ladyship' at every instant and bowed most deferentially, which very much amused me; it required all my self-control to keep my countenance, which however I did and I feel exceedingly majestic. All my silver concerns I had put out in grand style and on the whole I have been a very respectable 'Ladyship'.

This is a nice little spot just under Boxhill with a little quiet garden into which our sitting room opens. Sir Matthew sends you his best love and desires Papa will let him know soon whether he has heard about the dogs. He—that is Sir Matthew—is quite a pet and you have no idea how happy I feel, dearest Mama, although it was a bitter pang to me to leave my dear home.

> *Thursday morning, 23 September 1841, Shoreham*

You have no idea of anything half so charming as this dear little place. I verily believe it was made on purpose for us, it is so exactly what we like in every way. We arrived here for luncheon yesterday and had a most energetic greeting from Mrs. Malloch, [housekeeper] who poured out a great deal of Scotch talk and seemed very anxious and fussy. She had been to Worthing in a light cart to bring a few essentials, she said, which I believe consisted in foot tubs and sponge cakes, but alas she has altogether omitted tin tubs which we both think very essential to our happiness, so two have been summoned from Carlton Terrace and will soon arrive I hope. She has made the house look quite snug and comfortable but still she keeps apologising for the want of smartness. She was very anxious to know what *My Lady* liked for breakfast and got me some prawns. She is in a great rage with the oilman in town for not having sent some scraped beef which was ordered and she declares she *will* make him pay the carriage of it to punish him.

Lady Ridley has sent down her own teapot and coffeepot and

silver candlesticks by the Housekeeper, which I think very nice and kind of her.

We have read a little of Schiller and a little of Milton and I am rather pining for my small wee Coleridge which I have left behind by mistake: however I can do without it till we go back to Ampthill. I must tell you that those of my gowns which have been seen have been *excessively* approved—viz my Indian muslin and two lilac silks. I have made myself very smart with rings and chains and feel an extraordinary pleasure in decking myself out. What do you think of that?

If you have not cut the Blagdon [her husband's home] pine[apple] yet pray do so forthwith, for we had ours yesterday and it was delicious. I think there was never anyone so fortunate, so blessed as I am. I do not mean because of the pine.

25 September 1841, Shoreham

Dearest Mama, I did not write yesterday, feeling idle and having nothing particular to say and some other epistles to concoct. Mrs. Morier [a cousin] had written to me from Brighton begging that we would go over and lunch with her, but we both felt so much averse to it that I was e'en obliged to sit down and compose as amiable an apology as best I could—and indeed I felt that Mrs. M. ought not to expect us to show ourselves in so public a way so very soon. I hope she will not be offended and withhold her gracious favour from us. Yesterday we went to Worthing to do some shopping and take a quiet stroll on the seashore. I am overjoyed that we are here instead of there, for there are quantities of folks there and it is all public and staring. We bought pigeons, a rabbit, candles and all manner of oddments and were rather puzzled as to whether the rabbit should be skinned and prepared by the man or be done at home. Sir M. looked very grave and judgelike when the question was propounded and with due pomp decided at length to his own satisfaction and I have no doubt to that of the rabbit and the poulterer also.

From Sir Matthew to Lady Parke:

29 September 1841, Shoreham

I intended writing you at an earlier hour than an hour before post, but a heavy northern post requiring attention has forestalled you and you may now not get much. In addition to the post Cecilia has been so arch, and so full of 'quips and cranks and wanton wiles' for some time, that my attention has been somewhat distracted.

Two beings more happy in each other's society than we are no imagination could picture and no reality supply. My appreciation of your dear child daily increases, as does my conviction of my capability of ensuring her happiness, and I can write you in the fullest and most confident reliance on this most important and interesting topic. By the way Cecilia desires I will say *the tip of her nose is quite cool*. This I have impressed her is a sure sign of health. I am certain you would think her looking remarkably well. I am not quite sure about her being a Madonna—sometimes she is a Sunny Landscape in fair Italy, sometimes a Symphony in Music, sometimes an exquisitely harmonious picture—a glowing but tempered Claude, sometimes like one from another world, but at all times your dear and darling child and my sincerely and truly loved companion.

From Cecilia to her mother:

30 September 1841, Shoreham

There has been a small affair of honour about towels. I found only very fine smooth ones in my room and requested that I might be permitted to have rough ones, which I discovered was a great mortification to Mrs. Malloch who had had these fine articles especially woven for me. I therefore mean to have some for my face and hands, which will be a desirable arrangement I think. Mrs. M. makes capital orange marmalade and excellent barley water which rivals Papa's yellow bottle.

Would you like to have a specimen of our dinners? Enter first two whitings. They are devoured all but their heads and tails, which depart bereaved of their bodies. Enter next a roast partridge which is placed before me and a small wee bit of lamb before Sir Matthew. We both offer each other some of our respective dishes in the civillest manner and end by each eating our own. N.B. very hot roasted potatoes. Departed the first course. Then enters a smoking pudding which we both look at but, feeling that duty to ourselves and each other forbids our eating any more, we send it away. Enter the cheese—after which the fifth and last act of the play, a sumptuous dessert—grapes, pine[apples], brandy cherries, cakes, French plums. Here, as in all dramas, is the chief interest of the day centred and here are many of the characters put an end to.

I have made various discoveries, amongst which is that I see Sir Matthew's nose is crooked—a fact which I believe even Lady Ridley is not aware of. I forgot to mention, as one of the ornaments of our room, an elegant little extinguisher the handle of which is a beautiful frosted fox creeping up and looking wistfully at a cock perched at the top. It is a dear little funny thing and was a present of Lady Ridley to *Matt*, for I mean to call him so now IF I can summon courage.

Monday, 4 October 1841, Shoreham
I am sorry you miss my Milton, but he is not leading an unprofitable life here, for we read him very often with great satisfaction. All our books have had their turn, and we have bought a small *Childe Harold* that I may be introduced to the beauties of Byron. I assure you we spend our time in a sensible reasonable manner and keep very early wholesome hours: indeed in that respect we are quite an example to you at Ampthill. We had a visit from Mrs. Chatfield, our landlady, the other day and tried to make ourselves very agreeable to her. She is a rich old farmer dame, very fat and in deep mourning, poor thing. She sat on a chair in the middle of the room, very much puzzled about her hands and arms, which appeared to be very much in the way and were very large and conspicuous. She seemed quite pleased with us on the whole and she testifies her regard by bringing offerings of flowers or partridges whenever she comes.

October 1841, Shoreham
Sir M. and I are in a state of feud and discord about the clergyman, to whom I take great objection for many weighty reasons. First because he preaches the same sermon at his two churches the same day. Second because he reads carelessly and looks indifferent. Thirdly because he is always going out shooting, and fourthly—

because I do not like his looks. I see plainly we shall never agree about him. Is it not shocking that we should differ so?

Today after an early lunch we sallied forth for a down ride. We went up to the nearest point and cantered on and on for many miles till we got to a place called Amberley. Some of the squires in the neighbourhood were shooting rabbits on the heights with a pack of beagles and I thought it seemed most tempting sport. It is astonishing how little the *inhabitants* of this country seem to go up on the downs. We have never seen a single gentleman there until today when, besides the *beaglers*, there was a horseman in white trousers.

October 1841, Shoreham

Bismillah, how it rains! There is a sort of reservoir over the portico which is now brimful of water just under Sir Matthew's dressing room window and he experiences every morning a sore temptation to jump into it, only unfortunately he *might* be seen by the Worthing coach for about a minute from the road. He says he should only be taken for a statue, but on the whole we think it advisable and respectable not to do it, so I think he will resist.

From *Larry's Party*

Carol Shields

It is not only the new spouse who becomes more familiar during the honeymoon. Sometimes there are things about oneself that become apparent for the first time.

ON FRIDAY AFTERNOON – blizzards, high winds – Larry and his folks, and his girlfriend, Dorrie, and her family, went downtown to the Law Courts and got married. Dorrie (Dora) Marie Shaw and Laurence John Weller became the Wellers, husband and wife. And on Saturday morning the bridal couple boarded an Air Canada jet for London, England.

Most of the passengers on the plane were wearing jeans and sweaters, but Dorrie had chosen for her travel outfit a new rose-colored polyester blend suit. Now she regretted it, she told Larry. The suit's straight skirt was restrictive so that she couldn't relax and enjoy the trip, and she worried about the hard wrinkles that had formed across her lap. She should have invested in one of those folding travel irons she'd seen on sale. And she'd been a dope not to bring along some spot-lifter for the stain on her jacket lapel. By the time they got to England it would be permanently set. They put dye in airplane food, coloring the gravy dark brown so it looked richer and more appetizing. One of the salesmen at Manitoba Motors, where she works, told her about it. He also told her not to drink carbonated drinks on the flight because of gas. People pass a lot of gas on planes, he'd informed her. It had to do with air pressure. Also, one alcoholic drink on land equals three in the air. This is important information.

If only someone had filled her in about what to wear for a trip like this. She'd never been on a plane before – neither had Larry for that matter – but somehow she'd got the idea that air travel was dressy, especially if you were headed for an international destination, such as London, England. She was all for being casual, as she told Larry, she loved comfortable clothes, he knew that, but wouldn't you think people would make an effort to look nice when they went somewhere important?

'Not everyone's on their honeymoon,' he reminded her.

And that was the moment they heard a special announcement over the P.A. system, the pilot's chuckly, good-sport voice coming at them from the cockpit. 'Ladies and gents, we thought you'd like to know we've got a brand-new married couple aboard our flight today. How about a round of applause, everyone, for Mr. and Mrs. Larry Weller of Winnipeg, Manitoba.'

A stewardess was suddenly standing next to the bride and groom with a bottle of champagne and two glasses and also a corsage to pin on Dorrie's shoulder, compliments of Air Canada.

'Ohh!' Dorrie gave a little shriek. She glowed bright pink. She squirmed in her seat with pleasure. 'This is fabulous. How did you know? Baby roses, I love baby roses, and, look, they match my outfit. It's perfect.'

'I almost died of embarrassment,' Dorrie would tell Larry's mother two weeks later, back home in Winnipeg. 'I bet you anything I was blushing from head to foot. Everyone was just staring at the two of us, and then they started cheering and clapping and peering around their seats at us or standing up so they could see who we were and what we looked like. Was I ever glad I had my new pink outfit on. And Larry with his hair restyled. The newly-weds!'

The champagne sent Dorrie straight to sleep, her feet tucked up under her on the seat, and her head flopped over on Larry's shoulder. The sweet perfume of the roses, which were already darkening, got stirred in with the drone of voices and the dimmed cabin lights and the steady, sleepy vibrations of the plane as it nosed through the night sky.

A little drunk, stranded between the old day and the new, between one continent and another, Larry felt the proprietorial pleasure of having a hushed and satisfied companion by his side. He and Dorrie had boarded the plane under a weight of anticlimax, worn out after the wedding and the wedding lunch at the Delta and from moving his things over to Dorrie's apartment. And they were hollowed out too – that's how it felt – after a long, ecstatic night of sex, then the alarm clock going off at five-thirty, the last-minute packing to do, and Larry's folks arriving, too early, to drive them out to the airport. It was a lot to absorb. But now this unexpected tribute had come to them, to himself and to his wife, Dorrie. A wife, a wife. He breathed the word into the rubbery patterned upholstery of the seat ahead of him – wife.

A daze of contentment fell over him, numbing and fateful, and he shook his head violently to clear his senses – but in the excitement of the last few hours he had forgotten about his recent haircut. Instead of the movement of soft hair flying outward and then landing with a bounce on his neck, that comforting silky familiar flick against his cheek, he sensed only the abruptness of his cold, clean face, how exposed it was beneath the tiny cabin light and how stupidly rigid.

An hour ago he had felt the tug of drowsiness, but now he pledged himself to stay awake. Grief was involved in this decision, and possibly a crude form of gallantry. Staying awake seemed a portion of what was expected of him, part of the new role he had undertaken a mere thirty-six hours earlier, standing in front of a marriage commissioner at the Law Courts with his family and Dorrie's family looking on. 'Marriage is not to be entered into lightly, but with certainty, mutual respect, and a sense of reverence.' These words had been part of the civil ceremony, printed on a little souvenir card he and Dorrie had been given.

He was a husband now, and his chattering, fretful Dorrie, no longer a girlfriend but a wife, was slipping down sideways against his arm, her face damp, pared-down, and sealed shut with sleep. He felt her shoulder lift on every third or fourth breath, lift and then fall in a catching, irregular way, as though her dreams had brought her up against a new, puzzling form of exhaustion, something she would soon be getting used to.

For her sake he would stay alert. He would keep guard over her, drawing himself as straight as possible in his seat without disturbing her sleeping body. He'd clamp his jaw firmly shut in a husbandlike way, patient, forbearing, and keep his eyes steady in the dark. He would do this in order to keep panic at a distance. All that was required of him was to outstare the image in the floating black glass of the window, that shorn, bewildered, fresh-faced stranger whose profile, for all its raw boyishness, reminded him, alarmingly, of – of who?

His father, that's who.

'The very image of his mother,' people used to say about Larry Weller. Same blue eyes. The freckled skin. Dot's gestures. That mouth.

Larry could not recall any mention of a resemblance to his father. He was his mother's boy. Heir to her body, her intensity, and to her frantic private pleasures and glooms.

But now, twenty-seven and a half years into his life, he found that his father had moved in beneath his bones. That nameless part of his face, the hinged area where the jaw approaches the lower ear – he could see now what his flowing hair had hidden: that his father's genes were alive in his body. Even his earlobes, their fleshiness and colour. What was that colour? A hint of strawberry that spread from the ears up the veins to the cheeks, his father's cheeks, curving and surprisingly soft in a man's hard face.

His father's solid, ruddy presence. It arrived, sudden and shocking, and stayed with him throughout the two weeks of his and Dorrie's honeymoon. He met it each morning in the shaving mirror of the various modest hotels where they stayed. What kind of trick was this? He'd turn his eyes slowly toward the mirror, creeping up on his face, and there the old guy would be, larger and more substantial than a simple genetic flicker. His father's flexible loose skin pressed up against the glass, a fully formed image, yawning, hoisting up his sleepy lids, dressed in his work clothes with the bus factory's insignia on the pocket, Air-Rider, his broad shoulders and back bunching forward under Larry's pajamas, and his large red hands reaching out, every finger scarred in one way or another from the upholstery work he did at the plant. And Larry could hear the voice too, his father's high, querulous voice, with the Lancashire notes still in place after twenty-seven years in Canada.

Stu Weller. Master upholsterer. Husband of Dot, father of Midge and Larry.

Homecoming

Mary Clive

In the nineteenth century it was traditional, when a squire returned home from honeymoon with his new bride, for his tenants and employees to meet the carriage some way from the big house, take the horses out of the traces and pull the carriage home themselves. This happened, together with other ordeals, in November 1834 when Charles and Mary Wicksted came back to Betley in Staffordshire, as Mary recounted to her mother, Mrs Meysey-Wigley.

M Y DEAREST, dearest Mammy,
Mr Tollet wrote you a long account of our reception which

really was sublime. I still feel more like Julius Caesar than like my own self after having travelled with thirty men in hand instead of four horses. Charles did his best when it came to the point but they would not hear of a refusal and it really was not near so formidable an operation as I expected. There seemed not to be the least difficulty in drawing the carriage and they were all very orderly. One man used the English Shibboleth once and was called to order immediately by his fellow centaurs who cried out immediately 'No swearing!' and with that exception there was no sound heard except cheering which they stopped every now and then to perform. The village was filled with people from one end to the other—they say there must have been nearly a thousand—and every house had a party assembled. Most of the young élégantes were crowned either with roses or laurels. One horrid thing happened, but happily without injury. One man fell and we Juggernauted him. We felt the jolt of the carriage going over him but most providentially he was not much hurt. . . .

I should have written to you yesterday as I asked Mr Tollet to tell you, but from eleven o'clock to half-past three I was SITTING to an unintermitting influx of visitors and even after that others arrived whom I only avoided by rushing headlong with Charles to go duck shooting. Seventeen souls in all came and I am sorry to say the custom rages so of giving cake and wine in this country that it was necessary to administer it. Lady Egerton was the grandee amongst the callers yesterday and par parenthèse she gave cake and wine when her son married, so anyhow it is only doing like one's fellow creatures to give it also.

Nothing can exceed the kindness of the whole party here. One and all, short and tall, do their utmost, and dear, kind old Mr Tollet still stands pre-eminent le bon des bons. . . .

I went to the Kennels with Charles yesterday and was received with high honours. Old Wells had put on his new coat and had a sprig of laurel in his button-hole. The kennel itself was adorned with laurel and there was a white wand prepared for me to defend myself from the dogs. Wells carried a little white banner by the side of the carriage all through the village on Saturday. . . .

Matrimonial Catechism

Honoré de Balzac

XXXIII. The husband's interest, quite as much as his honour, prescribes that he shall never allow himself a pleasure for which he has not had the wit to awake a longing in his wife.

XXXIV. Pleasure is caused by the union of excitement and affection, hence one can hardly pretend that pleasures are solely material.

XXXVII. If there are differences between one moment of his pleasure and another, a man can always be happy with the same woman.

XXXVIII. The genius of the husband lies in deftly handling the various shades of pleasure, in developing them, and endowing them with a new style, an original expression.

XXXIX. Between two people who do not love one another, this genius is wanton; but the caresses over which love presides are never lascivious.

XLII. When two mortals are joined together by pleasure, all social conventions sleep. This situation conceals a rock on which many ships have struck. A husband is lost if he but once forget that there is a modesty which is independent of veils. Married love should take off and put on the eye-bandage only at the proper time.

XLIII. Power does not lie in striking hard or often, but in striking true.

XLIV. To bring to birth a desire, to feed, develop, foster, excite and satisfy it – is one long poem.

XLV. Pleasures go from distich to quatrain, from quatrain to sonnet, from sonnet to ballad, from ballad to ode, from ode to cantata, from cantata to dithyramb. The husband who begins with the dithyramb is a fool.

LII. The husband who leaves nothing to be craved for is lost.

III Confessions

From *Tolstoy: A Biography*

A. N. Wilson

Honesty, it seems, is not always the best policy when it comes to a new spouse. Here, in his biography of Leo Tolstoy, A.N. Wilson describes how shortly before they were married the writer decided to give his future wife Sofya his diaries to read.

H E WANTED to keep nothing hidden from her. Dr. Bers's [her father's] permission was sought before the notebooks were presented to his daughter, and he gave it. What can he have been thinking of, to give his consent? Did he hope that, when she learnt of Tolstoy's notorious (to Bers and his circle) depravity, Sofya would call the whole thing off? She was an inexperienced eighteen year old. In 1890, twenty-eight years later, she was still poring over them, making fair copies and trying to keep them from the hands of his friends and disciples. 'I don't think I ever recovered from the shock of reading the diaries when I was engaged to him,' she wrote. 'I can still remember the agonising pangs of jealousy, the horror of that first appalling experience of male depravity.' Here it all was, in one great dollop: the early whoring and wenching, the repeated doses of V.D., the gypsies, the Cossack girls, the quasi-homoerotic devotion to his student friends, the flirtations in drawing rooms – a whole catalogue of active sexual life going back twenty years. What was worst was the discovery that he had, until only a month or two before, been besottedly in love with his peasant mistress Aksinya. Yet, the wedding plans went ahead. In their first private interview after she had read the diaries, Sofya was in tears. 'Does this mean that you won't forgive me?' he asked. 'Yes, I forgive you, but it's dreadful,' she said, as she handed the books back to him. Tolstoy had aroused in her a lifelong addiction which was an essential ingredient in their relationship. They did not keep diaries all the time, but in the years when they did so, it was an irresistible game. She had to read his diaries, however hurtful or shocking they were. And, to put the record straight, she had to write her own version of events. It was as though, with a part of themselves, they did not quite exist until they had become characters on a page. On any ordinary human level, Tolstoy's action in showing her the diaries was cruel. But Tolstoy did not live on the ordinary human level. Whatever he thought he was doing when he showed her the books, he was actually putting her to the most important test of all: not, would she forgive him? but, would she read him? She passed the test. With a profound, intuitive intelligence, which gave her no pleasure, she latched on immediately to Tolstoy's need for absolution through the written word. It was something which bound them together very deeply, even when they felt hatred and dread of one another. She was his reader. She survived all the ups and downs of married life until this fact came to be challenged, and rival readers tried to move in and take her place. Even less than most people on their wedding day can Sofya Andreyevna have known what she was doing when she married her husband. But it is wrong to think of her as a witless victim. It hurt her very much to be in love with the monstrous hero of her own short story. But it was his monstrosity that she loved. And from the very beginning, she knew that her reading of the diaries put her in a unique position in the world. It was a position of power which she could not resist.

After an agitated week in which she and her mother bought the trousseau and made the arrangements, the day dawned. First thing in the morning, Tolstoy himself called at the Bers apartment in a state of confusion and excitement. He doubted, after all, whether they were doing the right thing. 'I have come to say,' he said, 'that there is still time. … All this business can be put a stop to.' Sofya started to cry. Did it mean that he was coming to cancel the wedding? 'Yes, if you don't love me.' More tears. Lyubov Alexandrovna burst into the room to find Tolstoy trying to console her daughter. All three of them must in that moment have wondered whether or not he was right. It was a crazy situation. But

Lyubov Alexandrovna had the reputation of her daughter to think of. All Moscow had been told. The invitations had been sent out, the church had been booked, the presents had been received, the dresses chosen. 'You've chosen a fine time for upsetting her!' said the future mother-in-law, and banished Tolstoy from the house, reminding him of the time of the wedding that evening.

We do not know how Tolstoy spent the day. Far too late, he returned to his apartments to change, and was told by a despondent servant that there was nothing to change into. All his clean clothes, and all his linen, had been packed and sent ahead with Tolstoy's brother Sergey Nikolayevich to Yasnaya Polyana. There was not so much as a clean shirt to be found.

The wedding was scheduled for eight o'clock at night in the Kremlin church of the Nativity of Our Lady. By seven o'clock, Sofya Andreyevna was waiting in her wedding dress. The custom was for the groomsman to come and tell the bride that the groom was waiting for her at the church. An hour later, he had still not arrived. At half-past eight, she and her family had begun to despair. Tolstoy, who had seemed in the morning so wild and uncertain, had evidently decided to do a bunk. Just then, Tolstoy's manservant arrived to explain what had happened to the luggage and the shirts, followed not long after by the groomsman to say that a shirt had at last been found and that the groom was now awaiting the bride in church. An hour late, and in a state of great distress, Sofya Andreyevna went to greet her lord. As he led her to the altar, the choir sang 'Come O Dove'. There were three hundred guests, who had been waiting for over an hour to witness the extended nuptial celebrations, the lighting and snuffing of candles, the chanting, the holding of crowns over the heads of the bride and groom. Sofya Andreyevna cried during most of the service.

Afterwards, when she was about to get into the carriage and be driven away by her new husband, she turned to her mother, threw herself into Lyubov's arms, and sobbed like a child. 'If leaving your family means such great sorrow to you, then you cannot love me very much,' Tolstoy said to her, when the carriage was on the move.

They broke the journey at a place called Birulyevo. Tolstoy had already established in the coach that his bride knew the facts of life. The innkeeper opened up the best suite – 'The Emperor's chambers' – and the young Countess sat shy on a sofa, unable to speak. A servant brought in a samovar. Still, silence and gloom, and what Tolstoy regarded as morbid timidity. 'Well,' he said, as they sat silently and watched the steaming samovar, 'show that you are the mistress. Come on, pour the tea!' She was so shy with him that she did not even dare to call her husband by name.

She had already read the diaries. Had she noticed in Tolstoy how swiftly sexual gratification turned to feelings of intense 'morbidity' in himself? Had she noticed how self-hatred in this area so easily became hatred of the person who had first excited all these messy feelings? Or was she merely dreading becoming another name in that notebook, that sad catalogue?

The next day, after another long journey, the pair arrived at Yasnaya Polyana. It was only a couple of months since she had called there with her mother, a flirtatious schoolgirl. Now she returned as mistress of the place. Her brother-in-law Sergey Nikolayevich was waiting to greet them as the coach pulled up at the front door, and so was Tante Toinette who, Tolstoy noticed, was 'already preparing to suffer', now that her favourite little nephew had found himself a bride. Auntie, as the custom was, held up an icon and Sofya Andreyevna genuflected and kissed it, before greeting her new relations. Sergey stood offering them bread and salt on a tray. That night, Tolstoy had a bad dream. Whether by this he means a nightmare or a wicked dream, it is hard to tell, but two other words are added. 'Not her.'

From *Tess of the D'Urbervilles*

Thomas Hardy

Before marrying Angel Clare, Tess Durbeyfield tries to make a clean breast of her earlier relationship with, and child by, the unscrupulous Alec D'Urberville, in a letter which she slips under Angel's door. When she discovers that the letter has slipped under the carpet as well, and that Angel has not seen it, she loses her nerve, destroys the letter and takes her mother's advice to keep quiet about her past. Here they are on their wedding night, one of the most fateful in all English literature.

A STEADY GLARE from the now flameless embers painted the sides and back of the fireplace with its colour, and the well-polished andirons, and the old brass tongs that would not meet. The underside of the mantel-shelf was flushed with the high-coloured light, and the legs of the table nearest the fire. Tess's face and neck reflected the same warmth, which each gem turned into an Aldebaran or a Sirius—a constellation of white, red, and green flashes, that interchanged their hues with her every pulsation.

'Do you remember what we said to each other this morning about telling our faults?' he asked abruptly, finding that she still remained immovable. 'We spoke lightly perhaps, and you may well have done so. But for me it was no light promise. I want to make a confession to you, Love.'

This, from him, so unexpectedly apposite, had the effect upon her of a Providential interposition.

'You have to confess something?' she said quickly, and even with gladness and relief.

'You did not expect it? Ah—you thought too highly of me. Now listen. Put your head there, because I want you to forgive me, and not to be indignant with me for not telling you before, as perhaps I ought to have done.'

How strange it was! He seemed to be her double. She did not speak, and Clare went on—

'I did not mention it because I was afraid of endangering my chance of you, darling, the great prize of my life—my Fellowship I call you. My brother's Fellowship was won at his college, mine at Talbothays Dairy. Well, I would not risk it. I was going to tell you a month ago—at the time you agreed to be mine, but I could not; I thought it might frighten you away from me. I put it off; then I thought I would tell you yesterday, to give you a chance at least of escaping me. But I did not. And I did not this morning, when you proposed our confessing our faults on the landing—the sinner that I was! But I must, now I see you sitting there so solemnly. I wonder if you will forgive me?'

'O yes! I am sure that——'

'Well, I hope so. But wait a minute. You don't know. To begin at the beginning. Though I imagine my poor father fears that I am one of the eternally lost for my doctrines, I am of course, a believer in good morals, Tess, as much as you. I used to wish to be a teacher of men, and it was a great disappointment to me when I found I could not enter the Church. I admired spotlessness, even though I could lay no claim to it, and hated impurity, as I hope I do now. Whatever one may think of plenary-inspiration, one must heartily subscribe to these words of Paul: 'Be thou an example—in word, in conversation, in charity, in spirit, in faith, in purity.' It is the only safeguard for us poor human beings. 'Integer vitae,' says a Roman poet, who is strange company for St. Paul—

The man of upright life, from frailties free,
Stands not in need of Moorish spear or bow.

Well, a certain place is paved with good intentions, and having felt all that so strongly, you will see what a terrible remorse it bred in me when, in the midst of my fine aims for other people, I myself fell.'

He then told her of that time of his life to which allusion has been made when, tossed about by doubts and difficulties in London, like a cork on the waves, he plunged into eight-and-forty hours' dissipation with a stranger.

'Happily I awoke almost immediately to a sense of my folly,' he continued. 'I would have no more to say to her, and I came home. I have never repeated the offence. But I felt I should like to treat you with perfect frankness and honour, and I could not do so without telling this. Do you forgive me?'

She pressed his hand tightly for an answer.

'Then we will dismiss it at once and for ever!—too painful as it is for the occasion—and talk of something lighter.'

'O, Angel—I am almost glad—because now *you* can forgive *me*! I have not made my confession. I have a confession, too—remember, I said so.'

'Ah, to be sure! Now then for it, wicked little one.'

'Perhaps, although you smile, it is as serious as yours, or more so.'

'It can hardly be more serious, dearest.'

'It cannot—O no, it cannot!' She jumped up joyfully at the hope. 'No, it cannot be more serious, certainly,' she cried, 'because 'tis just the same! I will tell you now.'

She sat down again.

Their hands were still joined. The ashes under the grate were lit by the fire vertically, like a torrid waste. Imagination might have beheld a Last Day luridness in this red-coaled glow, which fell on his face and hand, and on hers, peering into the loose hair about her brow, and firing the delicate skin underneath. A large shadow of her shape rose upon the wall and ceiling. She bent forward, at which each diamond on her neck gave a sinister wink like a toad's; and pressing her forehead against his temple she entered on her story of her acquaintance with Alec d'Urberville and its results [his rape of her], murmuring the words without flinching and with her eyelids drooping down.

Her narrative ended; even its re-assertions and secondary explanations were done. Tess's voice throughout had hardly risen higher than its opening tone; there had been no exculpatory phrase of any kind, and she had not wept.

But the complexion even of external things seemed to suffer transmutation as her announcement progressed. The fire in the grate looked impish—demoniacally funny, as if it did not care in the least about her strait. The fender grinned idly, as if it too did not care. The light from the water-bottle was merely engaged in a chromatic problem. All material objects around announced their irresponsibility with terrible iteration. And yet nothing had changed since the moments when he had been kissing her; or rather, nothing in the substance of things. But the essence of things had changed.

When she ceased the auricular impressions from their previous endearments seemed to hustle away into the corners of their brains, repeating themselves as echoes from a time of supremely purblind foolishness.

Clare performed the irrelevant act of stirring the fire; the intelligence had not even yet got to the bottom of him. After stirring the embers he rose to his feet; all the force of her disclosure had imparted itself now. His face had withered. In the strenuousness of his concentration he treadled fitfully on the floor. He could not, by any contrivance, think closely enough; that was the meaning of his vague movement. When he spoke it was in the most inadequate, commonplace voice of the many varied tones she had heard from him.

'Tess!'

'Yes, dearest.'

'Am I to believe this? From your manner I am to take it as true. O you cannot be out of your mind! You ought to be! Yet you are not. ... My wife, my Tess—nothing in you warrants such a supposition as that?'

'I am not out of my mind,' she said.

'And yet—' He looked vacantly at her, to resume with dazed senses: 'Why didn't you tell me before? Ah, yes, you would have told me, in a way —but I hindered you, I remember!'

These and other of his words were nothing but the perfunctory babble of the surface while the depths remained paralysed. He turned away, and bent over a chair. Tess followed him to the middle of the room where he was, and stood there staring at him with eyes that did not weep. Presently she slid down upon her knees beside his foot, and from this position she crouched in a heap.

'In the name of our love, forgive me!' she whispered with a dry mouth. 'I have forgiven you for the same!'

And, as he did not answer, she said again—

'Forgive me as you are forgiven! *I* forgive *you*, Angel.'

'You—yes, you do.'

'But you do not forgive me?'

'O Tess, forgiveness does not apply to the case! You were one person; now you are another. My God—how can forgiveness meet such a grotesque—prestidigitation as that!'

He paused, contemplating this definition; then suddenly broke into horrible laughter—as unnatural and ghastly as a laugh in hell.

'Don't—don't! It kills me quite, that!' she shrieked. 'O have mercy upon me—have mercy!'

He did not answer; and, sickly white, she jumped up.

'Angel, Angel! what do you mean by that laugh?' she cried out. 'Do you know what this is to me?'

He shook his head.

'I have been hoping, longing, praying, to make you happy! I have thought what joy it will be to do it, what an unworthy wife I shall be if I do not! That's what I have felt, Angel!'

'I know that.'

'I thought, Angel, that you loved me—me, my very self! If it is I you do love, O how can it be that you look and speak so? It frightens me! Having begun to love you, I love you for ever—in all changes, in all disgraces, because you are yourself. I ask no more. Then how can you, O my own husband, stop loving me?'

'I repeat, the woman I have been loving is not you.'

'But who?'

'Another woman in your shape.'

She perceived in his words the realization of her own apprehensive foreboding in former times. He looked upon her as a species of impostor; a guilty woman in the guise of an innocent one. Terror was upon her white face as she saw it; her cheek was flaccid, and her mouth had almost the aspect of a round little hole. The horrible sense of his view of her so deadened her that she staggered; and he stepped forward, thinking she was going to fall.

'Sit down, sit down,' he said gently. 'You are ill; and it is natural that you should be.'

She did sit down, without knowing where she was, that strained look still upon her face, and her eyes such as to make his flesh creep.

'I don't belong to you any more, then; do I, Angel?' she asked helplessly. 'It is not me, but another woman like me that he loved, he says.'

The image raised caused her to take pity upon herself as one who was ill-used. Her eyes filled as she regarded her position further; she turned round and burst into a flood of self-sympathetic tears.

Clare was relieved at this change, for the effect on her of what had happened was beginning to be a trouble to him only less than the woe of the disclosure itself. He waited patiently, apathetically, till the violence of her grief had worn itself out, and her rush of weeping had lessened to a catching gasp at intervals.

'Angel,' she said suddenly, in her natural tones, the insane, dry voice of terror having left her now. 'Angel, am I too wicked for you and me to live together?'

'I have not been able to think what we can do.'

'I shan't ask you to let me live with you, Angel, because I have no right to! I shall not write to mother and sisters to say we be married, as I said I would do; and I shan't finish the good-hussif' I cut out and meant to make while we were in lodgings.'

'Shan't you?'

'No, I shan't do anything, unless you order me to; and if you go away from me I shall not follow 'ee; and if you never speak to me any more I shall not ask why, unless you tell me I may.'

'And if I do order you to do anything?'

'I will obey you like your wretched slave, even if it is to lie down and die.'

'You are very good. But it strikes me that there is a want of harmony between your present mood of self-sacrifice and your past mood of self-preservation.'

These were the first words of antagonism. To fling elaborate sarcasms at Tess, however, was much like flinging them at a dog or cat. The charms of their subtlety passed by her unappreciated, and she only received them as inimical sounds which meant that anger ruled. She remained mute, not knowing that he was smothering his affection for her. She hardly observed that a tear descended slowly upon his cheek, a tear so large that it magnified the pores of the skin over which it rolled, like the object lens of a microscope. Meanwhile reillumination as to the terrible and total change that her confession had wrought in his life, in his universe, returned to him, and he tried desperately to advance among the new conditions in which he stood. Some consequent action was necessary; yet what?

'Tess,' he said, as gently as he could speak, 'I cannot stay—in this room—just now. I will walk out a little way.'

He quietly left the room, and the two glasses of wine that he had poured out for their supper—one for her, one for him—remained on the table untasted. This was what their *Agape* had come to. At tea, two or three hours earlier, they had, in the freakishness of affection, drunk from one cup.

The closing of the door behind him, gently as it had been pulled to, roused Tess from her stupor. He was gone; she could not stay. Hastily flinging her cloak around her she opened the door and followed, putting out the candles as if she were never coming back.

From *The Stone Diaries*

Carol Shields

We should leave the last word on the subject of wedding-night confessions to Carol Shields. In her novel The Stone Diaries *(1993) Daisy Goodwill marries, for the second time, in 1936, Barker Flett, who is in his fifties. Flett is a scientist, by then head of Agricultural Research in Ottawa. His mother had raised Daisy after her own mother died, but he has not seen her since she was 11, though they have corresponded regularly.*

AT HIS AGE he could not face the fret and fuss and jitters of a full-scale wedding, and so they were married quickly, quietly, in a judge's chambers. August 17th, 1936. The telegram dispatched to

Cuyler and Maria Goodwill in Bloomington minutes before the ceremony was framed in the past tense: 'We have just been married. Letter to follow.'

Both Daisy and Barker Flett felt cowardly about this announcement, and awaited a reply with some embarrassment.

The erotic realm is our nearest approach to the wild half of our nature. So thinks Barker Flett. There is a part of the human self that is unclassifiable. This is what he must learn to accept. And to be open to visitations of ardor without the thought of shame stealing in through every window. Why must everything be flattened by the iron of goodness and badness? Why?

He confesses to Daisy that he has in the past paid money for the attentions of women. She, in turn, resting her fingers lightly on his hair, confesses her true state: that she is untouched (her word), that something went wrong in her brief marriage to Harold A. Hoad; she's not sure what it was, but she may possibly have been at fault in the matter. He does not want to hear this; at this time in his life he needs all Daisy's strong feelings for himself.

These kinds of confessions, these points of honour, are almost always comic when viewed up close – and equally comic when viewed from a distance. All that unnecessary humiliation and preening honesty. And afterward regret. Was any of it really necessary? Of course not.

Daisy and Barker Flett have three children.

IV Unusual Arrangements

Charles Kingsley

Victorian sexuality had many aspects which still surprise today. The wedding night and honeymoon of the Reverend Charles Kingsley, remembered today as the author of The Water Babies, *is a prime example. He was immensely influential in his own day, amongst other things because of his efforts to mitigate the impact of industrialisation on the quality of life in an age of laissez-faire capitalism. But his grip on reality deserted him when it came to his own love life. He was as highly sexed as he was high minded and no doubt the great amount of outdoor physical exercise in which he indulged, his 'muscular Christianity', was something of a safety valve. His fiancée Fanny Grenfell sounds to have been as keen on the physical side of their forthcoming marriage as him. Yet a few months before their marriage in January 1844 he was moved to write to her:*

I WISH TO show you and my God that I have gained purity and self-control, that intense though my love is for your body, I do not love it but as an expression of your soul. And therefore, when we are married, will you consent to remain for the first month in my arms a virgin bride, a sister only?

He went on to argue that such self-denial would lead to an eventual state of permanent coition in heaven.

Will not these thoughts give us more perfect delight when we lie naked in each other's arms, clasped together toying with each other's limbs, buried in each other's bodies, struggling, panting, dying for a moment. Shall we not feel then, even then, that there is more in store for us, that those thrilling writhings are but dim shadows of a union which shall be perfect?

Fanny agreed; a little later Kingsley gave a more prosaic reason for their mutual abstinence.

I have been thinking over your terror at seeing me undressed, and I feel that I should have the same feeling in a minor degree to you, till I had learnt to bear the blaze of your naked beauty. You do not know how often a man is struck powerless in body and mind on his wedding night.

There is no description of their wedding night but, next best, there is 'a long, wanton letter about what you will do to me and I will do to you at Cheddar', (where they were to honeymoon) which Kingsley had requested Fanny write some weeks before. The St Elizabeth referred to was a medieval saint but Kingsley's life of her never got much beyond an introduction, and a series of drawings often with an obviously sadistic element and often of naked women bearing a strong resemblance to Fanny.

After dinner I shall perhaps feel worn out so I shall just lie on your bosom and say nothing but feel a great deal, and you will be very loving and call me your poor child. And then you will perhaps show me your Life of St Elizabeth, your wedding gift. And then after tea we will go up to rest! We will undress and bathe and then you will come to my room, and we will kiss and love very much and read psalms aloud together, and then we will kneel down and pray in our night dresses. Oh! What solemn bliss! How hallowing! And then you will take me up in your arms, will you not? And lay me down in bed. And then you will extinguish our light and come to me! How I will open my arms and then sink into yours! And you will kiss me and clasp me and we will both praise God alone in the dark night with His eye shining down upon us and His love enclosing us. After a time we shall sleep!

And yet I fear you will yearn so for fuller communion that you will not be so happy as me. And I too perhaps shall yearn, frightened as I am! But every yearning will remind me of our self-denial, your sorrow for sin, your strength for repentance. And I shall glory in my yearning, please God!

When they did consummate the marriage, presumably sometime in February, Fanny immediately became pregnant. After Cheddar they went to stay with Kingsley's father who was rector of St Luke's in Chelsea. Twelve years later Kingsley found he still could not work in what had been their bedroom in the rectory there, because of the memories of their nights of passion.

From *Small Island*

Andrea Levy

In Andrea Levy's novel, Small Island, *Hortense suggests to Gilbert that she lend him her savings so he can go to England from the West Indies. 'We will be married and you can send for me to come to England . . . A single woman cannot travel on her own - it would not look good. But a married woman might go anywhere she pleased.'*

GILBERT CUT A SURPRISING smart figure at the wedding. We were both astonished to see the other looking so elegant. He in a grey double-breasted suit, his trousers wide, his cuffs clean, his shirt white, his tie secured with a dainty knot, his hair nicely oiled and waving. I, in a white dress with a frill at the hem, white shoes with heels and a hat trimmed with netting sitting at a fashionable angle on my head. Gilbert, taking my hand in front of the altar, whispered softly, 'You look nice.' …

On returning to the Andersons' house the family insisted on making Gilbert and I a party, no matter how I protested. Mr Anderson perused his records asking, 'Gilbert, you like Count Basie?'

'Basie is the best.' …

What did it matter to me that the tuneless music was so loud my head throbbed? Or that the man I had married was prancing around the room screeching while the two little Anderson boys stood one on each of his feet, clinging to his legs, calling out for everyone to watch them? I did not care that on eight occasions I had to find an excuse for why I would not dance as everyone else was. Or that Mrs Anderson painfully landed her abundant backside on me after a complicated step and spin from her husband.

'You like Ellington, Gilbert?'

'Ellington is the best.'

I only smiled when Mr Anderson, leaning on Gilbert, both of them drunk on rum and diddling like schoolgirls, finally said, 'Gilbert, you know nothing about jazz, do you?'

'Well you have me there. No.' Then, as they toasted each other, Gilbert, now leaning on Mr Anderson, said, 'And let me tell you one more thing—I caan dance. But, hush, do not tell Hortense. You see how this woman likes a party? She will regret marrying a man who has two left feet.'

So when I said, 'Gilbert, don't you have to get ready for your trip tomorrow?' and everyone looked at me, I was not as embarrassed as I might have been.

Even when Mr Anderson winked at Gilbert, slapped his back and said to me, 'Of course, Hortense, you want to get your husband on his own on your wedding night.' And Mrs Anderson clapping her hands squealed with amusement.

Gilbert came to the room with two boys still clinging to his legs. 'You must go, boys. I have to play with my wife now.'

He tried to peel them off but they clung tighter, rattling with childish laughing. Mrs Anderson had to be called. She came into the room, grabbed the boys and tucked one under each of her arms. 'Come, we must leave,' she told them. Looking to me she smiled, saying, 'Hortense has something she must show Gilbert.' Then, with both boys howling, she took them from the room.

'So we are alone,' Gilbert said.

He had just one small bag. One small bag for someone travelling so far to start a new life in England. 'Is that all you have?'

He looked to his meagre luggage, then said, 'And I have you, of course, Hortense.'

I took a breath before asking, 'You will call for me? You won't get to England forgetting all about me and leave me here?'

He came closer to me from across the room. He put his hands on my shoulders. 'Of course not – we have a deal. You are my wife.'

'There may be women who will turn your head in England.'

'Hortense,' he said, holding me firmer, 'we have a deal. I give you my word I will send for you.'

Then, for the first time, he kissed me gently on my mouth. His breath smelt of rum but his lips were warm and soft against mine. I closed my eyes. When I opened them again he kissed me once more but this time the man poked his wet slippery tongue into my mouth. I choked finding myself on his wriggling organ. I could not breathe. I backed away from him, panting with the effort of catching my breath.

Turning away, I took off my hat to place it delicately in the cupboard. I could have been no more than five seconds but when I turned back Gilbert stood before me as naked as Adam. And between his legs a thing grew. Rising up like a snake charmed – with no aid, with no help – it enlarged before my eyes, rigid as a tree trunk and swelling into the air. I could do nothing but stare.

'Come to me, Hortense,' this man said, holding out his arms for me.

I was going nowhere near this thing. 'What is that?'

'What this?' he said, modelling it for me like it was something to be proud of. 'This is my manhood.'

'Keep that thing away from me!' I said.

'But, Hortense, I am your husband.' He laughed, before realising I was making no joke. The fleshy sacks that dangled down between his legs, like rotting ackees, wobbled. If a body in its beauty is the work of God, then this hideous predicament between his legs was without doubt the work of the devil.

'Do not come near me with that thing,' I screamed.

Gilbert crossed the room in two steps to place his hand over my mouth. 'Ssh, you want everyone to hear?'

I bit his hand and while he leaped back yelping I, trembling, ran to the door.

'Hortense, Hortense. Wait, wait, nah.' He sprang at the door, closing it with a slam. And as he stood panting before me I, terrified, could feel that thing tapping on me as a finger would.

But Gilbert's hands surrendered into the air and that wretched ugly extremity began deflating, sagging, drooping, until it dangled, flip-flopping like a dead bird in a tree. He held his palms up, 'Okay, okay, I will not touch you, see,' then, glancing down cupped his hands over his disgustingness. 'It's gone, it's gone,' he said.

He struggled into his trousers hopping round the room like a jackass while saying, 'Listen, listen to me.' Buttoning his trousers he tried to look into my face. 'Look at me, Hortense, look at me, nah.' When I finally looked on him he let out a long breath. Calming himself he began, 'Good now listen. You listening to me?' As I turned my face away, he tenderly took my chin and moved it back to him. 'You sleep in the bed and I will sleep here on the floor. I will not touch you. I promise. Look – I will give you my RAF salute.' He stepped back saluting his hand to his forehead, smiling, showing me his gold tooth. 'There, that is a promise from a gentleman. I will sleep on the floor. And tomorrow I will rise early, go to the ship and sail to the Mother Country for us both. Because, oh, boy, Miss Mucky Foot,' he shook his head slowly back and forth, 'England will need to be prepared for your arrival.'

From *Thy Hand Great Anarch!*
Nirad Chaudhuri

In this sequel to his autobigraphy, Nirad Chaudhuri, the Bengali writer, describes his marriage in 1932 to Amiya Dhar, who went on to be a writer herself. An eccentric intellectual whose books infuriated many in India, Chaudhuri lived the last thirty years of his life in Britain and died in Oxford in 1999 at the age of 101.

A NYWAY, IN THE afternoon I presented myself in my brother's house in all my splendour or rather elegance, and waited for my friends, who were to form the bridgroom's party. I think they were to be about thirty, Bibhuti Babu being one of them. He arrived and had a good look at me, and expressed his admiration for my clothes. But he did not even wink at me to reassure me about the loan.

The evening approached, and the cars, lent or hired, were ready. But Ashoke Babu with his decorated car had not arrived. Message after message came from the *Modern Review* office which was nearby, to inform us that he was delayed at the florist's and he asked us to wait until he arrived. I was unwilling to go before he came and sacrifice so much grandeur. But my father got very impatient, because the wedding time fixed by the priests astrologically was rather early. I do not know how for once I lost my will and did not resist when I was shuffled into the car lent by my dentist friend. Off we went, to my dismay.

But when my car, in which my nephew accompanied me, was going along Wellington Street I saw Ashoke Babu's decorated limousine going along in the opposite direction. I looked at my nephew, pointed in that direction, making an unintelligible sign to follow the car, so that I could change over and get into the other car. But my nephew did not understand, and I could not be articulate. We sped on and I got down at the bride's house in high dudgeon. I looked very peevish, not knowing that the womenfolk of the house were peeping at me from a vantage point. When my father came I told him that I had seen the car and he should apologize properly to Ashoke Babu. He arrived later, and after the banquet took some of my friends on a jaunt in the decorated car. The next day he took me and my bride home in the same car, but it was not decorated.

For the time being, I lost touch with my family and friends, being taken over by the bride's family. Only a servant who was accompanying me as valet remained behind to give change of clothes, bathing and shaving things, etc. The ceremony was gone through with great *éclat*, my friends shouting all the time when my bride was going round me seven times. I must confess that after the ceremony was over, I was more pleased with the goods and chattels I had got than with my wife. In the way of furniture I got a complete bedroom suite in solid teak (no veneer), mahogany finished, as I learned later, according to the bride's wishes. For myself I got a desk, chair, and revolving bookshelf. I was given silk clothes, including even silken underwear, and a pair of claret-coloured patent leather pumps. All this was supplemented by 22 carat gold cuff links and studs, a ring, and an 18 carat gold wrist watch. I felt very happy and soothed. My wife, I should add, came with over one kilogramme of solid 22 carat gold.

It was near midnight when, after breaking my fast, I was taken to the room where the bedroom suite had been placed. At first I was alone, and looked at the bed. I had never slept in a bed like that. There were obviously two mattresses on which was spread a very fine bedsheet. There were two big and deep pillows with fringed pillowcases for each of us. I also noticed a bedspread of linen embroidered in silk thread folded nearby. The room was fragrant with bunches of tuberose and garlands of jasmine. The mild fragrance of the creeper *Quisqualis indica* was coming up through a window, which was open to brilliant moonlight.

I was terribly uneasy at the prospect of meeting as wife a girl who was a complete stranger to me, and when she was brought in by my eldest sister-in-law and left standing before me I had nothing to say. I saw only a very shy smile on her face, and timidly she came and sat by my side on the edge of the bed. I do not remember how after that both of us drifted to the pillows, to lie down side by side.[1] Then the first words were exchanged. She took up one of my arms, felt it and said: 'You are so thin. I shall take good care of you.' I did not thank her, and I do not remember that beyond noting the words I even felt touched. The horrible suspense about European music had reawakened in my mind, and I decided to make a clean breast of it at once and look the sacrifice, if it was called for, straight in the face, and begin romance on such terms as were offered to me. I asked her timidly after a while: 'Have you listened to any European music?' She shook her head to say 'No.' Nonetheless, I took another chance and this time asked: 'Have you heard the name of a man called Beethoven?' She nodded and signified 'Yes.' I was reassured, but not wholly satisfied. So I asked yet again: 'Can you spell the

---

1. Of course, fully dressed. We Hindus (at least as long as we remain Hindu) consider both extremes – fully clad and fully naked – to be modest, and everything in between as grossly immodest. No decent man wants his wife to be an *allumeuse*.

92

name?' She said slowly: 'B, E, E, T, H, O, V, E, N.' I felt very encouraged. After that we talked about other things aimlessly and dozed off...

During the first few days I walked on air. I was married on a Thursday. The banquet at our house, for which supplementary money had to be borrowed from Bibhuti Babu, was given on the next Sunday. It went off very well. All my friends, including Bibhuti Babu and Ashoke Babu, came. I presented myself to them in all my glory, dressing myself this time with the clothes and jewellery given to me from the bride's side. I went up to Ashoke Babu and asked: 'How do I look?' He examined me from head to foot and said in his usual truthful manner: 'Like chewing gum wrapped up in gold leaf.' On that occasion he and my other colleagues presented my wife with a pair of gold earrings or rather ear pendants and a fine sari, all packed in a box covered with Indian handwoven silk, and with a greeting card which had a large design in colours taken from one of the painted ceilings of the Ajanta caves.

Three in a Marriage, 1802

Dorothy Wordsworth

In August 1802 the poet William Wordsworth took advantage of the brief Peace of Amiens to go to France with his sister Dorothy. His object was to see his daughter Anne-Caroline, born ten years before to his French lover Annette Vallon. He had not seen them in the intervening years of war though he had provided financial support. When brother and sister returned, they did not go straight back to their home at Grasmere in the Lake District, but to their friends since childhood, the Hutchinson family, now farming near Scarborough on the Yorkshire coast. William was to marry Mary Hutchinson, who would not so much replace his sister Dorothy in his life as be in addition to her. Many find it hard to accept the depths of devotion and empathy between brother and sister before his marriage or the triangular relationship formed by them and his new wife after it. But Dorothy Wordsworth's Grasmere Journal testify to both, particularly in the following passage covering the journey the three of them then made by post chaise back to Grasmere. For Dorothy there was an added poignancy because their route retraced the one she had taken with William when they had first set out to live at Grasmere in the winter of 1799.

POOR MARY was much agitated when she parted from her brothers and sisters and her home. . .

We had sunshine and showers, pleasant talk, love and cheerfulness. . . Before we reached Helmsley our driver told us that he could not take us any further, so we stopped at the same inn where we had slept before. My heart danced at the sight of its cleanly outside, bright yellow walls, casements overshadowed with jasmine and its low, double gavel-ended front. . . Mary and I warmed ourselves at the kitchen fire. We then walked into the garden, and looked over a gate up to the old ruin [of Helmsley castle] which stands at the top of a mount, and round about it the moats are grown up into soft green cradles, hollows surrounded with green grassy hillocks and these are overshadowed by old trees, chiefly ashes. I prevailed upon William to go up with me to the ruins. We left Mary sitting by the kitchen fire. The sun shone, it was warm and very pleasant. One part of the castle seems to be inhabited. There was a man mowing nettles in the open space which had most likely once been the castle court. There is one gateway exceedingly beautiful. Children were playing upon the sloping ground. We came home by the street.

After about an hour's delay we set forward again, had an excellent driver who opened the gates so dexterously that the horses never stopped. Mary was very much delighted with the view of the castle from the point where we had seen it before. I was pleased to see again the little path which we had walked upon, the gate I had climbed over, and the road down which we had seen the two little boys drag a log of wood, and a team of horses struggle under the weight of a great load of timber. We had felt compassion for the poor horses that were under the governance of oppressive and ill-judging drivers, and for the poor boys who seemed of an age to have been able to have dragged the log of wood merely out of the love of their own activity, but from poverty and bad food they panted for weakness and were obliged to fetch their father from the town to help them. Duncombe House looks well from the road—a large building though I believe only two thirds of the original design are completed. We rode down a very steep hill to Rievaulx valley, with woods all round us. We stopped upon the bridge to look at the abbey and again when we had crossed it. Dear Mary had never seen a ruined abbey before except Whitby! . . . Before we had crossed Hambleton hills and reached the point overlooking Yorkshire it was quite dark. We had not wanted, however, fair prospects before us, as we drove along the flat plain of the high hill, far far off us, in the western sky, we saw shapes of castles, ruins among groves, a great, spreading wood, rocks, and single trees, a minster with its tower unusually distinct, minarets in another quarter, and a round Grecian temple also—the colours of the sky of a bright grey and the forms of a sober grey, with a dome. As we descended the hill there was no distinct view, but of a great space, only near us, we saw the wild and (as the people say) bottomless tarn in the hollow at the side of the hill. It seemed to be made visible to us only by its own light, for all the hill about us was dark.

Before we reached Thirsk we saw a light before us which we at first thought was the moon, then lime kilns, but when we drove into the market place it proved a large bonfire with lads dancing round it, which is a sight I dearly love. The inn was like an illuminated house—every room full. We asked the cause, and were told by the girl that it was 'Mr John Bell's birthday, that he had heired his estate!' The landlady was very civil. She did not recognise the despised foot-travellers. We rode nicely in the dark, and reached Leeming Lane at eleven o'clock. I am always sorry to get out of a chaise when it is night. The people of the house were going to bed and we were not very well treated though we got a hot supper. We breakfasted the next morning and set off at about half past eight o'clock. It was a cheerful sunny morning. We soon turned out of Leeming Lane and passed a nice village with a beautiful church. We had a few showers, but when we came to the green fields of Wensley, the sun shone upon them all, and the Eure in its many windings glittered as it flowed along under the green slopes of Middleham and Middleham Castle. . .

[At Leyburn] The Landlady was very civil, giving us cake and wine but the horses being out we were detained at least two hours and did not set off till two o'clock. We paid for thirty-five miles, i.e. to Sedbergh, but the landlady did not encourage us to hope to get beyond Hawes. A shower came on just after we left the inn and while the rain beat against the windows we ate our dinners which M. and W. heartily enjoyed – I was not quite well. When we passed through the village of Wensley my heart was melted away with dear recollections – the bridge, the little water-spout, the steep hill, the church. They are among the most vivid of my own inner visions, for they were the first objects that I saw after we were left to ourselves, and had turned our whole hearts to Grasmere as a home in which we were to rest. The vale looked most beautiful each way. To the left the bright silver stream inlaid the flat and very green meadows, winding like a serpent. To the right we did not see it so far, it was lost among trees and little hills. I could not help observing as we went along how much more varied the prospects of Wensley Dale are in the summer time than I could have thought possible in the winter. This seemed to be in great measure owing to the trees being in leaf, and forming groves, and screens, and thence little openings upon recesses and concealed retreats which in winter only made a part of the one great vale. The beauty of the summer time here as much excels that of the winter as the variety, owing to the excessive greenness of the fields, and the trees in leaf half concealing, and where they do not conceal, softening the hard bareness of the limey white roofs.

One of our horses seemed to grow a little restive as we went through the first village, a long village on the side of a hill. It grew worse and worse, and at last we durst not go on any longer. We walked a while, and then the post-boy was obliged to take the horse out and go back for another. We seated ourselves again snugly in the post chaise. The wind struggled about us and rattled the window and gave a gentle motion to the chaise, but we were warm and at our ease within. Our station was at the top of a hill, opposite Bolton Castle, the Eure flowing beneath. William has since wrote a sonnet on this our imprisonment – 'Hard was thy durance Queen compared with ours.' Poor Mary! [Mary, Queen of Scots, had been imprisoned at Bolton Castle at one stage] Wm fell asleep, lying upon my breast and I upon Mary. I lay motionless for a long time, but I was at last obliged to move. I became very sick and continued so for some time after the boy brought the horse to us. Mary had been a little sick but it soon went off.—We had a sweet ride till we came to a public house on the side of a hill where we alighted and walked down to see the waterfalls. The sun was not set, and the woods and fields were spread over with the yellow light of evening, which made their greenness a thousand times more green.

There was too much water in the river for the beauty of the falls [at Aysgarth], and even the banks were less interesting than in winter. Nature had entirely got the better in her struggles against the giants who first cast the mould of these works, for indeed it is a place that did not in winter remind one of God, but one could not help feeling as if there had been the agency of some 'Mortal Instruments' which Nature had been struggling against without making a perfect conquest. There was something so wild and new in this feeling, knowing as we did in the inner man that God alone had laid his hand upon it, that I could not help regretting the want of it, besides it is a pleasure to a real lover of Nature to give winter all the glory he can, for summer will make its own way, and speak its own praises. We saw the pathway which Wm and I took at the close of evening, the path leading to the rabbit warren where we lost ourselves. The farm with its holly hedges was lost among the green hills and hedgrows in general, but we found it out and were glad to look at it again. When William had left us to seek the waterfalls Mary and I were frightened by a cow.

At our return to the inn we found new horses and a new driver, and we went on nicely to Hawes where we arrived before it was quite dark. Mary and I got tea, and William had a partridge and mutton chops and tarts for his supper. Mary sat down with him. We had also a shilling's worth of negus [hot spiced port and lemon] and Mary made me some broth for all which supper we were only

charged two shillings. I could not sit up long. I vomited and took
the broth and then slept sweetly. We rose at six o'clock—a rainy
morning. We had a good breakfast and then departed. There was a
very pretty view about a mile from Hawes, where we crossed a
bridge, bare, and very green fields with cattle, a glittering stream.
cottages, a few ill-grown trees, and high hills. The sun shone now.
Before we got upon the bare hills there was a hunting lodge on our
right exactly like Greta Hall, with fir plantations about it. We were
very fortunate in the day, gleams of sunshine, passing clouds, that
travelled with their shadows below them. Mary was much pleased
with Garsdale. It was a dear place to William and me. We noted well
the public house (Garsdale Hall) where we had baited and drunk
our pint of ale and afterwards the mountain which had been
adorned by Jupiter in his glory when we were here before. It was
mid-day when we reached Sedbergh, and market day. We were in
the same room where we had spent the evening together in our road
to Grasmere. We had a pleasant ride to Kendal, where we arrived at
about two o'clock. The day favoured us. M. and I went to see the
house where dear Sara had lived, then we went to seek Mr
Bousfield's shop but we found him not—he had sold all his goods
the day before. We then went to the pot woman's and bought two
jugs and a dish, and some paper at Pennington's. When we came to
the inn William was almost ready for us.

The afternoon was not cheerful but it did not rain till we came
near Windermere. I am always glad to see Staveley. It is a place I
dearly love to think of—the first mountain village that I came to
with Wm when we first began our pilgrimage together. Here we
drank a basin of milk at a public house, and here I washed my feet
in the brook and put on a pair of silk stockings by Wm's advice
[presumably in 1799]—Nothing particular occurred till we reached
Ing's chapel. The door was open and we went in. It is a neat little
place, with a marble floor and marble communion table with a
painting over it of the last supper, and Moses and Aaron on each
side. The woman told us that 'they had painted them as near as they
could by the dresses as they are described in the Bible', and gay
enough they are. The marble had been sent by Richard Bateman
from Leghorn. The woman told us that a man had been at her

house a few days before who told her he had helped to bring it down the Red Sea and she had believed him gladly! It rained very hard when we reached Windermere. We sat in the rain at Wilcock's to change horses, and arrived at Grasmere at about six o'clock on Wednesday evening, the 6th of October 1802. Molly was overjoyed to see us, for my part I cannot describe what I felt, and our dear Mary's feelings would I dare say not be easy to speak of. We went by candlelight into the garden and were astonished at the growth of the brooms, Portugal laurels, etc. etc. etc. The next day, Thursday, we unpacked the boxes. On Friday 8th we baked bread, and Mary and I walked, first upon the hill side, and then in John's Grove, then in view of Rydale, the first walk that I had taken with my sister.

From *Munby: Man of Two Worlds*
Arthur Munby

Arthur Munby (1828–1910), a lawyer who worked for the Ecclesiastical Commission and as a Christian Socialist helped out at the Working Men's and Women's Colleges, had a penchant for working-class girls, particularly when they had their sleeves rolled up and their hands and forearms well dirtied. In 1854 he met a lowly servant girl called Hannah Culwick whom he eventually secretly married in 1873, since she wanted to continue as a servant and not be 'ladyfied'. Munby thought that, once married, he would win her round to adopting the dress, manners and speech of his class, but she became increasingly angry at his promptings, and his continued demand that the marriage remain secret. In 1877 she went back to live among her own people in Shropshire. Here is a description of the first few days of their married life from the diary that he kept.

Saturday, 18 January

AT 2 P.M. I took Hannah from London Bridge to Dorking and Holmwood; for it had been a brilliant morning, and we were to sleep at Ockley. But leaving Holmwood station about 3.15, the sky was clouded and wind and rain approaching: so we simply walked by the field roads, under the lee of the fair brown woods, round to the pretty hamlet and picturesque church of Holmwood, and then the 3 miles back to Dorking, across the Common, in driving rain. We had good fare and warmth at the White Horse, & Hannah played her part very fairly, by dint of natural sweetness. But now that she was drest in black silk, her shapely hands looked somewhat large and laborious, and her dear complexion somewhat coarse: whereas her face looks ladylike and her hands delicate, when she is in her own servant's dress. *C'est sélon.* We returned to London, to Charing Cross, by 8.

Sunday, 19 January

And soon after one o'clock, I went down to the kitchen, and found her busy doing them . . . singing at her work, for joy, while smoothfaced ladies, coming from church, swept across the courtyard above her. 'I'm *cook* today, Massa!' said she, smiling; 'and I enjoy it.'

. . . I went to Lincoln's Inn, and dined in Hall . . . home by 8, and found my Hannah . . . on her knees relighting the parlour fire; wearing her cap & apron with her black silk 'frock'; and her sleeves down in token that it was Sunday evening: for a servant bares her arms for work and hides them at times of leisure, whilst a lady covers hers in the morning time, and bares them at evening, for show. In due course Hannah had her supper; but insisted on going down to the kitchen & eating it there; and returned almost directly. She is so used to getting her meals anyhow and feeding on broken victuals, that I can hardly persuade her to eat leisurely and sit down by me: even now, she acts on the pathetic assumption that only my leavings are for *her*! She read to me a few chapters of Thomas à Kempis, and the Psalms for the day; and so to bed . . .

Sunday, 26 January

For reasons of prudence as well as of courtesy, I asked three men to breakfast with me today: my neighbours Josiah Rees and Capt. Batten of the 8th. Foot, and Colonel Pearson. Of course I consulted my Hannah first; and she highly approved: 'I can wait on them quite nicely,' said she who ought to have presided and been waited upon. But when I say 'How I wish you could sit with us at the table!' she answers ironically 'Oh yes, I fancy I see myself sitting down to breakfast with four gentlemen and pouring out tea for them—oh Massa, how *can* you be so silly!' Such is her view, who used to look on a parlour-maid's place as something too smart and fine for her. And so she brought the breakfast up, and set out the dishes, and cleared them away; silently and meekly; unnoticed, like any common servant, and drest like a servant in cotton frock and apron: but she did not stay in the room to wait; the other was trying enough, but that would have been intolerable. That is one thing my darling wife did for me. Not quite unnoticed, however. 'What a very nice person your servant seems to be!' said Capt. Batten. I slipped down afterwards to the kitchen, where she was washing up, and kissed & thanked her. 'You are very welcome!' said this strange sweet spouse.

Australia in the 1850s

Rev J. D. Mereweather

The Rev. J. D. Mereweather described marriage customs among successful prospectors during the Australian Gold Rush in his Diary of a Working Clergyman in Australia and Tasmania: kept during the years 1850–53.

AFTER THE CEREMONY is over and the officiating minister has received generous proofs of the prodigality of the contracting parties, the couple and their friends drive to St. Kilda or Brighton with a suite of fortuitous applauding acquaintances. The toilette of the ladies is something preposterously extravagant. Their blue satin bonnets and white ostrich feathers oppress their heads; their crimson satin dresses blaze upon squat bodies, which have been submitted for the first and probably the last time to the screwing-in process of powerful stays. Next to the dress, come the heavy boots laced up in front. The coachman wears blue and white ribbons, so do the horses, so even does the whip, nay even the spokes of the wheels.

During the journey, which takes half an hour to an hour, English porter beer and champagne are drunk by the driven and the drivers. On their reaching the inn an expensive banquet is served and the most expensive liquors which the colony affords are circulated in profusion. Night arrives and the whole party gallop back to Melbourne in the most hopeless state of intoxication, having squandered a sum which I dare not here name, for fear of encountering incredulity. A week is spent by the married pair in all these delicate outpourings of first love, and then satiety having intervened and the gold-bag having diminished, the new bride awakes one morning without her partner at her side and discovers that he has bolted to his diggings. She suffers great misery and ultimately discovers that her partner, having got more gold, has married again in some other place and that in fact he has kept two or three consorts before herself. So she too, partly out of spite and partly from destitution, resolves to marry again. And thus the lower classes go on setting the marriage laws at defiance to the utter despair of the clergymen who see the inextricable social confusion prevailing round them, without the power to remedy it. In the midst of all this social turmoil, the Colonial Government, although a little taken aback, acts on the whole with the firmness and good sense which British gentlemen always show in cases of emergency.

V Royal Weddings

Queen Victoria & Prince Albert

In the words of the Queen herself, taken from her journal covering her wedding night and the first days of her honeymoon.

A S SOON AS we arrived [at Windsor] we went to our rooms; my large dressing room is our sitting room; the 3 little blue rooms are his . . . After looking about our rooms for a little while, I went and changed my gown, and then came back to his small sitting room where dearest Albert was sitting and playing; he had put on his windsor coat; he took me on his knee, and kissed me and was so dear and kind. We had our dinner in our sitting room; but I had such a sick headache that I could eat nothing, and was obliged to lie down in the middle blue room for the remainder of the evening, on the sofa, but, ill or not, I NEVER NEVER spent such an evening!!! My DEAREST DEAREST DEAR Albert sat on a footstool by my side, & his excessive love & affection gave me feelings of heavenly love & happiness, I never could have hoped to have felt before! He clasped me in his arms and we kissed each other again and again— really how can I ever be thankful enough to have such a Husband! He called me names of tenderness, I have never yet heard used to me before—was bliss beyond belief! Oh! this was the happiest day of my life!—May God help me to do my duty as I ought and be worthy of such blessings.

11 February 1840

When day dawned (for we did not sleep much) and I beheld that beautiful angelic face by my side, it was more than I can express! He does look so beautiful in his shirt only, with his beautiful throat seen. We got up at 1/4 p. 8. When I had laced I went to dearest Albert's room, and we breakfasted together. He had a black velvet jacket on, without any neckcloth on, and looked more beautiful than it is possible for me to say . . . At 12 I walked out with my precious Angel, all alone—so delightful, on the Terrace and new Walk, arm in arm! Eros our only companion. We talked a great deal together. We came home at one, and had luncheon soon after. Poor dear Albert felt sick and uncomfortable, and lay down in my room . . . He looked so dear, lying there and dozing.

12 February 1840
Already the 2nd day since our marriage; his love and gentleness is beyond everything, and to kiss that dear soft cheek, to press my lips to his, is heavenly bliss. I feel a purer more unearthly feel than I ever did. Oh! was ever woman so blessed as I am.

13 February 1840
My dearest Albert put on my stockings for me. I went in and saw him shave; a great delight for me.

The diarist Charles Greville, secretary to the Privy Council, obviously drew the wrong conclusions when he recorded that:

'She and Prince Albert were up very early on Tuesday morning, walking about, which is very contrary to her former habits. Strange that a bridal night should be so short; and I told Lady Palmerston this was not the way to provide us with a Prince of Wales.'

Lord Melbourne, the Prime Minister, on the other hand can have been left in little doubt since Queen Victoria sent him a note the day after the marriage in which she wrote of her 'most gratifying and bewildering' night:

'The Queen cannot conclude without telling Ld Melbourne how very, very happy she feels. She never thought she could be so loved as she is by dearest, dear Albert.'

This street ballad, Married at Last, *was composed on the occasion by one H. Paul of 22 Brick Lane, Spitalfields, cheaply printed and sold for a penny or so.*

I am a damsel gay and bright,
Who like to do the thing that's right,
The secret I don't like to mince,
I have married a buxom German prince,
He brought me sausages so fine,
He kiss'd me well and used me kind,
Thirty thousand pounds[1] he has got a year
I am married at last and I don't care.

CHORUS
Tiddle tol lol tol lol tol le
I am a damsel young and gay,
Who married a German prince so glad
And danced and sung old Mol in the wad.[2]

I bought him a dandy shirt so fine,
A pair of boots; and four and nine,[3]
A three cock'd hat and a feather all right
A great cow heel and a pound of tripe,
I bought him a watch as big as St Paul's,
And a slashing dashing pair of smalls,[4]
I bought him a gun like Oldgate Pump,
And he fired a shot a tiddle le bump.

I am a damsel gay and free,
The world may say what it likes of me,
I am the Queen of all the land,
And I can't do without a man;
Prince Albert is the man for me,

1. Albert's allowance from the Exchequer
2. Maybe the name of the tune intended for the song
3. A hat
4. Underpants

He is devilish fond of skilligalee,[1]
There is nothing like a wedded life,
I can't forget my wedding night.

Prince Albert came to marry me,
From mother's land of Germany,
Stark naked miles for me he'd run,
For I've got money though he's got none,
Thirty thousand is not much I'm sure,
Old Farmer Bull must find some more,
Since I got married I will make it right,
And fry the sausages day and night.
I to my lovely Albert said,
When we got married and went to bed,
I will buy you a three cock'd hat,
Sing burn the bellows and drown the cat;
Like turtle doves we'll happy dwell,
Then he tun'd his tingalaro[2] well,
Of whiskey he had eleven goes;
Singing Jack's the lad and off she goes.

If I was single I'd live in pain,
And if I was a widow I'd marry again,
If Albert died today for sorrow,
Blow'd if I wouldn't get married tomorrow,
There's nothing like a wedded life,
I was never so happy as since a wife,
My ladies look'd with jealousy,
'Cause they couldn't get married as well as me.

My marriage tale is nearly done,
I will bet the nation two to one,
My Albert will not go from me,
Unto the land of Germany,
And if I thought he'd bolt away,

1. Gruel. There is clearly a sexual double meaning intended here
2. Possibly some form of musical instrument

I would lock him up all night and day,
Aye, and keep his guarded well, oh 'fegs
With a great padlock on his legs.

George IV & Caroline of Brunswick

In 1795 things were rather different when Queen Victoria's uncle, George Prince of Wales (later George IV), undertook to marry his cousin Princess Caroline of Brunswick in return for having his debts settled. (This meant he was committing bigamy since he was already married to Mrs Fitzherbert.) His reaction on first meeting the uncouth Princess was to say to the diplomat who had accompanied her from Germany, 'Harris, I am not well; pray get me a glass of brandy', and then leave the room. The Princess exclaimed, 'My god! Is the Prince always like that? I find him very fat, and nothing like as handsome as his portrait.' Matters obviously went on as they had begun because Princess Caroline later recalled, 'Judge what it was to have a drunken husband on one's wedding day, and one who passed the greatest part of his bridal night in the grate where he fell down and where I left him.'

Charles I & Henrietta Maria

Here is an anonymous letter describing the first meeting of King Charles I with his French wife, Henrietta Maria, to whom he had already been married by proxy, 1625.

THE KING CAME from Canterbury thither [to Dover] to visit her, and though she were unready, so soon as she heard he was come, she hastened down a pair of stairs to meet him, and offering to kneel down and to kiss his hand, he wrapped her up in his arms and kissed her with many kisses ... At dinner being carved pheasant and venison by his Majesty (who had dined before) she ate heartily of both, notwithstanding her confessor (who all this while stood by her) had forewarned her that it was the Eve of St John Baptist, and was to be fasted, and that she should take heed how she gave ill example or a scandal at her first arrival.

The same night having supped at Canterbury her Majesty went to bed; and, some space of time after, his Majesty followed her; but being entered his bedchamber, the first thing he did, he bolted all the doors round about (being seven) with his own hand, letting in but two of the bedchamber to undress him, which being done, he bolted them out also. The next morning he lay till seven of the clock, and was pleasant with the Lords that he had beguiled them; and hath ever since been very jocund.

In stature her head reached to his shoulder: but she is young enough to grow taller. Those of our nation that know best her dispositions are very hopeful his Majesty will have power to bring her to his own religion. Being asked, not long since, if she could abide a Huguenot! 'Why not?' said she, 'was not my father one?' [Henri IV had become a Catholic to secure the throne of France.]

Napoleon & Marie-Louise of Austria

In 1808 Napoleon was able to take advantage of a previous proxy marriage in the same way as Charles I, when he met Marie-Louise of Austria for the first time. Here is Mme. de la Tour du Pin's description:

THE EMPEROR WAS then at Compiègne with the new Ladies of Honor of the Empress and was in a state of boundless impatience to see his new wife. A little calèche was waiting all hitched up in the court of the Château to take him to meet her. When the advance courier came, Napoleon rushed to the calèche and set out to meet the berline which was bringing the spouse so much desired. The carriage stopped. The door was opened and Marie-Louise prepared to descend, but her husband did not give her the time. He entered the berline, embraced his wife, and then having pushed her sister, the Queen of Naples, without ceremony onto the front seat of the carriage, he seated himself beside Marie-Louise.

Arriving at the Château he descended first, offered her his arm and conducted her to the salon de service, where all the invited guests were assembled. It was already evening. The Emperor presented, one after another, all the ladies of the mansion, and then the men. This presentation over, he took the Empress by the hand and conducted her to her apartment. All of us thought that the Empress was proceeding with her toilette. We waited for an hour and then commenced to be very anxious to have our supper. At this moment, the grand chamberlain came to announce that Their Majesties had retired. The surprise was great, but no one ventured to let it be seen, and we went to supper.

Philip II & Elizabeth of France

The French had much experience of proxy marriages. Philip II of Spain married Elizabeth, daughter of Henri II of France, as his second wife after the death of Mary Tudor in 1558. The Venetian ambassador, Giovanni Michiel, reported how the Duke of Alba stood proxy, not merely at the marriage ceremony but also on the wedding night.

THE QUEEN RETIRED to bed, and after her there entered, by the light of many torches, the King her father in company with the Duke of Alba. That Duke, having one of his feet bare, lifted the coverlet of the Queen's bed on one side and, having inserted his foot beneath the sheet, advanced it until it touched the naked flesh of the Queen; and in such manner the marriage was understood to have been consummated in the name of King Philip through the agency of a third person – that which was never afterwards to be understood by anyone.

Ferdinand IV & Maria Carolina

In 1768 King Ferdinand IV of Naples, Bourbon ruler of what was called the Kingdom of the Two Sicilies, married the Austrian Princess Maria Carolina, elder sister of Marie Antoinette, the future Queen of France. He had been kept virtually uneducated for fear that he might otherwise go mad like his brother, so was an ugly uncouth youth, interested only in hunting. The British ambassador in Naples, Sir William Hamilton, future husband of the notorious Emma, reported that Maria Carolina might not be really handsome, but had many charms. The Neapolitans, however, quickly gave her the nickname Polpett Mbocca (rissole-in-the-mouth) because her Habsburg jaw made her mumble.

FERDINAND MANIFESTED on his part, neither ardour nor indifference for the Queen. On the morning after his nuptials, when the weather was very warm, he rose at an early hour and went out as usual to the chase, leaving his young wife in bed. Those courtiers who accompanied him, having inquired of His Majesty how he liked her; *'Dorme come un' ammazzata,'* replied he, *'e suda come un porco'* ('She sleeps as if she had been killed, and sweats like a pig'). Such an answer would be esteemed, anywhere except at Naples, most indecorous; but here we are familiarized to far greater violations of propriety and decency. Those acts and functions which are never mentioned in England, and which are there studiously concealed, even by the vulgar, here are openly performed. When the King has made a hearty meal, and feels an inclination to retire, he commonly communicates that intention to the noblemen around him in waiting, and selects the favoured individuals, whom, as a mark of predilection, he chooses shall attend him. *'Sono ben pranzato,'* says he, laying his hand on his belly, *'Adesso bisogna una buona panciata'* ('I have dined well, and now I need a good easing of the belly'). The persons thus preferred then accompany His Majesty, stand respectfully round him, and amuse him by their conversation during the performance.

VI Honeymoon Journeys

On Board a Warship, 1797

Betsey Fremantle

In 1796, as the French advanced down Italy, an English family called Wynne was evacuated from Leghorn on Captain Thomas Fremantle's ship HMS Inconstant. *The captain then fell in love with the eighteen-year-old Betsey Wynne. When the* Inconstant *reached Naples they were married on 12 January 1797 at the house of the British ambassador, Sir William Hamilton (see page 112). The honeymoon was afloat, aboard the* Inconstant, *as described in* The Wynne Diaries.

Inconstant. Monday, January 16th

WE SAILED LAST night, had fair weather and pretty good wind all day. I find it quite odd to be alone here. I dare not think on those I left at Naples for it makes my heart swell with anguish, however I can make no complaints for I am as happy in my situation as it is possible to be. Fremantle is all attention and kindness. I have got a comfortable little cabin where I can do what I like.

Porto Ferrajo, Elba. Sunday, January 22nd

We had a long and tedious passage. Very blowing weather, poor Pozzo de Borgo[1] very seasick, Sir Gilbert[2] not very well. It did not affect me, it increased my appetite and I laughed at everybody else. We only came to an anchor this morning at three o'clock. I begin to get accustomed to the life I lead and find myself comfortable and happy.

1. A Corsican in the service of Britain
2. Elliot, British Viceroy of Corsica

The general report here is that this place is going to be evacuated but General de Burgh and the Viceroy are against it, a council of war is to be held in the evening to determine. I walked ashore with Fremantle met Captain Hope, Cockburn, Giffard, all very civil and the *sposa* received so many fine compliments of congratulation that she was quite at a loss. The weather delightful quite pleasant, Commissioner Coffin and Captain Elphinston dined with us. I spent the evening alone and I amused myself very well with my Harpsichord and books. It has been determined that Fremantle will remain here with the command l'Utile, Blanche and other small vessels all the rest go down to Gibraltar with Commodore Nelson. For a thousand reasons I prefer staying here to going immediately to England. Fremantle likes it as well, we are both contented. I daily think more and more that I have ensured my future felicity by marrying one who so well deserves my love and regard nothing on my part will be wanting for us both to be happy.

Monday, January 23rd

Commodore Nelson, the commissioner, Captain Hope and Cockburn dined with us. Very noisy. Commissioner Coffin is very good humoured and pleasant but sometimes makes a fool of himself. Old Nelson very civil and good natured, but does not say much.

Tuesday, 24 January

Took my usual walk, had Mde Granets and her daughters to dinner. Fremantle dined on board the *Minerve* where they had a drinking party. He assured me when he returned on board at nine that he was tipsy but I found him perfectly sober and even had he been tipsy he behaved so kind and good humoured to me, begged I should forgive him with so much good grace, that it could not have given me the least uneasiness.

Wednesday, 25 January

The weather was bad and in general this, a dismal day and unlucky. Last night the ship's company all got drunk and behaved horridly ill. Much flogging this morning which made Fremantle ill and broke my heart. I could distinctly hear the poor wretches cry out for mercy, from the cabin. A man broke his leg. After all this misery I was glad to get out of the ship and went over to the town. It rained.

Thursday, 26 January

A court martial to try three mariners of this ship. The weather so bad that I could not go on shore, stayed quietly on board with Fremantle, who spent the evening with me. He gives me daily new proofs of his attachment and gains more and more in my affections.

Saturday, 28 January

I was quite miserable all the morning as the three mariners were punished and flogged along side of every ship, some men flogged likewise on board and in the cabin I hear all that is going on quite distinctly. The two Miss Granets dined with me. A noisy supper in the evening. Colonel Drinkwater, Mr Hardman the commissioner, and Captain Cockburn at the head of the rioting party of all the other captains. They are going tomorrow.

Sunday, 29 January

The Viceroy [Sir Gilbert Elliot] was kind enough to come on board before he left from here. Commodore Nelson and all of them got under way in the morning.

Tuesday, 31 January

I had a rendezvous at Cantines with the French curate, breakfasted there and was tired to death of that good person. I walked round the bay with Fremantle and went to Pleasant Prospect, a delightful day, came on board to dress then went to dine with General Horneck; Col. Stephens, his lady and Lord Proby were there. An excellent dinner but long and stupid. The general is not very talkative until he has had double allowances of wine. I was glad when it was time for the ladies to retire and had a long tête-à-tête with old Mother Stephens, pleasant enough.

I was quite miserable all the morning as the three mariners were punished and flogged.

Wednesday, 1 February

Fremantle attacked me for some nonsense or other, I am too inanimate, but we were very good friends at last. I see that very little is required to make him uneasy and must be still more on my guard.

Thursday, 2 February

Sailed at noon, the *Blanche* and *Pettrel* with us.

Friday and Saturday

Beautiful weather, a westerly breeze, were off Marseilles Saturday evening, took a Spanish fishing boat in the night. The *Pettrel* could not sail and was sent back to Porto Ferrajo.

Sunday, 5 February

Took a prize in the morning, a ship under American colours laden with grain from the coast of Barbary bound to Marseilles. Though the master, Captain Richard Smith swears he was going to Genoa, his papers and letters prove the contrary. A great bore to examine these papers, translate jews letters. The ship comes from Bona, is named *La Vittoria*, was formerly an English transport, we cannot make out who she belongs to now, it is a great confusion and potheration.

Tuesday, 7 February

The weather continues charming, even too fine. Smith begins to acknowledge that he was going to Marseilles and the cargo will be condemned as French, probably belonging to a Jew, Jacob Bacri, an Algerine agent at Marseilles for the French company at Marseilles, but nothing very clean about the ship. The fishing boat sent back in the night.

Wednesday, 8 February

I behaved very foolishly towards Fremantle, caused him much uneasiness and made myself very unhappy, certainly not intentionally. I was very angry with myself afterwards but it was too late, all for a trifle and nonsense.

Thursday, 9 February

Was unhappy all the morning as I saw I had given F. real cause to be angry with me, however it was better explained and we were friends again. The *Blanche* is going to Porto Ferrajo with the prize.

Friday and Saturday

Continually in chase but did not take anything. I find time passes very quick, and I like being at sea almost better than Porto Ferrajo. The honeymoon is over but it finished almost better than it began, I flatter myself that the months that are to come will all be *honeymoons* for me.

Italy, 1838

Samuel Palmer

The painter Samuel Palmer married Hannah, daughter of his fellow-artist John Linnell, in 1837 and the couple set out for a working honeymoon in Italy almost immediately. In various letters to his friends written from Italy in 1838, he described the impact of first Rome and then Naples. Linnell had commissioned them to make copies of various pictures for him, and these were undertaken by Hannah while Palmer mostly worked out-of-doors.

BUT WHAT SHALL I say of Rome, of whose wonders a tenth part I have not seen, yet have seen what would fill a volume? Its churches are cathedrals, and its Vatican larger than the city of Turin within the walls. Rome is a thing by itself which, once seen, leaves the memory no more—a city of Art which one had dreamed of before, and can scarce believe that one has really seen with these ocular jellies—to which London seems a warehouse, and Paris a trinket-shop. What must it have been in its antique glory? You can only look at its dazzling palaces, blazing in Italian sunshine, with your eyes half shut. Indeed, Italian air and Italian light, and the azure of an Italian sky, can scarcely be imagined in England. It spreads its magic over streets and houses, and invests the commonest objects with a peculiar beauty: but the people do not, I fear, plunge into the Tiber after athletic games as heretofore, or wash their carcases as we do every morning in cold water; for they leave a wake of unsavoury odour behind them as they walk the streets, which are strewed with filth.

We saw the grand Easter ceremonies, and were several times within a yard of the Pope. We saw him wash the feet of the thirteen priests (whom he afterwards waits on at dinner, girding himself with a napkin), and after singing mass, bless the immense assembled multitudes from the façade of St. Peter's. This is a sublime spectacle—thousands of country people in their picturesque costumes, beating their breasts, holding out strings of beads, and awaiting, in breathless silence, the great benediction. When the Pope appears, all is hushed. He spreads out his arms over the people and blesses them; and then, all in a moment, the great guns of St. Angelo fire, the martial bands distributed over the piazza, strike up, and the bells of the city, which are silenced through Passion Week, ring out a peal. Before this, at the grand mass at St. Peter's, at the moment when the elements are consecrated and all are prostrate, a slow, sublime harmony of wind instruments peals along from over the great western door, softened in this immense vault as in the open air. The dome, though much higher and vaster than St. Paul's, is not, in my judgment, nearly so sublime; and in sublimity and musical effect I think the grandest ceremonials of the Vatican are far short of our cathedral worship.

The weather was for months very rainy, and (we being without a fireplace) so cold that I wore a waistcoat lined with flannel, and Mrs. Palmer wrapped up like a mummy. To me, our December was nothing like it, and it seemed rather strange, in a climate which, I had been told, ripened strawberries at Christmas. However, I bore it with an allowance of English grumbling, and learned in time to wade along the streets, avoiding the water-spouts which concentrate the rain on the tops of the houses, and hurl it down in torrents to scour away the filth. When the sun burst forth, out I popped, like the lady in the weather-box, and tried to draw white palaces so sunny that the white paper seemed 'double smut' against them. Mrs. P., meanwhile, went every morning about two miles by herself to the Vatican, to copy the Bible subjects in the Loggia; being occasionally annoyed a little on the way; people calling after her 'Piccola Inglese' &c. Then we met at our room in the twilight, and turning down a dark passage and opening a little door, found ourselves at our dinner-table, with Messrs. Gibson, Williams, &c., where the hour passed very pleasantly after our labours, in chewing, chattering, and laughing. *Conversation* you know, in the true sense of the word, is banished from civilized society.

I think I have made quite sure of my drawing of ancient Rome and the moment I cast my eyes on these mountains and on Capri, which looks like an enchanted island, I said to Naples, 'I think I can grapple with you' . . . We have a little room which commands the bay, Vesuvius, Capri, and the whole chain of mountains, and which is quite cool at three in the afternoon. Indeed though we were all day yesterday lodging-hunting (a most sudorific employment), and had both slept the night before in a pestiferous little den with only a thin roof between us and the sun, in a bed not large enough for one person, with a window opening inwards to the shaft or funnel of the house, ventilated only by blasts from drains and kitchens, and in one of the most filthy streets, I do not, in this blessed climate, suffer at all from heat; but enjoy, rather, the perspiration of walking, like a tepid bath; and feel as if the sun were only ripening me like the plums and peaches.

I quite agree with you that the interior of Naples is filthy and uninteresting; but surely on the shores of this bay one feels that one has at last discovered the climate and the land of joy and of enchantment. But what shall I say of Monte St. Angelo? Surely all the mountains we have seen would kick the beam if weighed against its ripe convexity, and yet clifted sides. The right wing of the bay, certainly, though cultivated, is tame. But I should fear that such a bay, such mountains, and such a climate, are rarely to be found elsewhere. From the very little I have seen, I should think that here may be found united the grandest mountains with the richness of Devonshire valleys.

We lived a month in Pompeii, dining in one of the antique vaults, and living for the first time in a room with an unglazed window: we had only to step out, and we were in the 'city of the dead'. Here Mrs. P. made thirteen sketches of the antique pictures, and we saw a slight eruption of Vesuvius. We then stayed two months at Corpo di Cava, commanding the finest distant mountains I have seen, and are now in Naples once more, to get a second view of Baiæ, intending, in a day or two, to trace its beautiful shores.

I will, if possible, get a sketch of that white temple you saw while anchoring in the bay. How I should enjoy a long talk over it, and over a large cup of tea—pure terra-vert! When shall we join again by an English fireside, over that intellectual, social, but long untasted beverage?

. . . I have been thinking a great deal about the principles and practice of art, and endeavouring very much to increase my acquaintance with the phenomena of nature, as well as working hard and incessantly, with the exception of time consumed in travelling; so I am in full energy, with my will and determination not a whit unstrung by time, and hope to bring forth fruit in my old age. Travelling, so far from unsettling me, has, I am sure, limited and concentrated my desires and on a few points, calmed my mind most sweetly. I never had a [Benjamin Robert] Haydonish rage for big pictures; but now I have seen how even Raffaelle was set to paint dark chambers like a house-decorator, with a window coming in the middle of one of his finest; how an altar is fixed up for months against the Charon group in *The Last Judgement* in the Sistine Chapel, and how the same kind of homage is paid to works of genius in most of the Churches which are fortunate enough to possess them, I look upon a kit-cat panel head-and-shoulders portrait as, after all, the most enviable field for exertion. Besides, I think the Great Masters themselves, with very few exceptions, distilled more of their intensity into little cabinet pictures than upon great walls and altar-pieces. Such wrought and polished gems as Mr. Mulready's *Seven Ages*, the half of which I was fortunate enough to see, leave a deeper dent in my memory than many of the great Jupiters and St. Jeromes sprawling over large ceilings and saloons.

It is moonlight, and the Bay of Naples fills up our window, sparkling like diamonds on ebony: what a pretty thing to do with our blue-black flake-white!

India, 1837

Honoria Lawrence

Honoria Lawrence married Henry Lawrence in Calcutta in 1837. They were both from northern Ireland and had met when he came home on sick leave from India in 1827 after taking part in the Burmese War. They fell in love but did not declare it to each other, in Henry's case because he was too poor to be able to support a wife. This changed in 1833 when he was seconded from the Bengal Army to become a revenue officer, but by then Honoria was engaged to a clergyman. Only after Honoria had broken off this engagement did a cousin reveal to her Henry's enduring love. In 1836 she wrote to him to say that she would marry him. So, nine years since they had last met, they came together again in India. Both strong in their Christian faith, they were to make a formidable but much loved team – loved both by Lawrence's English subordinates, but also by the Punjabis whom he governed with rectitude and swift justice. His four brothers were also out in India. Three were in the army like him and he and they all became generals. The other brother, John, was to become Viceroy. Honoria died in 1854 and Henry was killed at the start of the siege of Lucknow during the Indian Mutiny in 1857. Honoria's journal written to Henry, describes their journey up the Ganges by boat as far as Revelganj, to the west of Patna, and then overland to Gorakhpur where Henry was stationed.

Monday, August 21
[Their wedding day]

I WAS ASTIR before six. At eight you came to me. We went down to breakfast. At nine thirty we left this house. And then Harry! – we came home, and thank God, our first hour of our union was given to Him.

We remained in the drawing room till eleven that night.

Saturday you and Dick went to Calcutta. I rummaged your papers, looked over your clothes, and enjoyed my new privilege so to do very much.

August 23rd

We rather made fools of ourselves. We rose early and went out boating. And in the evening went out again.

Tuesday August 29th

We went to Dum Dum. Came back very tired, found the Hutchinsons returned. Began to be on our good behaviour.

Wednesday August 30th

We were working at the Theodolite, very hot. You went to Calcutta. On your return you found me in bed and ill with fever. Of Thursday I remember little.

Tuesday September 5th

We embarked on the pinnace, and then, dearest we fairly felt that we were afloat together, that we had each other and no one else to look to for comfort. We shall neither of us forget how we sat that evening and looked at the banks of the river, talking of the past, the present, and the future.

Tuesday September 12th

Wrote a tragedy this morning.

September 22nd

Time passes, I know not how. 'One long sunshine holiday' of happiness.

September 30th

Arrived at Seeta Khoond. Several small tanks walled in. One is filled by a hot spring of very clear pure water. On our way home climbed a rocky eminence. Came back to the pinnace, heartily glad to be in our own place again.

Henry inserts a description of this tiring day and ends:

Mrs. Lawrence is requested in future not to be so frisky and to take any opportunities, when fatigue is before her, to spare herself by lying down when she can, shutting her eyes and opening her stays. There are a hundred ways of making the best of a bad bargain and she's the cleverest cook who makes the best broth out of the fewest materials.

October 7th

I shall not without pain leave our little ship where we have passed so many hours. We are entering afresh the cares and duties of an active life; you to resume old habits, only modified by the addition of a wife; I to try my steps in a new path under your guidance. We have here learned that we can be all in all to one another, but have recognised the Giver of our precious gifts.

Letter to a friend

We are in a pinnace. It is fifty-five feet long but not drawing above two feet of water, with two masts, and rigging somewhat like a yacht, but ruder. It has sixteen oars, but we proceed chiefly by sailing and tacking. The pinnace has a poop, covering about two-thirds of its length, and forming the cabins. One fifteen feet square; the other fifteen by twenty feet and about seven feet high. These two rooms venetianed all round, having a purdah or curtain let down from the outside during the heat of the day. The heat has been oppressive, the thermometer being 90° and 92°. We have had one rather severe squall, but I have not yet seen anything like the violence of the elements that I expected in this climate. Indeed I think our western ideas of the horrors of India are vastly exaggerated. I have not yet seen a snake, except one in the water, though I am not yet reconciled to the great cockroaches which creep out from the crevices of an evening. Nor was I much pleased to see a scorpion walk deliberately across the floor a few days ago, nor to find a centipede making a bed of the slipper I was about to put on. One of my greatest annoyances is the prickly heat, which is a red rash breaking out over the body with an infinity of little watery specks excessively irritating.

We are, on board, about forty souls, ourselves, our servants, the manjee (commander) and crew. The boatmen are called dandees, from dand, an oar, and the profession is followed by both Hindus and Mussulmanns. Our men are dark, spare and active, most of them young, for their work does not favour long life. They wear mainly a waist-cloth and small skull cap of white or coloured cotton. The manjee is in no way distinguished from those under him, except that instead of pulling the ropes, he steers and gives orders, which he delivers in a sort of loud, prolonged chant audible at a good distance.

There is no part of the costume where the natives shew such variety of taste as in the arranging of the hair. And this does not as far as I can see depend on religious distinction. Some cover the head with a load of folded cloth, others wear no covering on it, and have the hair cropped close. Some wear little caps and the hair reaching down to the shoulders, where it is cut square across. Others have a broad line shaven from the forehead to the nape of the neck, and others cut off the hair above the forehead from ear to ear. And it is not uncommon to see the whole head shaven except one long tuft on the crown. The Mussulmanns have generally fine beards. But the Hindoos almost always shave theirs.

You would be astonished what absolute rags are the sails of country boats, and still more so that these tatters do carry along the vessel. Except in boats that are partly of European build, the bamboo is one of the chief materials, forming masts, helms, oars, spars, anchors. If there be no wind, we track by a rope fastened to the mast and pulled by a set of the *dandees*, who walk on the bank. Sometimes they are obliged to go through the water, and even to swim a considerable distance. They seem to feel neither heat nor moisture and they roll about in the river, their grinning black faces appearing above the water.

Often have I seen a man wash in the stream the piece of cloth that forms his dress, wring it out and then wrap it round his body, while the *manjee* shouts to them calling them his '*babas*', or children.

They are all a most loquacious race, and their chief pleasure seems to be smoking a '*hubble-bubble*' or pipe, a cocoa-nut shell or small hollow globe of wood which has a long tube inserted at the upper part, with a little earthen saucer on the top, where the lighted tobacco is placed. The globe is filled with water and from one side of it projects another tube, to which the mouth is applied and thus the smoke is inhaled through the water. The *hubble-bubble* is the chief refreshment of all the hard working classes, as the *hookah* is the grand recreation of the idle. We sail or track along until sunset, when we lie to, close to shore, and anchor, or rather *lagao*. That is: several ropes are put out from the boat, each having at the end a strong bamboo stake which is driven into the ground, and so we are secured for the night.

As soon as we are fairly *lagaoed* all hands are at work; some chopping firewood, intent on improving their supper; some going into the water carrying a net stretched between two bamboos shaped like the letter Y, and on his head a light basket into which he puts the little fishes as he catches them; others who are further advanced, lying down after supper to rest. The strong red glare of the fire, falling on their bronzed figures, and lighting up their bright black faces looking very picturesque. Of a moonlight night they sometimes sit up very late, talking and laughing; the wit among them telling stories, or the whole group discussing the price of grain.

We get up about daylight and after a cup of coffee go on deck, where we sit till the sun drives us in. We then dress and are ready for breakfast at nine o'clock. During the day we read, write and otherwise occupy ourselves till towards five o'clock, when we dine, and afterwards go on deck. When the pinnace comes to, we land and ramble or sit on the shore till eight o'clock. Then we have tea, and busy ourselves till ten o'clock. I should like our voyage to last for months, it is so free from care, so unshackled, so independent of any enjoyment beyond what we have in each other's society, intellectual pursuits and the fair face of Nature.

Journal continued:
October 10th

10.30 a.m. In a *palkee* [a palanquin, a box-litter for travelling in, carried by servants] contrived from my sea cot in a most Robinson Crusoe like fashion. We left the pinnace and continued *daking* [being carried by relays of men] till 8.30 a.m. this morning, having missed our bearers, left behind our *petarrahs* [luggage] forgotten to put tea in the *palkee* and divers other moving accidents. But, darling, why should these things ruffle us? These are our appointed trials sent to teach us forebearance and self-government. Excuse the lecture, my own Harry. Roads in places very bad, sometimes over morasses and *jheels* [flood waters], sometimes merely a path through a field.

Burra Ganj, October 11th

Alas darling, too soon does the teacher require to be taught. Before many hours I was peevish and irritable, and that to your dear self. We started at 3 p.m. and at four got to the house of a charitable indigo planter, who gave us a cup of tea. Reached Meerganj at six, got into a buggy and had a delightful drive by moonlight to the bungalow which we are now in. The furniture consists of a table, a cot, and two chairs, but there is a good roof to keep out the sun. We have *khana panee* [a wash house], soap and water, clean clothes, books and writing materials. Above all we have each other.

Henry replied:

Our dawn trip was a most disastrous one, the bearers at no stage of the tour being ready, and then being vile jawing fellows. I feel that I was more like a maniac than aught else for twenty-four hours. But instead of peevishness I saw nothing but the utmost sweetness and gentleness in you, my darling.

Hatimpore, October 13th

Reached the Jurie where we were ferried over in a most primitive manner. Two boats, each hollowed from a single trunk were lashed together, and on this the buggy was placed. We afterwards crossed in the same way. The bend of the stream looked like a lake with steep banks overgrown with jungle. On the banks were some travellers seemingly waiting to be ferried over. As we came in sight, the boat pushed off from the opposite side, the men standing up in it and shoving it along by tall bamboo poles. The water like a mirror reflecting the whole, beautiful butterflies and birds flying about and the wood-pigeons cooing from the surrounding thickets. The jungle consisted chiefly of Mimosa, three species. Long running creepers festooned many of the bushes, and the ground was enamelled with wild flowers. There we were, darling, the only two Europeans, and all the world to each other.

As the sun went down the moon shone out and we had a lovely drive in the clear night, passing through patches of wood and lanes bordered with bamboos all sparkling with fireflies. The native villages among the trees very picturesque. Their low thatched roofs overgrown with gourd-like creepers. The inhabitants standing and sitting in groups outside in the moonlight. Here and there a large single tree, under which lay a herd of cattle, seeming to enjoy the cool evening as much as we did. We reckoned on finding a tent, and at 8 p.m. we saw among the trees at sunset our servants seated and fires lighted. All this was very pretty but we were somewhat aghast to find no tent and a *charpoy* [bed] spread under the canopy of heaven. However, you found in the *tope* [spinney] a matted shed where our bed was placed. We got a fine plump *moorghie* [chicken], and we have been very comfortable but for the swarms of insects, which even the mosquito curtains did not exclude and which bite me unmercifully.

Yesterday the 12th we were up before sunrise, and after perfunctory ablutions and summary toilette, performed after most rural fashion under a tree, we got into the buggy and went over such a road 'if road it might be called, which road was none'. Joke the first was your getting out and carrying me over some *jheels*, and afterwards walking through such places that your clothes were all wet except your *banian* [undershirt]. When we came halfway, you took off your own clothing, girded the *Pushmina* [shawl] round your loins and put on my cloak to the great astonishment apparently of the niggers, who stared at seeing a sahib so attired.

Here we got letters and papers. Before nine we crossed the

Ghagra, and after half an hour's driving reached the tent at Kussur Thana. Here we were made amends for all our troubles, finding all comfortable; and after breakfast and bath we were very snug.

Henry interposes:

At 11.00 p.m. while you are snoring like a young rhinoceros, I again take up the book to testify how good a traveller you are, how courageous by land and water, and how gentle and forbearing to your cross husband.

Puttrah, October 15th

Yesterday read, wrote, and at 4.30 p.m. set out for Pycowly. The road a wheel track through fields or no track at all through swamps and *nullahs* [water-courses]. 'Crackskull Common and Featherbed Lane' were nothing to it, but we got safely to our tent, which was cheerful and where all was bright and right.

Started this morning at five thirty. After we had gone a little way I was astonished at the politeness of the natives, who showed us the way, smoothed the road and shoved on the buggy. I soon learned this was not all disinterested benevolence.[1] As we came near the village you pointed out the old Fakir's abode. When we got to our own tent, the traps were not there. And funny enough, we were immediately greeted by an envoy of his holiness, asking permission to send a breakfast. We pushed on however, to Reade's camp,[2] quite a Canvas City, which we reached about nine, and here we are, at home and busy. I do not recollect ever feeling better than for the last few days.

1. They had reached the district in which Henry had authority.
2. E. A. Reade, the Collector of Gorakhpur, was a lifelong friend.

Switzerland, 1858

Stopford Brooke

Stopford Brooke (1832–1916) was a clergyman and man of letters. A notable preacher, he became one of Queen Victoria's chaplains before leaving the Church of England in 1880. Thereafter he preached in Unitarian chapels and wrote many books on English literature.

To his brother William Brooke

Ouchy, sur Lac de Genève
Sunday, April 5, '58

I AM SITTING on the shores of the lake, with a pocket ink bottle and a pen, smoking my morning cigar. I am only allowed two a day, which is very short commons to me, who used to smoke so much, but with E. it can be borne. The mountains are all unclouded this morning, but are sleeping in a sunny haze which lessens their height, and softens their ruggedness. . . As far as I have gone into Switzerland, I have seen nothing to equal Snowdon. But we intend to go on to Chamonix and see the Mont Blanc range and the glacier. Then, I suppose, I shall feel satisfied, if such a thing is possible. The eye is never satisfied with seeing. Byron wrote 'The Prisoner of Chillon' in the Inn we are staying at, Hôtel de l'Ancre; and it is a fit place for a poet. The scenery is not too grand to strip a writer of his self-consciousness, and is noble and tender enough to wake up all poetic power and delicacy. . . I have either not settled down into realized married life, or I have settled down too completely—I cannot tell which. Time will show. Sometimes I am immensely happy—at other times I am as downcast and ennuyé as ever I have been, but with my character I shall be for ever subject to these continued alterations of feeling. . .

Yesterday we attended the English Church here, a hideous edifice, where I heard the service very badly read, and a sermon by a friend of the rector's, which had the peculiarity of shaving close to good points, and yet never touching them. Emma and I stayed for the Sacrament which we liked, and afterwards took a most lovely walk by the shores of this blue, blue water. I have so often wished for you, even with my wife and in the honeymoon I want a man to talk to now and then... I felt so thoroughly inclined to rush out of my seat yesterday and mount the pulpit... Tomorrow I think we leave this place for Bex in the valley of the Rhône, from thence to Martigny or Chamonix, certainly to Chamonix in the end, and then homewards by the Belgian towns.

Switzerland & Italy, 1873

Lady Monkswell

Mary Josephine Hardcastle married Robert Collier in 1873. She was the daughter of an MP and her husband's father, Sir Robert Collier, was a judge, and a former MP and Attorney-General. He was later created the 1st Lord Monkswell, a title to which her husband, a lawyer, succeeded in due course. Their honeymoon was that of an archetypal upper-middle-class high-Victorian couple, progressing from Paris to the Swiss Alps, then to Milan, Florence and Rome.

Monday, 1 Sept.

WE DEPARTED IN pouring rain for Dover, Paris, Lucerne & the Italian lakes &, let us trust, Rome! When we hove in sight of the sea I tremblingly observed that it was what I call very rough, & as we are all three extremely bad sailors the lookout was cheerful. However Bob got me a deck cabin, & at 10.30 Call [her maid] & I tucked ourselves up & waited upon fate. I in a recumbent, Call in a fiercely upright position. I had disquieted myself in vain; we had a capital passage, during which I slept. We went to bed at the Hôtel Dessin, Calais, about 2 a.m.

Tues., 2 Sept. [Paris]

Bob & I are amused at the distressed behaviour of various brides & bridegrooms; we flatter ourselves we are taken for brother & sister! I was at Paris last in June '63 with Mama, Miss Pyman & Emily, on our way back from Rome. We are at the Hôtel Meurice. After dinner we took a stroll along the Rue Rivoli, & saw a soupçon of ruins [i.e. after the siege of Paris and Communard riots, 1870–1] in the moonlight.

Monday, 8 Sept. [At Meiringen]

Bob walked & I rode over to Rosenlaui, about 2 hours alongside of the Reichenbach. Rosenlaui consists of an hôtel right under the glacier, the Welhorn, Wetterhorn & Dossenhorn (up which latter Bob has been), & some splendid jagged rocks called Engelhörner.

Sat., 13 Sept.

I sketched the waterfall behind the house very badly. A friend of Bob's in the person of Sir Henry Thompson, the great surgeon, rode in with his daughter from Meiringen. He is a most agreeable man. I sat next to him at table d'hôte, and we talked a great deal. He, like Sir Robert Collier [her father-in-law], exhibits when he may in the Royal Academy, & I have reason to believe that they draw from the same live model on Sunday afternoons.

Sunday, 14 Sept.

We attended a grand exhibition of sketches by an artist (one Croft) up in his bedroom. It was a most impressive ceremony; Sir Henry Thompson, his daughter, Bob & I each collected our candles & marched upstairs with them till we looked like a religious procession. Once caught there was no getting away again till Sir H.T., who knows the habits & customs of artists, cut us a way of escape.

Tuesday, 16 Sept.

Start at 8—over the (great) Scheidegg to Grindelwald. My, the cold! snow lying at the top, two shawls availed nothing—Drove from Grindelwald to Lauterbrunnen, & tried Bob's naturally sweet temper to the uttermost by my variety of exclamations of surprise & delight over the Jungfrau & party. Rode up to Mürren.

Wednesday, 17 Sept.

I had a delicious run down to Lauterbrunnen with Bob at about 8—The view of the Jungfrau through the fir trees was something quite beyond everything. We drove from Lauterbrunnen to Interlaken then along the lake of Thun; the colours were exquisite, green, blue & purple shadows. At Frutigen it began to rain. We reached Kandersteg at 6.30.

Thursday, 18 Sept.

Bob walked & I rode over the Gemmi. We ought to have seen an enormous view from the top but the clouds kept steaming up so we only caught glimpses of several rows of purple & snow mountains. We drove from Leukerbad along a most delightful valley into the Rhône valley, where we were rather bored it was such a long straight road, tho' there was a nice group of snow mountains just in front of us. We were obliged to take refuge in 'Gil Blas' (which improper novel Bob is reading with immense enjoyment). We also feared our horse might drop down dead, but he survived to carry me up the Visp-Zermatt valley the next day.

Monday, 22 Sept.

Who should come into lunch but Master Willy Gladstone [the Prime Minister's eldest son] as Bob calls him, & a younger brother.

I did my first & last snow pass, we went over the S. Théodule. We intended to have started about 4.30 a.m., but fate in the shape of S. Maurice's fête stept in, & nothing would persuade the guide & porters to start before 7. We began with three hours' rather steep ascent to the edge of the glacier, this I performed on the back of a horse. Then I got off &, with the guide shoving one side, & Bob the other, I embarked on the long slightly inclined snow slope. There was a very good track all the way, & the snow was quite hard so it was plain sailing enough, but how anyone could find his way with no track & in a mist is beyond me. We took two hours getting to the little inn perched on some rocks at the top. Here we rested a half hr.

& watched Master Willy Gladstone toiling up the snow down below in a rope & a mask. We had about three-quarters of an hr. more snow & rocks, then we got down to Breuil at the head of the Valtornanche. Here we rested & ate, & then walked slowly down the valley looking back constantly at the Matterhorn. Master W.G. caught us up & we walked some way together; he now understands that I have 'changed my situation'. We put up at the funniest little inn in the village of Valtornanche. We were waited upon with immense dignity by the host & hostess. Mr. Justice Lawson & son & daughter, & the two Master Gladstones, were the only people there.

Thursday, 25 Sept. [At Châtillon.]
We drove to Courmayeur—6 hours, to see the view of the S. side of Mont Blanc. We passed a romantic shooting château of King Victor Emmanuel's, & got to a most picturesque village called Villeneuve, & then we had a long piece under walnut trees down a narrow gorge with the cliff one side & river deep down on the other. After about 4 hours we suddenly came upon an opening at the end of the valley, & the edge of a snow mountain which kept on disclosing itself higher & higher. (Driver) 'Voilà le Mont Blanc'.—I can not imagine a more beautiful shaped mountain, it beats all I have seen before.

Saturday, 27 Sept.
We drove to Châtillon—3 hours—& then on 6 hours more to Ivrea along a beautiful valley full of villages & mixed castles & vines. I looked up at the very nick of time & saw Mont Blanc about 40 miles off. You can only see it for 200 or 300 yards, & Bob was just then taking his usual nap. I'm sorry to say that the word *einspanner* [a one-horse carriage] sends my 'Lord & Master' to sleep! I should think no tourist had been to Ivrea since the flood. We saw some pretty costumes on the road—a girl in a deep red garment with white sleeves & white drapery on her head. We also saw some delightful dun coloured cattle yoked together drawing great weights. The population of the valley seemed a half-grown miserable race.

Monday, 29 Sept.

At Milan. We went over the Cathedral which I enjoyed very much, but Bob I am sorry to say does not enjoy anything but country, & thinks towns a bore. We also saw Leonardo's 'Last Supper'. I was very much struck by that beautiful ruin, there is more fire in its ashes than in the best copy I have ever seen. We went to the Brera & saw L. da Vinci's sketch of Our Lord's head for his big picture; it was extremely touching. The women actually walk about in Milan with black lace veils over their heads—I would not have believed it. We went by train to Como, & there found to our horror there was no corresponding steamer, so we had to go in a little boat to Villa d'Este, an hôtel about an hour off.

Tuesday, 14 Oct.

We started from Florence at 8.30, and did not get into Rome till 6.30, a good long journey. We passed Perugia, Assisi & Foligno, most picturesque towns; the train passed through beautiful rugged hills covered with bay trees. At Arni there was a beautiful huge broken bridge '*o'er the pale waves of Na*', & other Norman remains. We also passed lake Trasimeno with the old Etruscan Cortona looking down upon it. My excitement waxed more & more as we approached the Eternal City, Arturo & Madge [her husband's sister] who were waiting for us. We had first to pass through a stand in a fumigated hall till we were nearly choked. Arturo is very tall & slim, with a rather small but handsome & refined face & small hands & feet; he was in a blue uniform. Madge is about as big as Emily [i.e. small], rather fatter & not in the least like Bob. They came with us to the hotel Constenzi, & sat by while we ate our supper. The principal medium of conversation is fluent but Anglican French.

Thursday, 16th Oct.

We went to the Palace of the Caesars where they have been making vast excavations. With help of Bob's classical learning, which is but scanty, & explanations from Arturo who does not know much about it, & old Chute whom we found prowling round Baedeker in hand, & the two plain sisters in tow—I succeeded in understanding that the two principal 'pieces' were the Emperor's

Palace & the House of Livia. The paintings on the wall astonished me less by the brightness of their colour than by the capital way in which they were drawn. I never appreciated before how the world must have gone back after the invasion of the Goths—compare these walls with the mosaics of the 7th century, the latter, as Bob irreverently but justly remarked are like drawings by a child.

Friday, 17 Oct.

We had a happy day in the baths of Caracalla where I sketched for 2 hours while Bob read *Waterloo* to me with admirable patience; then we walked to the Colosseum, which we have vowed to see every day, tried to find out some baths of Claudia, got into a *ligno* & drove down the Via Appia. I marked down a charming little view of St. Peter's & 2 stone pines, but human nature cannot sketch for more than a certain time. We gave a dinner party in the evening—Madge, Arturo & Mr. & Mrs. Grove, he a feeble imitation of Mr. Merivale, she pretty & gentle & half Italian. I talked a great deal to Arturo; he told me how the country is being stirred up everywhere.

Saturday, 25th Oct.

We went down to our National Church & I enjoyed the service very much after so many broken Sundays. In the afternoon Bob & I went on to the Pincio & observed the Roman world. They have an absurd custom of walking about in families—1 & 2 proud Father & Mother, 3 a nurse with a red frill round her head & silver pins carrying what looks generally like the eldest & only hope. There really were a certain number of smart carriages with very *outré* toilettes.

Monte Carlo, Rome & Naples, 1873

Emily Birchall

Emily Jowitt was the daughter of a well-to-do Quaker merchant in Leeds. At the age of 20 she got first class honours in the Cambridge Examination for Women. In January 1873, the following year, she married Dearman Birchall, a wealthy Leeds cloth merchant, aged 44, widowed with a daughter. The disparity in ages was no bar to their devotion to each other. After a few days in Browns Hotel, Albemarle Street, London W1, they left for the Continent. We catch up with them and their characterful Italian courier Perrini in the South of France.

Tuesday, 4 February

THIS HAS been one of the red letter days of my life, having been signalized by a glorious walk, in magnificent scenery, on an absolutely perfect day, and with a most congenial companion. What more could be desired? After a long discussion on ways and means yesterday with Perrini, we suddenly started the brilliant idea that we would walk to Mentone [from Nice], whilst he and the luggage came by train. Our faithful Italian threw up his hands and eyes, gasped for breath, and all but fainted on the spot. At last, after having vainly tried to dissuade us from so suicidal an enterprise, he resigned us to our fate, washing his hands of us, and evidently regarding us as a couple of amiable lunatics.

So this morning we started directly after breakfast, i.e. at 11 a.m. by Nice time (an hour later than ours) and had a most exhilarating and delightful walk, intensely enjoyed by both of us. The steep first part of the ascent was the only place where we really found the sun excessively hot. There I mounted parasol and veil, and doffed gloves and all doffable garments, and Dearman peeled to his shirt sleeves, greatly exciting my envy of his cool and airy appearance. The heat was however by no means oppressive, as there was all the time a most delicious breeze. The views the whole way were of course perfectly enchanting, and delighted me even more than they did three years ago, for one sees them so much more satisfactorily when on foot than from a carriage. As we mounted the Turbia, the long stretch of blue sea, with all its charming bays and capes, Villa-franca below us to our right, beyond that Nice, then the Cap d'Antibes running far out to sea, beyond again the islands opposite Cannes, further still the exquisite Esterels with their grand outlines, and farthest of all the hills just on this side of Marseilles, while looking inland, our eyes feasted on the lovely snowy peaks of the Maritime Alps, and, nearer, on the olive covered hills, the terraced vineyards and the scattered cottages of the country round Nice – all this made up a superb picture, seen as it was on a day of such brilliance.

We reached the excessively picturesque village of Turbia [Turbie] soon after 2.30, and remained there nearly an hour, baiting ourselves. We ventured to enter an awfully seedy-looking restaurant, where we found an untidy but amiable landlady who covered the little wooden table with a clean white tablecloth, and gave us knives and plated forks and even dinner-napkins, and, by and by, very good hard-boiled eggs, bread and nice sweet vin du pays which last exactly suited my taste, and to all of which fare we did full justice …

The latter part of the walk was made in the darkening twilight, for we did not reach Mentone till nearly six. We were received by Perrini, who was anxiously looking out for us, having evidently expected either to hear of our demise, or to see us brought in on litters, in a state of collapse. We have taken up our quarters at the Hotel Victoria.

Wednesday, 5 February

Monte Carlo was unusually gay, owing to a pigeon shooting match that was going on there so we saw it under its most gorgeous aspect, crowded with the fast and fashionable, the ladies in toilettes of the most magnificent description conceivable, and all under the cloudless bright blue sky.

We watched the pigeon-shooting for a little while, but thought it very poor sport. The birds were shut up, one at a time, in little traps, about 20 yards from the sportsmen, and on a string being pulled, the trap opened, and the pigeon flew out, to be immediately brought down, for it hardly ever rose a yard into the air before it was hit, though one or two birds managed to get clear away untouched. We soon had seen as much of this as we wished, and repaired to the Casino, there to become very soon absorbed in the intense interest either of watching the different faces round the tables, or else of following the fortunes of some one man. We found those who played highest the most attractive, and there certainly was a great deal of high play going on. We watched one very handsome young man for a long time; he won at first, very largely indeed, and had no end of notes, rouleaux and napoleons before him, but then the luck turned, and he lost each coup, every time turning paler, and biting his lips, till at last all was gone, he had not a single napoleon left, and then he rose and walked away. Another quite old man, English, played desperately and apparently without any system or plan, and we saw him do nothing but lose, note after note, always 1000 francs at least; he seemed to be terribly unlucky, but we were told he had won far more than he had lost. We stood for hours watching an English gentleman at rouge et noir, with the deepest interest. He played evidently on a regular system, entering everything in a book, and very high too, for we several times saw him stake as much as £200 at once. He won 20,000 francs whilst we watched him.

We dined at the *table d'hôte* in the handsome dining hall; about 300 there, and a very good dinner.

Afterwards we watched the play again, and then left at 9.50, or ought to have done, but the train was half an hour late, so we had another long wait at the station. We hear that the tables made £9,000 sterling one day last week. The whole affair is kept up in the most luxurious style, reading rooms, concert rooms, &c.; but it certainly must pay the Prince very well.

Saturday, 8 February

Perrini is a source of perpetual amusement to us, he indulges in considerable exaggerations, and the strongest expressions, but always with the same genial face, and he never loses his temper in the slightest degree. He frequently uses the threat 'if he doesn't do it, I will break his neck' and profusely bestows such mild epithets as vagabond, rascal, scoundrel, &c &c. Whilst we were in France, he found a reason for every ill that befell us, in the fact that the country enjoyed the Republican form of government; if a hotel-keeper made an exorbitant charge, he was a republican, if the candles would not light, they were revolutionary, if the coffee was smoked, a republican had prepared it. We thought his spirits would rise on crossing the Pont St. Louis frontier, and entering a Kingdom, but no, Italy is no better, 'Sir, we are in Italy' is thought sufficient explanation for any misadventure, 'a nation of liars' he calmly calls his own compatriots, for he is a Genoese by birth. He *considers* himself English, however, and such is the strength of his devotion that he 'would rather be dead in England than alive in any other country'. So much so, that he has invested his little all in the purchase of 'some land in England – a small freehold, – at Brompton, – I pay no taxes for it, – it is *in the cemetery*, Sir'! He said this afternoon, 'This is a charming country, so enlightened, so intelligent, I daresay I might find in it somewhere a *newspaper of last year*'. He was able to console himself for the horror of our walking to Mentone the other day only by the reflection that 'these English, they have legs of steel', and when I remarked 'it is not so very far; it is a good walk', 'Yes, Madame, you are perfectly right, it is a good walk, a *very* good walk. I call it not walking; I call it killing'. When he heard that Dearman had taken off his coat for the walk, he nearly expired. 'Thank you Sir, I am very much obliged to you – Oh! yes, an excellent thing, Sir, an admirable thing, if you want to get an inflamation.' His accent, and manner of speaking, are irresistibly comic, and he amuses us endlessly.

Wednesday, 12 February

Who could be twelve hours in Rome and keep away from her Cathedral? We walked to it, guided by Perrini over the Ponte di S. Angelo whence the first glimpse of the Dome came to us, and far from feeling the least touch of that disappointment which, so many say, accompanies the first sight of it, it filled me with wondering admiration. It was grander, huger, vaster than my dreams of it. We walked on till we stood in the glorious Piazza, with S. Peter's in front of us, its splendid colonnade on either side, and the Vatican to our right. We went into the Cathedral, and we stood still in sight of its vastness, breathless with awe and wonder. Dearman says he never felt so excited by anything in his life, and my feelings were certainly beyond description. The glorious majesty of the whole impresses one more than anything else, but besides this there is the individual beauty of every inch of roof and wall, pillar and floor, the exquisite taste of the decoration, the richness of the marbles, the loveliness of the frescoes, and the great beauty of the sculpture. The vastness of the scale of S. Peter's can only be appreciated when one sees in the distance at the other end of the nave, how tiny men and women look, and how small those statues or other objects, which one knows to be really of great size, appear at that distance. We were disgusted with the irreverence of one vulgar English tourist, who had seated himself, Murray [guidebook] in hand, on the top step of the High Altar itself, and just in front of the very altar.

Thursday, 13 February

At five we took a most recherché Victoria we saw in the Piazza, with silver mountings, showy horse, very showy driver, quite a dazzling little turn-out (compare with our London cabs, and confess the superiority of Rome!), and drove to the Mamertine Prison, which was specially lighted up, we were told. Our driver stopped in a small square filled with carriages evidently waiting for their occupants. We got out, and as our driver told us to go straight on, we wandered on, seeing nothing at all like an entrance to a prison or to anything at all, but pointed onwards by the men, who all seemed to know what we wanted without our appealing to them, till we came to what looked like the back way to a mews. Here we did hesitate, but the numerous ostlers and coachmen about said we were all right, and we went on, through a little door, and down a dark passage till we suddenly found ourselves in the midst of a large party of English and American tourists, all carrying torches, and listening to a sort of lecture which Mr. Parker (whom Dearman knows) was giving. To them we joined ourselves, and we all went through the five vaults of the prison, where Jugurtha and Catiline, and St. Paul were, almost certainly, confined, and, tradition says, St. Peter also. From the main part of the prison to St. Peter's cell, we had to go down a narrow low little passage just like a drain, and more than 100 yards long, which, creeping slowly along, almost on hands and knees, as we were, seemed *interminable*, and was most fearfully hot and stifling. The laughter and merriment with which it was entered, soon changed into silence, or groans, or gasps, or anxious inquiries, 'Shall we have to come back the same way, Mr Parker?' &c. This passage much resembles a drain in size and form, and has only just now been discovered and cleared. When at last we emerged, we found ourselves in the cell said to be Peter's, and we all drank out of the well which sprang up miraculously in order to enable him to baptize his jailors, and then we slowly made our way, up and up, out into the fresh air of heaven once more, having been nearly asphyxiated, but immensely interested.

After dinner we paid a most delightful moonlight visit to the Colosseum, and most glorious it was, but the lovely evening had drawn thither numbers of tourists, and their voices and laughter were so little in harmony with the noble silence of the great still amphitheatre, and one heartily wished them all away, it was so entirely a case where 'only man was vile'.

From the Colosseum we went to the Pantheon, but found it all locked up for the night; however, on going round to the back, we succeeded in finding the sacristan, an old monk, who admitted us. He was by no means remarkable for symmetry of feature, a fact which Perrini instantly observed, and when we were absorbed in the contemplation of the large dimly-lighted mysterious-seeming rotunda, he drew our attention to the shadow of light cast by the moon on the interior of the dome; 'Oh! how very remarkable! look sir, how wonderfully like the profile of the old monkey at the door! What a strange coincidence! I will call him, that you may see for yourselves.' He then proceeded to go back for the monk, and returned with him, politely asking him something about the church in Italian, and then turning to us, just as if translating the holy man's answer, and gravely saying 'Now sir, you see the resemblance I spoke of. Look at the nose of this rascally old monkey, and observe how exact its portrait. Then too the chin' – but at this point we were both compelled to turn our backs precipitately on the monk and bury ourselves and our mirth in the dark recesses of the church. Perrini's absolute imperturbability of visage, and the calm way in which he alternately does the polite on such occasions, to the priests, in Italian, and then abuses them to us in English, are a constant trial to our gravity. His hatred to the priests is something tremendous, and he seems to have seen a good deal of their dark side.

Thursday, 20 February

We came to the edge of the Tiber, and there I saw just below, the remains of an *old bridge*. My heart leaped for a sure instinct told me 'that must be all that is left of the Bridge of Horatius!' It was this that I had longed to see, more perhaps than anything else in Rome. I had read it up in Murray, and found it there prosaically called the Sublician bridge, so now, when I think I see its foundations before my eyes I wish to make assurance doubly sure; and before giving free course to my emotions, I make a desperate effort to rally the scattered forces of my Italian vocabulary, I arrange a sentence in hot haste, I rush to the guardhouse, dash open the door, and find myself in the midst of a body of soldiery, at whom I discharge my volley '*E quello il ponte Sublicio, vi prego di dirmi?*' The 'captain of the gate' (a stalwart youth, successor to Horatius) steps forward, and replies politely '*Si, signora, il ponte di Horatio.*' I nearly faint at the words, I gasp out a syllable of thanks, I dart out again. I lean over the low wall, I look down on the basements of the piers of Rome's oldest bridge, I look up and across the 'broad floods' to the 'further shore' where brave Horatius stood alone and where the thrice thirty thousand, all Etruria's noblest shrank back 'from the ghastly entrance where those bold Romans stood', I gaze on the yellow river, as tawny now as then, my feet are on the very spot where 'now he feels the bottom, now on dry earth he stands', and the grand heroism of twenty four hundred years ago seems clear and real before my eyes.

Monday, 24 February

This afternoon we have been strolling about for three hours, visiting the ghastly, grotesque, but curious, interesting, and certainly unique, cemetery below the church of the Capuchins, which is decorated entirely with the bones of departed monks, all arranged in fantastic patterns, while others, more recently taken up from the holy earth of Jerusalem, in which each one rests only till his place is wanted for another, stand in niches, fully dressed and bearing in their withered hands their crucifix and rosary. The bones of 5000 dead Capuchins repose – no, anything but *repose*, to be set up and exposed to the gaze of the curious to the end of time – have their abode here, and one wonders at the coolness with which the living ones, habited exactly like those brown skeletons in the niches, can gaze on their dead brethren, whose fate must, sooner or later, be theirs.

Wednesday, 15 March, Naples

Dearman had an ardent longing to see one of the craters that, he had heard, had suddenly opened in the side of Vesuvius and poured forth volumes of lava. Asking the guide if there was such an opening near San Sebastiano, he replied that he could shew us one, an hour's walk thence. We decided at once to go thither, thinking it a nice unhackneyed sort of thing to do, and rather out of the beaten track and golden visions floated before our minds of the credit we should derive from our discovery of the wonderful side-crater, which should hence-forth appear in all the Baedekers and Murrays. So we left the carriage and Perrini at San Sebastiano, fortified ourselves against the pangs of hunger by some oranges and apples, and started on our walk at 1.15. We found it a long tiring affair, first over rough lava, for a long distance, decidedly hard walking, then up and up, along a narrow path between huge high banks – almost cliffs, and here it was *intolerably* hot. We walked mounting always for an hour and a quarter, when we suddenly perceived the hermitage just above us. Knowing that this was the last point, on the way up Vesuvius, that can be reached by carriages, we began to suspect that we had been sold, for we didn't want to come up here at all, as we meant to make the regular ascent of the mountain another day. Appealing to the guide, however, we were assured that, Yes he understood; there was a little crater that we should see, only one '*piccolo momento*' more. But our suspicions increased, and were finally confirmed when a few minutes afterwards, we reached the Hermitage, and unmasked the villainy of our guide who it appears only meant that we should have a good view of the big crater! Dearman pitched into him in good sound English, which I sought to translate for the culprit's benefit, into very mild Italian, till I found all the force of vituperation was evaporating in the process. At last the happy thought struck us 'why should we not, as we *were* so near, go on up to the top then and there', and the idea was stimulated by our suddenly perceiving a party of 3 young Englishmen, riding past us on ponies, the last of whom was Prince Arthur. This seemed to prove that it was not utterly demented to begin the ascent at 3 p.m., so we set to work, sent off the crafty guide with a note to Perrini, telling him to meet us at Resina with the carriage, ordered some ponies, arranged terms with the nice guide (a government official, not a promiscuous vagabond like him of San Sebastiano) gulped down part of an omelette, as Dearman said we must have 'something to walk on' and finally mounted our little steeds at 3.10. After 20 mins, rough but not steep riding, we reached the Atrio dei Cavalli, at the foot of the mountain proper, which looked as we approached it somewhat like an Eastern encampment, with its little band of horses feeding leisurely on the scanty herbage, surrounded by swarthy picturesque ragamuffins of all ages. From this point up to the summit is a very very stiff walk of an hour or an hour and a half, all the way excessively steep, and on soft cinders, very small almost like black sand, on which one sinks in and slips back at every turn, so that the fatigue of the ascent is immensely augmented. I had 3 guides to help me; the two in front were really of some use, the one behind of none. Dearman had one, and we were, on starting, seized by about a dozen more volunteers, who descanted on the enormous difficulties of the way, which rendered at least 5 guides necessary for each person!! as well as by the 6 bearers of a *chaise à porteurs*, who almost forced me into it 'it is too far for a lady – La signora would be much better in a chair; ladies never walk all the way.' At last we shook ourselves free of these wretches, and proceeded on our way. The sun was intensely hot, and the walk was certainly tiring whilst it lasted, but it seemed soon accomplished, and then, when we – quite suddenly – reached the summit, a sight burst upon our view that would have repaid a thousandfold, ten times the toil. Right before us, shelving away from beneath our very feet, lay the deep hollow, with romantic jagged edges, in which darkly yawn the three great craters. The smoke cleared off most opportunely, as if on purpose to give us a perfect view of all the grand scene, merely curling upwards in soft filmy beauty, which added greatly to the picturesqueness of the view, and leaving clear to our eyes all the richly tinted sides of the vast hollow, bright with sulphurous hues of yellow, red and green. I had expected *thrilling interest*; for the *beauty* I was not prepared. The smoke came up beneath our feet as we walked, the ground was *burning* hot to the touch of our hands, and almost painful even through our boots, and we realized how literally we were on a volcano, when the guide pointed out to us, in several places, crevices or little apertures through which we could see the red-hot lava glowing not one foot from the surface. I pushed in a stick, and drew it out *in flames* and the guide offered to cook us eggs, which we declined, as we thought they would taste strongly of sulphur, and then he poked a bit of lava out of a hole, and gave it to Dearman to light his cigar on, which he did. We stayed up at the top about an hour intensely enjoying the glorious panorama of all the surrounding country, and the marvellous scene immediately before us, which every movement varied, according as the smoke augmented or diminished, blew on this side or on that. Sometimes the hot white sulphurous cloud swept all round and over us, but the fumes of brimstone were not so overpowering as I should have expected, though near the fire crevices the sulphur smell was tremendously powerful.

From *The Rainbow Comes & Goes*

Diana Cooper

Lady Diana Manners, the most beautiful girl of her generation, had a long engagement to Duff Cooper during the First World War. While she nursed, he was in the Foreign Office before going to France with the Grenadier Guards in 1918, where he won the DSO for bravery and survived, unlike most of their male friends. They married in 1919 and their honeymoon was largely a tour of plutocratic houses and hotels. Formal peace was declared on 29 June 1919, the same day that Archduke Ferdinand had been assassinated at Sarajevo in 1914.

PHILIP SASSOON HAD LENT us his house at Lympne, and from there we crossed to France and so to Paris. We were rich with presents and cheques and stayed at the Ritz, and I liked being called Madame and wearing a wedding-ring and being happy all the time. We 'déjeuné sur l'herbe', dined under trees and loved the French and the whole generous world. From Paris we went to Florence, where my old friend Ivor Wimborne had taken Berenson's famous villa, *I Tatti*. There I first saw fire-flies in their millions. We were shy because we were so newly married and not alone. From Fiesole we motored to Rome, with a night at Orvieto, where we didn't know that 'Orvieto sings', and ordered bad champagne. In Rome we lived in grandeur at the Grand Hotel (a wedding present from Marconi) and we bathed in the Specchio di Diana and planned to live there. Our destination was the heaven of Lord Grimthorpe's Villa Cimbroneon the mountain height above Ravello. Thirty years ago it was a day's journey from Naples. We drove, accompanied by dear faithful Wadey [her maid], for three hours in a bus and a few hours in a fiacre, and then a long climb, followed by our boxes on bowed peasant shoulders. The house, set in its vast hanging gardens of lemons and olives and statues and quotations from Omar Khayyam carved on stone seats, seemed all that mortal lovers could demand. With too much zeal we ran down the two miles of hill and steps to the sea, bathed, lay rocking in a boat in the June sun and came back in the evening glow to our dinner cooked by the butler who was also Mayor of Ravello. He gave us a fish curled like a scythe holding a branch of honeysuckle in its poor gills, and wine made on the estate that fizzed a little and intoxicated a lot.

The next day, crippled by stiffness and raw from sunburn, I could move only on a donkey, and on its back the Mayor led me into the churches and round the altars. We could not bear it to end and thought foolishly that the return would be less prosaic, and also less hot, if we took a ship from Naples to Marseilles. Green as saplings we took berths in the ship that sailed on the day that suited us. It turned out to be a Rumanian troopship packed past its plimsoll line with soldiers. A violent Mediterranean storm blew up as we left. The troops were laid all over the decks and passages and were sick to a man. It was a dreadful journey, but at Marseilles the guns were banging away, not for war but for peace, which that day was declared.

From *Travels with Myself and Another*
Martha Gellhorn

In Travels with Myself and Another, *Martha Gellhorn describes travelling to China in the company of an 'Unwilling Companion' – Ernest Hemingway. They had married on the 21st November 1940 in Cheyenne, Wyoming and set out to report on the war in China via Hawaii. He called their 'super, horror journey' a honeymoon.*

EARLY IN FEBRUARY 1941, we set out from San Francisco for Honolulu by boat. We imagined this trip would be like the already distant good old days when one crossed from New York to France, on a French ship, wallowing in delicious food and drink and luxury. UC always had the right idea about pleasure which is: grab it while you can. Instead of hoped for delights, we were batted about the decks like ping-pong balls, hurled into nailed-down furniture unless unnailed-down furniture hurled itself into us until finally, incapable of standing upright, we retired to our berths where we lay eating and drinking and trying not to be flung from berth to floor.

Trays crashed off our laps, bottles spilled; the ship proceeded with the motion of a dolphin, lovely in a dolphin and vile in a ship. UC muttered a lot: why had nobody warned us, if he had known the

Pacific was this kind of ocean he would never have set foot on it, a man should stick with the waters he knew, as a matter of fact, he knew and respected many lakes and rivers too, and look at it any way you want, M, this is a bad sign. The sea voyage lasted roughly forever. Somewhere, over the detestable grey waves, Honolulu would be a haven of sun, swimming, peace and stationary land. Nobody warned us about the traditional aloha-welcome either.

I made a full airmail report to my mother:

'There were finally eighteen leis on each of our necks. UC had a face of black hate. He said to me "I never had no filthy Christed flowers around my neck before and the next son of a bitch who touches me I am going to cool him and what a dung heap we came to and by Christ if anyone says aloha to me I am going to spit back in his mouth." You get the feeling?'

You Hated Spain

Ted Hughes

For thirty-five years after her suicide in 1963, Sylvia Plath's former husband kept silent on the subject of their marriage. Then, in 1988, he published Birthday Letters, *a collection of eighty-eight poems, most of them addressed directly to her. Here, he remembers their honeymoon, about which Plath, in her journal, had this to say: 'Never in my life have I had conditions so perfect: a magnificent, brilliant husband ..., a quiet large house with no interruptions, phones or visitors; the sea at the bottom of the street, the hills at the top. Perfect mental and physical well-being.'*

Spain frightened you.
Spain.
Where I felt at home.

The blood-raw light,
The oiled anchovy faces, the African
Black edges to everything, frightened you.
Your schooling had somehow neglected Spain.
The wrought-iron grille, death and the Arab drum.
You did not know the language, your soul was empty
Of the signs, and the welding light
Made your blood shrivel.
Bosch Held out a spidery hand and you took it
Timidly, a bobby-sox American.
You saw right down to the Goya funeral grin
And recognized it, and recoiled
As your poems winced into chill, as your panic
Clutched back towards college America.
So we sat as tourists at the bullfight
Watching bewildered bulls awkwardly butchered,
Seeing the grey-faced matador, at the barrier
Just below us, straightening his bent sword
And vomiting with fear. And the horn
That hid itself inside the blowfly belly
Of the toppled picador punctured
What was waiting for you. Spain
Was the land of your dreams: the dust-red cadaver
You dared not wake with, the puckering amputations
No literature course had glamorized.
The juju land behind your African lips.
Spain was what you tried to wake up from
And could not. I see you, in moonlight,
Walking the empty wharf at Alicante
Like a soul waiting for the ferry,
A new soul, still not understanding,
Thinking it is still your honeymoon
In the happy world, with your whole life waiting,
Happy, and all your poems still to be found.

From *Iris*

John Bayley

John Bayley's memoir of his novelist wife Iris Murdoch's life, and her descent into Alzheimer's, is inflected throughout with the sense of true companionship which is already evident in this description of their honeymoon in the 1950s. Theirs was not a conventional marriage, but to read the book is to realise the quality of their friendship.

R IVERS, AS I SAID, featured in our honeymoon, although not by intention. Our idea had been to take a cultural tour in a leisurely manner, down through France and over the Alps into north Italy, keeping clear of famous places like Florence and Venice, which we would leave for another time, staying instead at Urbino, San Gimignano and Arezzo, places earnestly recommended to Iris by a couple whom I thought of as her 'art friends' – Brigid Brophy and her husband Michael [Levey], who was later to become director of the National Gallery. Brigid had chided Iris for allowing herself to do anything so banal as to get married, but her sarcasms were weakened by the fact that she had, however reluctantly, taken the same step herself. She wanted the experience of having a child, and single mothers in those days had not yet acquired the glamour they would achieve later on.

Wisely we were not going in the Riley, but in a very small Austin van, which I had recently bought new for a modest sum. It was all the cheaper because being a 'commercial vehicle' it was exempt from what was then called Purchase Tax. The same Elaine Griffiths who had asked me to the party at St Anne's where I met Iris, had recently acquired one of these, and being a crafty lady had caused a garage to remove the metal side panels at the back, substituting neat glass windows. The vehicle now became officially a saloon car, and as such was not subject to the 30 mile an hour speed limit imposed in those days on all trucks and vans. She recommended this device, but after consideration we rejected it, unwisely as it turned out, because I was soon stopped and fined by an unsporting policeman for doing nearly forty miles an hour.

. . .

Half a century ago the roads of France were empty. Long straight poplar-bordered roads, still full of '*déformations*' as a result of wartime neglect, but wonderfully relaxing to buzz happily down in a *reverie à deux*. No trouble going through towns. A helpful sign promised 'Toutes Directions'; a bored gendarme blew his whistle unnecessarily; small restaurants advertised their *repas* with a sign on the pavement. France existed not for the tourist nor for its own people (where were they? who were they?) but for honeymoon couples like us, without much money, listening together to each poplar saying 'hush' as we drove past, as regularly as the telegraph wires of those days used to rise and fall beside the train. Then we would stop at one of the little restaurants, three-quarters empty, and have *charcuterie* and *entrecôte aux endives*, with unlimited quantities of red wine which never had to be uncorked or bought by the bottle. Cramped little hotels (*de la Poste* or *du Gare*) had scrubbed floors that smelt of garlic and Gauloises cigarettes. Natives were taciturn, speech formalised and distant; but I noticed that the severest French person (and to me all their faces looked austere, like those of monks and nuns) responded to Iris's smile.

Of course she knew France already – another France, inhabited entirely, in my eyes, by writers and intellectuals who sat in cafés and wrote books between drinks. It was not so long since Iris had been under the spell of Sartre's novel *La Nausée* and Raymond Queneau's *Pierrot Mon Ami*. She had met Queneau in Brussels cafés at the end of the war, and through him had heard of Samuel Beckett's pre-war novel *Murphy*. *La Nausée* had interested her philosophically, and *Murphy* had bequeathed to her own first novel *Under the Net* a notional spirit of Bohemia. Along with existentialism, and perhaps partly in response to it, there went at that time with Iris something less *engagé* and more irresponsible, something that made me think of the young person in Boswell's Johnson who wished to study philosophy, but 'cheerfulness kept breaking in'.

Our own cheerfulness found a perfect foil in quiet empty unresponsive France, which fed us so deliciously and so cheaply, and sent us on our way down endless roads on which one seemed to cover hundreds if not thousands of kilometres without any effort at all.

Our first swim was in a river of the Pas de Calais, a deep placid tributary of the Somme. Perhaps the place of the poem by Wilfred Owen, where hospital barges had been moored during those futile offensives of the first world war. The next was much further south, in a steep and wild wooded valley, with pine and chestnut growing up the mountains. The water was warm, and the stream so secluded that we slipped in with nothing on. Usually cautious, Iris may have felt that now we were in France Anglo-Saxon inhibition could be discarded. It was in this remote spot that my feet encountered a smooth round object in the shallows. It was half buried in the ooze, but I fished it up without difficulty and found an object like a Greek or Roman amphora, earth-coloured and cracked in one or two places. It was clearly not ancient – we found a trade name stamped on the base – and I was about to let it sink back into its underwater home when Iris, treading water beside me, vigorously demurred. Even at that date she wanted to keep everything she found. Wrapped in French newspapers it reposed in the bottom of the little van and lived on for years in a corner of our garden back home, until its cracks were found out by the frost and it came to pieces.

After setting it down on the bank we slipped in again for another swim. Iris seemed dreamy and absent. 'Suppose we had found a great old bell,' she said as we dried ourselves. I pointed out that this would hardly be likely in such a wild spot, far from any town or village. But her imagination was equal to that one.

'It could have been stolen from a belfry and buried in the river until they could dispose of it. People at home are stealing lead from country churches all the time, aren't they? Then the thieves here never came back.'

'Quite a recent event? Nothing legendary about it?'

'No, wait … The church was desecrated at the reformation by those – what did they call them in France?' she appealed as she stood beside me, an earnest figure streaked all over with river mud, which she was vaguely spreading over herself with the towel.

'Huguenots?'

'That's it. The Huguenots got down the bell and wanted to break it up or melt it or something, but some devoted worshippers of the old church managed to steal it away and bring it here for safe keeping.'

Although she had done ancient history in her exams, Iris was a scholar who had done her best papers in philosophy. So she had often told me; and her sense of the historical was certainly rather sketchy. But as her novels show, her imagination possessed its own brand of sometimes almost pedantic accuracy.

The most striking episode in her next novel *The Bell* certainly came out of that river. A great bell is found in an old abbey, now the centre of a modern religious community. The symbol of the bell is enigmatic: not so the penetrating and perceptive account of characters who wish to try to lead the religious life.

Next day we were in a mountain region, nearing the frontier. In order to make an early start for crossing the Alps we decided to stop the night at a small town with a railway junction. In the dead of night our bedroom door was suddenly flung open and a voice proclaimed in dramatic tones *'Georges! C'est l'heure.'* The unshaded light over the bed dazzled us, and when he saw how things were the young railwayman who had come to rouse his comrade hastened to switch it off again, muttering in a more subdued way, *'Ah – Madame, mille pardons.'*

As we negotiated the hairpins next day I could talk of nothing but Hannibal. I remembered the story told by Livy. Confronted in the pass with a wall of solid rock, perhaps the result of a landslide, Hannibal had great fires lighted and attempted to crack open the obstacle by pouring vinegar on it as the stone cooled. 'But where could he have got enough vinegar,' demanded Iris, 'and in any case would it work? Has any one tried it?' Her scepticism was an instance of the meticulous way she always planned the more outlandish episodes in her fiction, testing them in her mind with careful commonsense to make sure they really worked. *The Bell* itself was an example. I always felt there was something wonderfully literal about the discovery of the great bell, which reminded me of *Alice in Wonderland*, one of Iris's own favourite books.

We continued to debate the logistics of Hannibal's campaign, and the difficulties his quartermasters must have had with the vinegar supply. As we drove higher we came into mist, and there was a sound of cowbells. We had a bottle of sparkling burgundy with us in the van, bought with this ceremony in mind. At the top of the pass we drank it, and laid the bottle to rest under a stone beside the road. I marked the place carefully, as I thought, for our idea was to retrieve the bottle on our return journey. When it came to the point, Iris did not like to think of the bottle we had shared being left there. On our return we repeated the ceremony with a bottle of Asti Spumanti, from its home town, but try as I might, and I was sure I had the right place, I could not find the other bottle. So we put the Italian one in a similar place, Iris hoping they would keep one another company.

Safe down from the Alps, in Susa, we ate our first Italian spaghetti. It was sunny now, after the grey Alps, and hot, even though we were still high up. As we left Susa, full of spaghetti and red wine, a stout grocer, who had been standing at the door of his shop, stepped out in the road and held up his hand. Did we perhaps require any supplies? Wine? He could let us have jars of very good wine – his own. Lowering his voice he said we could have it all free in exchange for a few petrol coupons – *coupone*. Petrol was scarce in Italy and extremely expensive. Supplied by the travel agent at home with these coupons for the journey, the tourist motoring on the continent found himself a popular figure.

We would have liked to oblige, but we would be needing the coupons ourselves – how many we could not yet say. The friendly grocer appreciated the dilemma. If there were coupons over when we returned, then we would do business. A fortnight or so later we did so. Massive salamis a yard long were pressed upon us, and huge bottles of wine. When we stopped again on the way over the alpine pass Iris unearthed a vast smooth stone – perhaps it had been dislodged by Hannibal's experiment with the vinegar? She longed to take it home, so I heaved it on top of all the other rubbish that by now cluttered the floor of the van. It must have landed on top of one of the big wine bottles. Unknowing we descended into France with a gallon or so of red wine trickling through on to the road. Much remained behind. I still have an old vest, marbled, despite occasional washings over the years, in a delicate patterning of pink and Tuscan red.

Our appetite for *spaghetti pomodoro* was insatiable. We seemed to eat or want to eat nothing else on that honeymoon. And eating it very often in the open air, under what Shelley calls 'the roof of blue Italian weather'. In the afternoons we slept deeply after several lunch-time carafes of cold white wine, Chianti too. The white wine came in carafes beaded with condensation and with a little leaden seal on one side, certifying a *mezzolitro*. We persuaded the friendly maternal waitress of a *trattoria* to sell us one of them.

Our search for rivers continued, and the afternoon we left Susa for the south we found another one. As I later discovered from the map, it was the Tanaro, a branch of the Ticino, where Hannibal's Numidians had soundly beaten the Roman cavalry. In contrast to our last swim this now idyllic stream ran through the open sun-filled plain, reached after bumping for a mile along on a sandy track which instinct told me must lead to a river. No one was about: we had the whole landscape and the hot afternoon to ourselves.

Or so we thought. We were about to come out of the water when Iris gave a warning cry. The bank was lined with people – Italian farmers, a uniformed policeman. Some child must have spotted us and called his elders to come and see what these strange foreigners were up to. Conversing animatedly they gazed on us with friendly smiles, teeth flashing in their brown faces and under the policeman's fine black moustache. It was a frieze from a painting, perhaps the Baptism of Christ. But there we were in the water with nothing on and somehow we had to get out and get to our clothes. And without shocking any local susceptibilities.

Suddenly the policeman seemed to appreciate the problem. How did he do so? – it may have been the look on our faces. With authoritative gestures he drove the farmers and children – there were no women present – along the river bank and back to the road. When they were gone he remained where he was, just beside our belongings and bedraggled towel, and seemed to smile invitingly. There was nothing else for it. We emerged with what dignity we could, bowing our thanks and smiling graciously as if we were fully clad.

A day or so later we were in Volterra, the 'lordly Volterra' of Macaulay's *Lays*,

Where scowls the far-famed hold,
Piled by the hands of giants
For god-like kings of old.

The mountains were full of marble quarries and there were shops selling alabaster. We used to sit at a café in the square where the waiter looked exactly like photographs of the young Kafka. Iris took a great interest in him. Unlike most Italian waiters he moved with diffidence, as if uncertain of what he was carrying or where to put it. He seemed to like us, but his smile was distrait, a little tormented, as if he were planning some work he knew he would never finish. His head was always surrounded by wasps which he made no attempt to brush away, as if they were visible embodiments of the angst within him. 'Perhaps he will put us both in one of his stories,' said Iris.

It was while asking poor Kafka and his attendant wasps for *Punt e Mes*, the delicious slightly bitter Italian vermouth we had both taken a fancy to, that I realised a difference, suddenly seeming to me very important, between our sense of him and his interior troubles, and our growing sense of each other. If Kafka were really a troubled soul, and not just worried about the football results, there was nothing we could do about it, no way we could establish contact with him. His sadness, if it existed, was that of an unknown life, a part of life we were familiar with back home and took for granted, but which here had no existence we could enter into. Sitting at the sunlit table, the desolation of things, the tears of things of which Virgil's Aeneas was reminded in passing, seemed all around us, but in an inaccessible almost surreal form, that of young Kafka wandering in and out of the café carrying glasses of *Punt e Mes* and the tiny cups of espresso.

Iris seemed to be in a reverie too. I took her hand and it pressed mine. What was she thinking? I had no idea, any more than I had in the case of Kafka, and I knew very well there was no way to find out. But this realisation reassured me deeply: it made me as happy as the hypothetical woes of Kafka had made me feel sad. Such ignorance, such solitude! – they suddenly seemed the best part of love and marriage. We were together because we were comforted and reassured by the solitariness each saw and was aware of in the other.

The hotel we found in a back street was old and shabby; our room with its furniture and its dusty red velvet hangings might have been in a decaying palazzo. It gave no meals, and in the morning we returned to the square, where Kafka brought us coffee and buns. It was in Volterra, I think, that we began to feel really married, as if something in the old grand forbidding little town had reminded us of both good and bad fortune, of short time, and the long wearisomeness of history. It was in Volterra, too, that Iris's life of secret creation became a reality for me. I felt her at work, with no idea of what she was doing or how, and that gave me the same feel of safe and yet distant closeness. I think she realised then how much I was beginning to enjoy this, and would come to depend on it.

From *Shopaholic and Sister*

Sophie Kinsella

I'M SITTING ON a hillside in the middle of Sri Lanka at the Blue Hills Resort and Spiritual Retreat, and the view is spectacular. Hills and tea plantations stretch ahead, then merge into a deep-blue sky. I can see the bright colours of tea-pickers in the fields, and, if I swivel my head a little, glimpse a distant elephant padding slowly along between the bushes.

And when I swivel my head even further, I can see Luke. My husband. He's the one on the blue yoga mat, in the cut-off linen trousers and tatty old top, sitting cross-legged with his eyes closed.

I know. It's just unbelievable. After ten months of honeymoon,

Luke has turned into a totally different person from the man I married. The old corporate Luke has vanished. The suits have disappeared. He's tanned and lean, his hair is long and sun-bleached and he's still got a few of the little plaits he had put in on Bondi Beach. Round his wrist is a friendship bracelet he bought in the Masai Mara, and in his ear is a tiny silver hoop.

Luke Brandon with an earring! Luke Brandon sitting cross-legged! . . .

'Greetings, O Spiritual One,' says Luke, and I open my eyes to see him standing in front of me, holding out a glass of juice.

'You're just jealous because you don't have a beautiful spirit,' I retort, and casually smooth back my hair so the red painted dot on my forehead shows.

'Insanely,' agrees Luke. 'Have a drink.'

He sits down beside me on the ground and hands me the glass. I take a sip of delicious, ice-cold passion-fruit juice and we both look out over the hills towards the distant haze.

'You know, I could really live in Sri Lanka,' I say with a sigh. 'It's perfect. The weather . . . the scenery . . . all the people are so friendly.'

'You said the same in India,' points out Luke. 'And Australia,' he adds as I open my mouth. 'And Amsterdam.'

God, Amsterdam. I'd completely forgotten we went there. That was after Paris. Or do I mean before?

Oh yes. It was where I ate all those weird cakes and nearly fell in the canal.

I take another sip of juice and let my mind range back over the last ten months. We've visited so many countries, it's kind of difficult to remember everything at once. It's almost like a blur of film, with sharp, bright images here and there. Snorkelling with all those blue fish in the Great Barrier Reef . . . the Pyramids in Egypt . . . the elephant safari in Tanzania . . . buying all that silk in Hong Kong . . . the gold souk in Morocco . . . finding that amazing Ralph Lauren outlet in Utah . . .

God, we've had some experiences. I give a happy sigh, and take another sip of juice.

'I forgot to tell you,' Luke produces a pile of envelopes, 'some post came from England.'

The envelope is all thick and creamy white and has a crest on the back with a Latin motto. I always forget how totally grand Suze is. When she sent us a Christmas card, it was a picture of her husband Tarquin's castle in Scotland, with 'From the Cleath-Stuart Estate' printed inside. (Except you could hardly read it because her one-year-old, Ernie, had covered it with red and blue fingerpaints.)

I tear it open and a stiff card falls out.

'It's an invitation!' I exclaim. 'To the christening of the twins.'

I gaze at the formal, swirly writing, feeling a slight pang. Wilfrid and Clementine Cleath-Stuart. Suze has had two more babies and I haven't even seen them. They'll be about two months old by now. I wonder what they look like. I wonder how Suze is doing. So much has been going on without us.

I turn over the card, where Suze has written a scrawled message. 'I know you won't be able to come, but thought you'd like it anyway . . . hope you're still having a wonderful time! All our love, Suze xxx. PS Ernie loves his Chinese outfit, thank you so much!!'

'It's in two weeks,' I say, showing Luke the card. 'Shame really. We won't be able to go.'

'No,' agrees Luke. 'We won't.'

There's a short silence. Then Luke meets my eye. 'I mean . . . you're not ready to go back yet, are you?' he says casually.

'No!' I say at once. 'Of course not!'

We've only been travelling for ten months, and we planned to be away for at least a year. Plus we've got the spirit of the road in our feet now. We've become wandering nomads who gather no moss. Maybe we'll never be able to go back to normal life, like sailors who can't go and live on the land.

I put the invitation back in its envelope and take a sip of my drink. I wonder how Mum and Dad are. I haven't heard much from them recently, either. I wonder how Dad did in the golf tournament.

And little Ernie will be walking by now. I'm his god mother and I've never even seen him walk.

Anyway. Never mind. I'm having amazing world experiences instead.

'We need to decide where to go next,' says Luke, leaning back on his elbows. 'After we finish the yoga course. We were talking about

Malaysia.'

'Yes,' I say, after a pause. It must be the heat or something, but I can't actually get up much enthusiasm for Malaysia.

'Or back to Indonesia? Up to the northern bits?'

'Mmm,' I say noncommittally. 'Oh look, a monkey.'

I cannot believe I've got so blasé about the sight of monkeys. The first time I saw those baboons in Kenya I was so excited I took about six rolls of film. Now it's just, 'Oh look, a monkey.'

'Or Nepal . . . or back to Thailand . . .'

'Or we could go back,' I hear myself saying out of nowhere.

There's silence.

How weird. I didn't intend to say that. I mean *obviously* we're not going to go back yet. It hasn't even been a year!

Luke sits up straight and looks at me.

'Back, back?'

'No!' I say with a little laugh. 'I'm just joking!' I hesitate. 'Although . . .'

There's a still silence between us.

'Maybe . . . we don't *have* to travel for a year,' I say tentatively. 'If we don't want to.'

Luke passes a hand through his hair, and the little beads on his plaits all click together.

'Are we ready to go back?'

'I don't know.' I feel a little thrill of trepidation. 'Are we?'

I can hardly believe we're even talking about going home. I mean, look at us! My hair's all dry and bleached, I've got henna on my feet and I haven't worn a proper pair of shoes for months.

An image comes to my mind of myself walking down a London street in a coat and boots. Shiny high-heeled boots by L K Bennett. And a matching handbag.

Suddenly I feel a wave of longing so strong I almost want to cry.

'I think I've had enough of the world.' I look at Luke. 'I'm ready for real life.'

VII A Sense of Foreboding

Rollercoaster

Lynn Huang

THEY WERE GOING way too fast.

Andrew, usually the careful driver in Singapore, was behaving like a go-cart driver now that they were on the country roads of New Zealand. After another tailgate-and-overtake sequence – this time of a large RV – Lynn wished heartily that she had gotten her driving licence in time for their honeymoon.

'There are speed limits,' she offered. 'We'll get a ticket, if we don't get killed first.'

'Lots of Singaporeans get tickets,' Andrew said nonchalantly, ignoring the other possibility. 'Nobody I know has ever paid.'

They both agreed that such insouciance in the face of the law was totally unacceptable for two law-abiding Singaporeans. But then, this was not Singapore, and they were on honeymoon.

Still, Lynn wished Andrew would go slower. They were southbound on the west coast of the South Island, having stopped at Haast for lunch, and were heading inland through Haast Pass to Lake Wanaka. The surrounding beauty grew monotonous after a while. There were no other cars on the road for miles, besides their little Suzuki. Jet lag was setting in. They needed coffee badly.

So when the little wooden signboard of 'Coffee' appeared at the entrance of a side-road, Andrew had turned in immediately, no questions asked. They drove through forest for another 15 minutes, and were on the verge of turning back when they reached a gravelled clearing, with a small but solidly-built wooden cabin and some chairs and tables outside. A friendly golden retriever wagged his tail twice at the visitors, and went back to sleep.

The café was run by a couple, who could be anywhere between 40 and 60 years of age, with the muscular, weather-beaten frame of people who have spent their whole lives outdoors. There were no other customers in sight. Ravenous from the drive, Andrew and Lynn ordered coffee and hot burgers, and went outside for a walk while the woman went to work cooking behind the counter.

The café was ringed by trees, which appeared to provide thick forest cover. But that was deceptive. A small path at the back of the cabin led them quickly through the trees into a large clearing. There was a glint of water in the distance – perhaps they were nearer to Lake Wanaka than they thought? But in the foreground, there was an intricate wooden structure. It was less than two storeys in height, clearly disused, its white paint peeling, and with some of the supporting beams fallen to the ground. It was fenced up.

The café's ageless owner had joined them, golden retriever at his heels.

'Yeah, that's a rollercoaster,' he said, anticipating the question-mark in Lynn's mind.

'Came with the property when my grandfather bought it. Built in the 1930s, when folks still had the mind to build these things before they were all shipped off to fight in the war. A wooden one – same pedigree as the Giant Dipper in California.'

The man's Kiwi lilt made 'pedigree' sound like 'pea digree'. He went on to explain how the wooden rollercoaster worked, and how wooden ones had a certain charm compared to the prefab steel tubular ones nowadays, but Lynn was not really listening. Instead, she made her eyes trace the contours of the structure, where the car – presumably wooden too, but nowhere in sight now – would start, where it would accelerate, and then whoosh down along the slight bend. It was a strange feeling, like being the only visitors in a museum of medieval court jester costumes.

The waft of sizzling bacon and fries beckoned them. The man concluded by saying, 'It's too dear to take down now, but it's still good Kiwi rimu wood. You won't find another like her in Westland', and with his accent, Lynn thought he had said 'wasteland'.

Back in the café, Andrew proclaimed over cheeseburgers and fries that he liked rollercoasters, especially those '360-degree ones'.

I've married a speed demon, Lynn thought. She recalled her white-knuckled fear in Hong Kong's Ocean Park, riding the Viking, which had looked so tame from outside. She had kept her eyes tightly shut throughout the ride. She mentally set a threshold on what sort of theme park rides she'll go on with Andrew. Maybe a few tamer Disney rides, but no Six Flags.

'I always like to sit at the very front of the rollercoaster,' Andrew continued.

'Physics says that the G-forces are stronger at the back,' Lynn shot back, anxious to puncture some of Andrew's alarming bravado.

Ignoring her, Andrew was making large circular motions in the air with his coffee spoon, mimicking the 360-degree rollercoaster turns. To her consternation, a large blob of latte foam landed on Lynn's nose. Andrew collapsed in merriment.

They reached their motel on Lake Wanaka just as the sun began to set. As they brought their bags into the room, the setting sun lengthened their shadows to five-metre giants on the asphalt.

Andrew had promised 'no dull nights on our honeymoon', but after his shower, he fell asleep almost immediately, exhausted by the day's driving. Lynn stayed awake for a while, but there was nothing on TV except rugby and the news, and she soon feel asleep too.

In her dream, Lynn was in a different time and place. Andrew and her were in the car driving out to Tokyo Bay. It was night, and the neon lights in Odaiba shimmered in the distance at the far end of the Bay. Then she saw that they were not heading to Odaiba after all, but were instead driving on a rollercoaster track, which looked brand-new, paved with glistening asphalt. In the middle and at each side of the road, there were thoughtful luminous road markings. Just ahead the road heaved – it was the beginning of the 360-degree turn. Andrew said, we need to go fast now, or we'll fall like fridge magnets from the track. In her dream, Lynn grasped the physics of this as inevitable. Keep to your lane, she said soundlessly, as Andrew floored the accelerator, and they hurtled forward and crested the top of the turn. There was only the night-sky above and the neon lights below, and absolute silence.

Don't close your eyes now, Lynn told herself. Especially not now.

From *Earthly Paradise*

Colette

Colette was one of France's favourite novelists in the last century, creator of Gigi, Cheri, Claudine. In 1893, aged twenty, she married the notorious Willy Gauthier-Villars, a womaniser and exploiter of the talents of others, including her own. Their wedding breakfast took place at 6.30 in the evening, at her parents' home. Pierre Verber and Adolphe Houdard were the groom's best men; Sido was Colette's mother's name.

MANY RECOLLECTIONS of this bygone day have escaped me; all the people gathered around the festive board are now dead, except for the bride with the splash of red carnations on the bodice of her white wedding gown, and perhaps also the maid of honour in the shot silk dress. I believe the menu was quite simple and very good. But between the sea pike *sauce mousseline* and the sweets – *bastions de Savoie*, a moulded almond pudding capped with quivering pink spun sugar – my memory has bequeathed nothing to me. For, thanks to a few draughts of champagne, I dropped off into the sudden kind of doze that overwhelms tired children at the table. Apparently my head leaned against the back of my chair and stayed there. Madame N. had her second fit of indignation over this, Sido having insisted, in a vindictive tone addressed to everyone and no one, that I be allowed a moment's sleep. I slept for a few minutes and . . . [then Sido's] superstitious hand, as it slid a white shawl around my shoulders, plucked the carnations from my bodice and woke me up completely, just in time for me to be asked to perform the ritual of cutting the cake, deflating the nougat bastion, and ruining the moulded pink and green ice cream with a silver spade . . .

Next day I felt separated from that evening by a thousand leagues, abysses, discoveries, irremediable metamorphoses.

An hour before the departure, next day, Pierre Veber performed a mock bullfight in the middle of the street, using Sido's venerable red shawl as a matador's cape. I travelled to Paris in an old railway carriage that rattled along like a stagecoach, accompanied by three men who were all complete strangers to me, although I had just been married to one of them.

The thrilling idea of seeing Paris again—and also, I think, the farewell champagne—made them a bit hilarious. Corpulent and agile, as always, my husband performed amazingly deft acrobatics on the luggage racks. Houdard sang a few songs from the depths of his Sadi-Carnot [the then French President] black beard, and Pierre Veber patiently demolished the mechanism of the alarm bell. Then they calmed down and incautiously went to sleep as the night closed in.

Now and then I pressed my face to the window for a glimpse, on the horizon, of the indefinite glimmer that would announce our approach to Paris. But I encountered nothing except my blurred reflection and behind me the reflection of the three unknown men, who, with lolling heads, were sleeping. I suffered from thirst, and my heart was swollen with pain over a mental impression that remained with me. My mother had stayed up all night and at daybreak was still wearing her grand outfit of black faille and jet. Standing at the blue-and-white tiled stove in the little kitchen, Sido was pensively stirring the morning chocolate, her features, unguarded, betraying a look of terrible sadness.

From *Madame Bovary*

Gustave Flaubert

CHARLES WAS NOT of a facetious turn. He had not shone during the celebration of his wedding. He replied but tolerably to the witticisms, puns, remarks with double meanings, compliments and

Gaulish jests which it was considered to be a duty to level at him from the soup onward.

The next day, on the other hand, he seemed another man. It was rather he who might have been taken for the virgin of the day before, while the bride allowed nothing to appear in her manner from which anything at all could be divined. The most waggish knew not what to say, and they looked at her when she passed near them with an unmeasured intensity of mental application. But Charles dissembled nothing. He called her 'my wife', used 'thou' in addressing her, consulted every one about her, looked for her everywhere, and often drew her away into the grounds where he could be seen in the distance to pass his arm about her waist and continue walking half bent over her and ruffling the chemisette of her bodice with his head.

Two days after the wedding the newly married couple took their departure. Charles, on account of his patients, could not remain longer absent. Père Rouault directed that they should be driven home in his covered vehicle, and himself accompanied them as far as Vasson-ville. There he took leave of his daughter in a final embrace, got out and commenced his journey back on foot . . .

She occupied herself during the first days in meditating changes in her house. She removed the glass shades from the candlesticks, had new wall-papers hung, the staircase repainted, seats made in the garden all round the sun-dial. She even inquired how it might be contrived for her to have a little pond with a jet of water and fish in it. And, finally, her husband, knowing that she liked driving, picked up, second-hand, a phaeton which, once it had been provided with new lamps and splash-boards of grain leather, almost resembled a tilbury.

So he was happy and without a care in the world. A meal taken alone with her, a walk in the evening along the high-road, a gesture of her hand passed over the fillets of her hair, the sight of her straw hat hanging on the fastener of a window, and many other things besides, in which Charles had never suspected pleasure to lie, these made up now the continuance of his happiness. In bed of a morning, as they lay with heads side by side on the pillow, he would watch the sunlight as it quivered through the down of her fair cheeks, half covered by the scalloped flaps of her night-cap. Observed at such close quarters, her eyes seemed to him grown larger, especially when, as she awoke, she opened her eye-lids several times in succession; black in the shade and deep blue in a strong light, they possessed, as it were, layers of different colours that succeeded one another, and, from being duller deep down, grew brighter and brighter towards the surface of the enamel. His own eye would lose itself in those depths, and he saw there a reduced image of himself as far as the shoulders, with the silk kerchief he wore about his head and the half-opened upper part of his shirt. He rose. She used to go to the window to see him off, and remain with elbows resting on the sill, between two pots of geraniums, clad in her dressing-gown falling loosely about her. Charles, in the street, used to buckle on his spurs at the post; and she would continue to talk to him from above, breaking off with her lips and blowing towards him some sprig of flower or leaf which, after fluttering hither and thither, poising itself momentarily, describing half-circles in the air like a bird, ere it fell, would cling to the ill-combed mane of his old white mare standing motionless at the door. Charles, after mounting, used to throw her a kiss; she answered always with some gesture, closed the window, and he rode off. And then along the highway that stretched out endlessly its long ribbon of dust, by the hollow lanes where the trees bent over and made arbours, through the paths where the corn came up to his knees, with the sun on his shoulders, and the air of the morning in his nostrils, his heart full of the joys of the night, mind tranquil, flesh satisfied, he went musing upon his happiness like men who, after dinner, lick their lips again at the remembered taste of the truffles they are digesting.

Till now what had he had in existence that was good? Was it his school days, when he was there shut up within those high walls, alone in the midst of his school-fellows richer than himself or more clever in their class-work, boys whom he made laugh by his accent, who made fun of his clothes, and whose mothers came to the visitors' room bringing pastry in their muffs? Was it later, when he was studying medicine and never had a purse well-lined enough to pay the price of a quadrille for any little work-girl who had become his mistress? After that he had lived for fourteen months with the widow, whose feet in bed were cold as pieces of ice. But now he was the possessor for life of this pretty woman, whom he adored. For him the universe extended not beyond the silken circuit of her petticoat and he used to reproach himself for not loving her as she deserved, used to want to gaze upon her again, and he would make his way back quickly, and mount the staircase with beating heart. Emma, in her room, would be dressing, and with silent steps he would approach and kiss her on the back, at which she would utter a cry.

He could not keep himself from continually touching her comb, her rings, her neckerchief; sometimes he gave her loud smacking kisses on the cheeks; at other times gentle little kisses in rows all the length of her bare arm, from the tips of her fingers to the shoulder; and she used to push him away, half smiling and bored, as one does a child who is for ever dangling after one.

Before her marriage she had believed herself to be in love; but the bliss that should have resulted from that love not having come, she must have been mistaken, was her reflection. And Emma sought to learn what precisely one was to understand in life by those words 'felicity', 'passion', 'intoxication of delight', that had seemed to her so fine in books . . .

She reflected sometimes that those were, however, the most glorious days of her life, the honeymoon, as folk said. To enjoy their sweetness, 'twould have been necessary, doubtless, to journey to those regions with sonorous names where the morrows of marriage pass in a more delicate indolence! In post-chaises, behind blinds of blue silk, you ascend at foot's pace the precipitous roads, listening to the song of the postillion which the mountain echo sends back with the bells of the goats and the sullen noise of the waterfall. When the sun is setting, on the shores of gulfs you breathe the perfume of lemon-trees; then, in the evening, on villa terraces, alone and with fingers intertwined, you look up at the stars whilst you lay schemes for the future. It seemed to her as if certain places on the earth must produce happiness, like a plant indigenous to their soil and growing with difficulty in any other spot. Why was it not for her to lean her elbow on the balcony of Swiss chalets, or to imprison her grief in some Scottish cottage with a husband clad in a long-skirted coat of black velvet and wearing high soft boots, a sugar-loaf hat, and ruffles!

Perhaps she might have desired to unburden her heart of all these things in confidence to some one. But how express an unseizable disquietude that changes its aspect like the clouds, that whirls hither and thither like the wind? Words failed her accordingly, and the opportunity, and the courage.

If Charles had willed it so, however, if he had divined anything of it, if his look but once only had come to meet her thoughts, it seemed to her that a sudden and abundant outpouring would have burst from her heart, even as the wall-fruit falls from its tree when the hand is laid on it. But, as the intimacy of their life grew closer, even so an interior detachment proceeded which unbound her from him.

Charles's conversation was as dull as a street pavement, and everybody's ideas defiled through it in their ordinary dress, without exciting emotion, laughter, or reverie. He had never had the curiosity, he said, while he lived in Rouen, to go to the theatre to see the actors from Paris. He knew neither how to swim, nor to fence, nor to shoot with the pistol, and he could not explain to her one day a term of horsemanship with which she had met in a novel.

A man, on the contrary, should he not know everything, excel in multiple activities, initiate you into the forces of passion, the refinements of life, all the mysteries? But he taught nothing, that man, knew nothing, desired nothing. He believed her happy; and she bore him ill-will for that calm so secure, for that serene heaviness, for the very happiness which she gave to him.

From *Honeymoon*

Noel Blakiston

Noel Blakiston, a very cultivated civil servant high in the Public Records Office, published four collections of short stories in the 1950s and 60s. His youthful correspondence with Cyril Connolly was published under the title A Romantic Friendship.

THE YOUNG MAN and young woman, who were walking out of the castle of the Sforzas, were evidently tourists. Their clothes, his particularly, betrayed the fact that their travelling wardrobe did not include attire for use in cities that was different from that in which they walked on the hillsides or slept in trains. Mary, the girl, who, like Kenneth, the boy, was making her first visit to Italy, became increasingly conscious, as the days followed one another in the best dressed country in the world, how alien they made themselves appear by their bohemian look. In London, of course, their appearance showed them to be adherents of the arts, members of the intelligentsia and believers in a sophisticated, uninhibited love life. There they contrasted most favourably with the stuffed shirts, the business men, the philistines. Here, however, it was being every day borne in upon her that it was Kenneth and herself who were the barbarians.

'Why,' she said, 'we look just like Germans!'

Kenneth was nettled by the remark.

'No, we don't', he said. 'We don't just stand about gaping indiscriminately and saying "*wunderschön!*" We can criticize things intelligently. I'm sure our talk is better.'

'Honestly, Kenneth, what do you know about the talk of Germans? You don't know a word of their language, any more than you do of Italian.'

'You can see what they're saying.'

'Well, anyhow, I wasn't talking about talk. I was talking about our uncivilised appearance in Italy.'

'Good heavens! You surely don't care about what the macaronis think of your appearance?'

He gave a pitying laugh. Kenneth was an Italophobe. He was so before ever he had set foot in Italy. He had been confident that this country would not come up to Greece which he had visited with a friend the year before. At every turn he was being proved right. The tamed and pretty-pretty landscape, the simpering art, the babyish mother-worship, the scented dandies combing their hair in public places, the ubiquitous ices and orangeade—it was all exactly as he had foretold. Not a man's country!

It may be asked why he had brought his bride to Italy for their honeymoon.

'We are young,' he had said. This was certainly the case. He was just twenty-two and she was nineteen. 'We should tick off Italy before I take you to Greece.'

The observation, made one evening in a London coffee bar, had seemed to her profound. It had that quality of intellectual mastery that she found in so much of what Kenneth said and to which she submitted so gladly. The prospect of having her education so authoritatively taken in charge had not been the least of his attractions for her. He was certainly brilliant. His talk made play with all the great names in literature and the arts, and with many others that were new to her. She watched his friends, the others in their gang, listening to him with respect. How lucky she was to have caught him!

It was true that his genius had not yet had time to assert itself in any very material manner. He had got a job as an assistant master in a progressive private school in the north of London. He did not, of course, look on the job as anything but temporary, or indeed, though he had no further plans to divulge, as anything but the necessary prelude to a career of greatness. What great man, he said, has not started life as a schoolmaster?

Mary was the child of a broken marriage. Tossed from parent to parent and from school to school, she had not made much headway in conventional education. She had learned, however, to look after herself and when, two years ago, her father had died, leaving her a little money, she had taken a bed-sitting room in Chelsea and enrolled herself at an art school. Perhaps the most important date in her spiritual development up to the time of her marriage, had been the occasion when a white-headed man had said to her 'May I see some examples of your work?' The idea of regarding painting and drawing, the happiest occupations in the world, for which any child will hope for a wet afternoon, the idea of regarding this form of play as work seemed to make her suddenly adult. If they were prepared to take her as seriously as that, she would not fail them, and amongst the new friends she was making there was every encouragement to be serious. For whatever they might lack in collars and ties and a change of clothes, they did not lack the habit of conviction. There seemed to be no question under the sun on which she would not hear a confident, decisive and generally indignant, verdict. The intellectual excitement went to her head. When the brilliant Kenneth asked her to be his wife, she had no doubts about accepting him.

'I must of course tell uncle Oliver,' she had said. 'You will have to meet him. And I suppose you should meet my mother.'

The latter meeting was the occasion of a double introduction, for the young people were presented at it to the man whom the mother was about to marry as her fourth husband. The foolish creature made Kenneth drunk and pronounced him a darling.

'We needn't see them again,' said Mary.

The meeting with her uncle was a different matter. Uncle Oliver, her father's elder brother, was the only one of her family who meant anything to her now. 'He's like an old monk ploughing in my otherwise empty background,' she had said to Kenneth. 'He's always there.' Though he had no legal responsibility, he had assumed a kind of moral guardianship over his homeless niece, which she was glad to recognize. Himself childless, and recently a widower, he was happy to step into the role of father, which poor Andrew, sick, drunken, and demoralized by that wretched woman, had so inadequately filled. Moreover, his age had just forced him into retirement. With the plough taken from his hands, he had no strong attachment in life other than his Mary. He recognized, however, that at her age, and with her experience of the older generation, he could hardly expect her to do other than present him, for most of the time, with her back view.

The meeting with Kenneth had been a success. The boy had been on his best behaviour and uncle Oliver had taken no offence at the arrogance which showed itself only just below the surface. Meeting few young people, he had forgotten what it was to see the world in black and white. He found Kenneth full of promise. But when Mary divulged that they intended to get married in a few weeks, he was appalled.

'But you're still growing up so fast,' he said. 'You hardly know each other. Give it a year or six months, at least.'

His advice had not been taken and here they were, in the second week of their honeymoon, walking across the bridge over the dry moat that encircles the castle of the Sforzas. Beyond the bridge, they sat on a stone bench a few yards from the parapet of the moat, looking at the castle wall. Behind them there was the public park. From beyond the castle came the roar of the city of Milan. Against this muffled bass accompaniment, a shrill performance by the treble voices of several hundred swifts was being given just in front of them. As they shot and dived and glanced and swerved over the moat, the birds were shrieking with ecstasy. Occasionally one of them would stop to perch for a second in a crevice of the castle wall, occasionally one or two would soar away from the congregation of their fellows high up into the blue; but the multitude was entirely absorbed in its violent, rapturous interweaving, between the moat and the battlements, a few feet away from the brickwork of the castle.

The evening sun shining directly upon the wall threw the shadow of each swift streaking along the bricks. The result of this was that there appeared to be twice as many swifts as there actually were. Mary was about to comment on this phenomenon but withheld her observation. In her hand she had a picture postcard of the Michelangelo *pietà* which they had just been looking at in the museum of the castle. Kenneth was talking about Greek sculpture. He was describing the figures of Harmodius and Aristogiton. These were long names and Mary had never heard them before and knew nothing about Greek sculpture. Suddenly, to clinch the moral of his discourse, he pointed to her card.

'. . . whereas that yearns,' he said. Q.E.D.

She looked at the photograph.

'It doesn't yearn,' she said. 'Perhaps you could say, it droops, but then it's meant to.'

'All right—"droops". That's just as bad. But what can you expect from a pansy?'

How wrong he was, Mary thought. She looked at her card with love. This *pietà* seemed to her about the best of all the things they had yet seen. She decided to send it to uncle Oliver. Such an action would be breaking a compact made but ten days ago. 'Let's have no letters to families, no picture postcards to anybody!' Kenneth had said. 'It's just you and me!' 'Of course,' she had agreed enthusiastically, ten days ago.

The castle wall, like so many old walls in Italy, was punctured with untidy holes, as though the builders had had to leave before finishing their work. Kenneth was quite sure that these were the apertures where the scaffolding poles had been. The workmen had simply been too lazy to fill them in. 'How like these people!' he had said. Mary was not convinced. If that was the explanation, it seemed to her rather *un*like these people. However it might be, the holes had their uses. She had become aware that many of them were occupied by pigeons, watching, like dowagers, in staid detachment, the frantic revelling of the younger generation.

Kenneth was now talking about homosexuality, of the difference between the ancient and the modern varieties. 'Greek homosexuality was virile,' he said. 'The pansy came in at the Renaissance.'

The subject was one on which she had nothing to say. She listened suspiciously. Listening to Kenneth, now that she had him to herself all the twenty-four hours of the day and night, had become a most different experience from listening to him in London. How little, it seemed, they had been alone with each other before their honeymoon! How rarely they had looked at anything new together, to test their observation and their taste! Here, where all was new to them equally, and her opinion was as good as his, his talk had daily become for her less oracular. And it was not just in matters of taste that her confidence had been slipping away; his famous mastery of facts had been called in question too. The unwillingly acknowledged confusion of Mantegna and Montagna the other day had filled her with doubts on both scores. She had begun to ask herself whether, on the subjects about which she knew nothing, he was always right.

He was talking about Socrates and his pupils. '. . . whereas these people,' he was saying, and with a comprehensive gesture of the arm he included all Milan, all Italy, 'they don't begin to be moral adults. Of course their religion doesn't give them a chance. Permanent adolescents.'

A loving couple, sauntering hand in hand over the bridge from the castle, now passed between them and the parapet. It was possibly speech that was coming from the mouth of the girl. It sounded more like a cooing. The pair looked as though they knew all the rules of love. No bungling there. A little further on, there was another stone seat, unoccupied. The man, with his spare hand, brushed a place on it for the girl to sit upon. As he did so, he evidently observed that the stone was warm (the sun had indeed only just left it), for the girl, with her spare hand, felt it. She then sat down, lifting her skirt, with her spare hand, in order that her flesh might receive the warmth through one less layer, perhaps through no layer, of clothing. The act was performed with simple, ungiggling decorum. How at home in the world! thought Mary.

Kenneth was back at her postcard.

'It's all emotion and thought,' he said. 'He'd given up using his eyes by the time he did that.'

'Bosh!' she said. 'Absolute bosh! And as for using eyes, we've now been sitting here for twenty minutes and you haven't yet even noticed the swifts!'

She got up and went to the parapet. Lucky swifts, happily screaming all together! Presently she would scream, and it would be the unhappiest and loneliest scream in the whole world.

Two or three weeks after receiving the postcard from Milan, Oliver was sitting in the club one evening. Leo sat down next to him.

'By the way,' said the latter, 'how's that niece of yours getting on? Is she back from her honeymoon yet?'

'As a matter of fact, she had lunch with me today.'

'How's it going?'

'Not too well, I'm afraid. After a certain amount of beating about the bush, she opened up. She said "Uncle, I wish I'd taken your advice. I find I've married a bore, an inaccurate bore. He notices nothing and he gets everything wrong."'

'What did you say?'

'What would you have said?'

'I don't know. I expect I would have advised her to get out as quick as she can. Did you?'

'I did nothing of the kind.'

The emphasis with which this was said surprised Leopold Hayward and caused him, as at a word of command, to sit up a little straighter in his chair.

'I said,' the other went on, '"he may be boring now, but he is still far too young to have taken on the definitive status of a bore. And it doesn't matter if he's wrong about things now. He'll get right. He's got the thing that matters at his age, impetus." I said, "Marriage, creative marriage, is not play, it's work. The rewards come at the end not at the beginning," I said. "It is for you to make him not a bore, to teach him to notice things. It is your life work. You have given yourself plenty of time. You should have a clear fifty years." I said.'

While Oliver was speaking, Leo imagined himself to be the niece listening. As the uncle struck and struck again, he experienced a kind of elation, for he felt himself being carried up into reality, almost into a book.

From *Here We Are*

Dorothy Parker

THE YOUNG MAN in the new blue suit finished arranging the glistening luggage in tight corners of the Pullman compartment. The train had leaped at curves and bounced along straightaways, rendering balance a praiseworthy achievement and a sporadic one; and the young man had pushed and hoisted and tucked and shifted the bags with concentrated care.

Nevertheless, eight minutes for the settling of two suitcases and a hat-box is a long time.

He sat down, leaning back against bristled green plush, in the seat opposite the girl in beige. She looked as new as a peeled egg. Her hat, her fur, her frock, her gloves were glossy and stiff with novelty. On the arc of the thin, slippery sole of one beige shoe was gummed a tiny oblong of white paper, printed with the price set and paid for that slipper and its fellow, and the name of the shop that had dispensed them.

She had been staring raptly out of the window, drinking in the big weathered signboards that extolled the phenomena of codfish without bones and screens no rust could corrupt. As the young man sat down, she turned politely from the pane, met his eyes, started a smile and got it about half done, and rested her gaze just above his right shoulder.

'Well!' the young man said.

'Well!' she said.

'Well, here we are,' he said.

'Here we are,' she said. 'Aren't we?'

'I should say we were,' he said. 'Eeyop. Here we are.'

'Well!' she said.

'Well!' he said 'Well. How does it feel to be an old married lady?'

'Oh, it's too soon to ask me that,' she said. 'At least—I mean. Well, I mean, goodness, we've only been married about three hours, haven't we?'

183

The young man studied his wrist-watch as if he were just acquiring the knack of reading time.

'We have been married,' he said, 'exactly two hours and twenty-six minutes.'

'My,' she said. 'It seems like longer.'

'No,' he said. 'It isn't hardly half-past six yet.'

'It seems like later,' she said. 'I guess it's because it starts getting dark so early.'

'It does, at that,' he said. 'The nights are going to be pretty long from now on. I mean. I mean—well, it starts getting dark early.'

'I didn't have any idea what time it was,' she said. 'Everything was so mixed up, I sort of don't know where I am, or what it's all about. Getting back from the church, and then all those people, and then changing all my clothes, and then everybody throwing things, and all. Goodness, I don't see how people do it every day.'

'Do what?' he said.

'Get married,' she said. 'When you think of all the people, all over the world, getting married just as if it was nothing. Chinese people and everybody. Just as if it wasn't anything.'

'Well, let's not worry about people all over the world,' he said. 'Let's don't think about a lot of Chinese. We've got something better to think about. I mean. I mean—well, what do we care about them?'

'I know,' she said. 'But I just sort of got to thinking of them all of them, all over everywhere, doing it all the time. At least, I mean—getting married, you know. And it's—well, it's sort of such a big thing to do, it makes you feel queer. You think of them, all of them, all doing it just like it wasn't anything. And how does anybody know what's going to happen next?'

'Let them worry,' he said. 'We don't have to. We know darn well what's going to happen next. I mean. I mean—well, we know it's going to be great. Well, we know we're going to be happy. Don't we?'

'Oh, of course,' she said. 'Only you think of all the people, and you have to sort of keep thinking. It makes you feel funny. An awful lot of people that get married, it doesn't turn out so well. And I guess they all must have thought it was going to be great.'

'Come on, now,' he said. 'This is no way to start a honeymoon, with all this thinking going on. Look at us—all married and everything done. I mean. The wedding all done and all.'

'Ah, it was nice, wasn't it?' she said. 'Did you really like my veil?'

'You looked great,' he said. 'Just great.'

'Oh, I'm terribly glad,' she said. 'Ellie and Louise looked lovely, didn't they? I'm terribly glad they did finally decide on pink. They looked perfectly lovely.'

'Listen,' he said. 'I want to tell you something. When I was standing up there in that old church waiting for you to come up, and I saw those two bridesmaids, I thought to myself, I thought, "Well, I never knew Louise could look like that!" Why, she'd have knocked anybody's eye out.'

'Oh, really?' she said. 'Funny. Of course, everybody thought her dress and hat were lovely, but a lot of people seemed to think she looked sort of tired. People have been saying that a lot, lately. I tell them I think it's awfully mean of them to go around saying that about her. I tell them they've got to remember that Louise isn't so terribly young any more, and they've got to expect her to look like that. Louise can say she's twenty-three all she wants to, but she's a good deal nearer twenty-seven.'

'Well, she was certainly a knock-out at the wedding,' he said. 'Boy!'

'I'm terribly glad you thought so,' she said. 'I'm glad someone did. How did you think Ellie looked?'

'Why, I honestly didn't get a look at her,' he said.

'Oh, really?' she said. 'Well, I certainly think that's too bad. I don't suppose I ought to say it about my own sister, but I never saw anybody look as beautiful as Ellie looked today. And always so sweet and unselfish, too. And you didn't even notice her. But you never pay attention to Ellie, anyway. Don't think I haven't noticed it. It makes me feel just terrible. It makes me feel just awful, that you don't like my own sister.'

'I do like her!' he said. 'I'm crazy for Ellie. I think she's a great kid.'

'Don't think it makes any difference to Ellie!' she said. 'Ellie's got enough people crazy about her. It isn't anything to her whether you like her or not. Don't flatter yourself she cares! Only, the only thing

185

is, it makes it awfully hard for me you don't like her, that's the only thing. I keep thinking, when we come back and get in that apartment and everything, it's going to be awfully hard for me that you won't want my own sister to come and see me. It's going to make it awfully hard for me that you won't ever want my family around. I know how you feel about my family. Don't think I haven't seen it. Only, if you don't ever want to see them, that's your loss. Not theirs. Don't flatter yourself!'

'Oh, now, come on!' he said. 'What's all this talk about not wanting your family around? Why, you know how I feel about your family. I think your old lady—I think your mother's swell. And Ellie. And your father. What's all this talk?'

'Well, I've seen it,' she said. 'Don't think I haven't. Lots of people they get married, and they think it's going to be great and everything, and then it all goes to pieces because people don't like people's families, or something like that. Don't tell me! I've seen it happen.'

'Honey,' he said, 'what is all this? What are you getting all angry about? Hey, look, this is our honeymoon. What are you trying to start a fight for? Ah, I guess you're just feeling sort of nervous.'

'Me?' she said. 'What have I got to be nervous about? I mean. I mean, goodness, I'm not nervous.'

'You know, lots of times,' he said, 'they say that girls get kind of nervous and yippy on account of thinking about—I mean. I mean—well, it's like you said, things are all so sort of mixed up and everything, right now. But afterwards, it'll be all right. I mean. I mean—well, look, honey, you don't look any too comfortable. Don't you want to take your hat off? And let's don't ever fight, ever. Will we?'

'Ah, I'm sorry I was cross,' she said. 'I guess I did feel a little bit funny. All mixed up, and then thinking of all those people all over everywhere, and then being sort of way off here, all alone with you. It's so sort of different. It's sort of such a big thing. You can't blame a person for thinking, can you? Yes, don't let's ever, ever fight. We won't be like a whole lot of them. We won't fight or be nasty or anything. Will we?'

'You bet your life we won't,' he said.

'I guess I will take this darned old hat off,' she said. 'It kind of presses. Just put it up on the rack, will you dear? Do you like it, sweetheart?'

'Looks good on you,' he said.

'No, but I mean,' she said, 'do you really like it?'

'Well, I'll tell you,' he said. 'I know this is the new style and everything like that, and it's probably great. I don't know anything about things like that. Only I like the kind of a hat like that blue hat you had. Gee, I liked that hat.'

'Oh, really?' she said. 'Well, that's nice. That's lovely. The first thing you say to me, as soon as you get me off on a train away from my family and everything, is that you don't like my hat. The first thing you say to your wife is you think she has terrible taste in hats. That's nice, isn't it?'

'Now, honey,' he said, 'I never said anything like that. I only said—'

'What you don't seem to realize,' she said, 'is this hat cost twenty-two dollars. Twenty-two dollars. And that horrible old blue thing you think you're so crazy about, that cost three ninety-five.'

'I don't give a darn what they cost,' he said. 'I only said—I said I liked that blue hat. I don't know anything about hats. I'll be crazy about this one as soon as I get used to it. Only it's kind of not like your other hats. I don't know about the new styles. What do I know about women's hats?'

'It's too bad,' she said, 'you didn't marry somebody that would get the kind of hats you'd like. Hats that cost three ninety-five. Why didn't you marry Louise? You always think she looks so beautiful. You'd love her taste in hats. Why didn't you marry her?'

'Ah, now, honey,' he said. 'For heaven's sakes!'

'Why didn't you marry her?' she said. 'All you've done, ever since we got on this train, is talk about her. Here I've sat and sat, and just listened to you saying how wonderful Louise is. I suppose that's nice, getting me all off here alone with you, and then raving about Louise right in front of my face. Why didn't you ask her to marry you? I'm sure she would have jumped at the chance. There aren't so many people asking her to marry them. It's too bad you didn't marry her. I'm sure you'd have been much happier.'

'Listen, baby,' he said, 'while you're talking about things like that, why didn't you marry Joe Brooks? I suppose he could have given you all the twenty-two-dollar hats you wanted, I suppose!'

'Well, I'm not so sure I'm not sorry I didn't,' she said. 'There! Joe Brooks wouldn't have waited until he got me all off alone and then sneered at my taste in clothes. Joe Brooks wouldn't ever hurt my feelings. Joe Brooks has always been fond of me. There!'

'Yeah,' he said. 'He's fond of you. He was so fond of you he didn't even send a wedding present. That's how fond of you he was.'

'I happen to know for a fact,' she said, 'that he was away on business, and as soon as he comes back he's going to give me anything I want, for the apartment.'

'Listen,' he said. 'I don't want anything he gives you in our apartment. Anything he gives you, I'll throw right out the window. That's what I think of your friend Joe Brooks. And how do you know where he is and what he's going to do, anyway? Has he been writing to you?'

'I suppose my friends can correspond with me,' she said. 'I didn't hear there was any law against that.'

'Well, I suppose they can't!' he said. 'And what do you think of that? I'm not going to have my wife getting a lot of letters from cheap traveling salesmen!'

'Joe Brooks is not a cheap traveling salesman!' she said. 'He is not! He gets a wonderful salary.'

'Oh yeah?' he said. 'Where did you hear that?'

'He told me so himself,' she said.

'Oh, he told you so himself,' he said. 'I see. He told you so himself.'

'You've got a lot of right to talk about Joe Brooks,' she said. 'You and your friend Louise. All you ever talk about is Louise.'

'Oh, for heaven's sakes!' he said. 'What do I care about Louise? I just thought she was a friend of yours, that's all. That's why I ever even noticed her.'

'Well, you certainly took an awful lot of notice of her today,' she said. 'On our wedding day! You said yourself when you were standing there in the church you just kept thinking of her. Right up at the altar. Oh, right in the presence of God! And all you thought about was Louise.'

'Listen, honey,' he said, 'I never should have said that. How does anybody know what kind of crazy things come into their heads when they're standing there waiting to get married? I was just telling you that because it was so kind of crazy. I thought it would make you laugh.'

'I know,' she said. 'I've been all sort of mixed up today, too. I told you that. Everything so strange and everything. And me all the time thinking about all those people all over the world, and now us here all alone, and everything. I know you get all mixed up. Only I did think, when you kept talking about how beautiful Louise looked, you did it with malice and forethought.'

'I never did anything with malice and forethought!' he said. 'I just told you that about Louise because I thought it would make you laugh.'

'Well, it didn't,' she said.

'No, I know it didn't,' he said. 'It certainly did not. Ah, baby, and we ought to be laughing, too. Hell, honey lamb, this is our honeymoon. What's the matter?'

'I don't know,' she said. 'We used to squabble a lot when we were going together and then engaged and everything, but I thought everything would be so different as soon as you were married. And now I feel so sort of strange and everything. I feel so sort of alone.'

'Well, you see, sweetheart,' he said, 'we're not really married yet. I mean. I mean—well, things will be different afterwards. Oh, hell. I mean, we haven't been married very long.'

'No,' she said.

'Well, we haven't got much longer to wait now,' he said. 'I mean—well, we'll be in New York in about twenty minutes. Then we can have dinner, and sort of see what we feel like doing. Or I mean. Is there anything special you want to do tonight?'

'What?' she said.

'What I mean to say,' he said, 'would you like to go to a show or something?'

'Why, whatever you like,' she said. 'I sort of didn't think people went to theaters and things on their—I mean, I've got a couple of letters I simply must write. Don't let me forget.'

'Oh,' he said. 'You're going to write letters tonight?'

'Well, you see,' she said. 'I've been perfectly terrible. What with all the excitement and everything. I never did thank poor old Mrs. Sprague for her berry spoon, and I never did a thing about those book ends the McMasters sent. It's just too awful of me. I've got to write them this very night.'

'And when you've finished writing your letters,' he said, 'maybe I could get you a magazine or a bag of peanuts.'

'What?' she said.

'I mean,' he said, 'I wouldn't want you to be bored.'

'As if I could be bored with you!' she said. 'Silly! Aren't we married? Bored!'

'What I thought,' he said, 'I thought when we got in, we could go right up to the Biltmore and anyway leave our bags, and maybe have a little dinner in the room, kind of quiet, and then do whatever we wanted. I mean. I mean—well, let's go right up there from the station.'

'Oh, yes, let's,' she said. 'I'm so glad we're going to the Biltmore. I just love it. The twice I've stayed in New York we've always stayed there, Papa and Mamma and Ellie and I, and I was crazy about it. I always sleep so well there. I go right off to sleep the minute I put my head on the pillow.'

'Oh, you do?' he said.

'At least, I mean,' she said. 'Way up high it's so quiet.'

'We might go to some show or other tomorrow night instead of tonight,' he said. 'Don't you think that would be better?'

'Yes, I think it might,' she said.

He rose, balanced a moment, crossed over and sat down beside her.

'Do you really have to write those letters tonight?' he said.

'Well,' she said, 'I don't suppose they'd get there any quicker than if I wrote them tomorrow.'

There was a silence with things going on in it.

'And we won't ever fight any more, will we?' he said.

'Oh, no,' she said. 'Not ever! I don't know what made me do like that. It all got so sort of funny, sort of like a nightmare, the way I got thinking of all those people getting married all the time; and so many of them, everything spoils on account of fighting and everything. I got all mixed up thinking about them. Oh, I don't want to be like them. But we won't be, will we?'

'Sure we won't,' he said.

'We won't go all to pieces,' she said. 'We won't fight. It'll all be different, now we're married. It'll all be lovely. Reach me down my hat, will you, sweetheart? It's time I was putting it on. Thanks. Ah, I'm so sorry you don't like it.'

'I do so like it!' he said.

'You said you didn't,' she said. 'You said you thought it was perfectly terrible.'

'I never said any such thing,' he said. 'You're crazy.'

'All right, I may be crazy,' she said. 'Thank you very much. But that's what you said. Not that it matters—it's just a little thing. But it makes you feel pretty funny to think you've gone and married somebody that says you have perfectly terrible taste in hats. And then goes and says you're crazy, beside.'

'Now, listen here,' he said. 'Nobody said any such thing. Why, I love that hat. The more I look at it the better I like it. I think it's great.'

'That isn't what you said before,' she said.

'Honey,' he said. 'Stop it, will you? What do you want to start all this for? I love the damned hat. I mean, I love your hat. I love anything you wear. What more do you want me to say?'

'Well, I don't want you to say it like that,' she said.

'I said I think it's great,' he said. 'That's all I said.'

'Do you really?' she said. 'Do you honestly? Ah, I'm so glad. I'd hate you not to like my hat. It would be—I don't know, it would be sort of such a bad start.'

'Well, I'm crazy for it,' he said. 'Now we've got that settled, for heaven's sakes. Ah, baby. Baby lamb. We're not going to have any bad starts. Look at us—we're on our honeymoon. Pretty soon we'll be regular old married people. I mean. I mean, in a few minutes we'll be getting in to New York, and then we'll be going to the hotel, and then everything will be all right. I mean—well, look at us! Here we are married! Here we are!'

'Yes, here we are,' she said. 'Aren't we?'

From *Wide Sargasso Sea*

Jean Rhys

Antoinette Cosway has married Mr Rochester – an arranged marriage – on Jamaica in the 1820s and now they are on honeymoon on one of the Windward Islands at a house called Granbois that she has inherited. Christophine, her 'da', her old nurse, is housekeeper there and Amelie is a maid.

SHE WAS SITTING on the sofa and I wondered why I had never realized how beautiful she was. Her hair was combed away from her face and fell smoothly far below her waist. I could see the red and gold lights in it. She seemed pleased when I complimented her on her dress and told me she had it made in St Pierre, Martinique. 'They call this fashion à la Joséphine.'

'You talk of St Pierre as though it were Paris,' I said.

'But it is the Paris of the West Indies.'

There were trailing pink flowers on the table and the name echoed pleasantly in my head. Coralita Coralita. The food, though too highly seasoned, was lighter and more appetizing than anything I had tasted in Jamaica. We drank champagne. A great many moths and beetles found their way into the room, flew into the candles and fell dead on the tablecloth. Amélie swept them up with a crumb brush. Uselessly. More moths and beetles came.

'Is it true,' she said, 'that England is like a dream? Because one of my friends who married an Englishman wrote and told me so. She said this place London is like a cold dark dream sometimes. I want to wake up.'

'Well,' I answered annoyed, 'that is precisely how your beautiful island seems to me, quite unreal and like a dream.'

'But how can rivers and mountains and the sea be unreal?'

'And how can millions of people, their houses and their streets be unreal?'

'More easily,' she said, 'much more easily. Yes a big city must be like a dream.'

'No, this is unreal and like a dream,' I thought.

The long veranda was furnished with canvas chairs, two hammocks, and a wooden table on which stood a tripod telescope. Amélie brought out candles with glass shades but the night swallowed up the feeble light. There was a very strong scent of flowers—the flowers by the river that open at night she told me—and the noise, subdued in the inner room, was deafening. 'Crac-cracs,' she explained, 'they make a sound like their name, and crickets and frogs.'

I leaned on the railing and saw hundreds of fireflies—'Ah yes, fireflies in Jamaica, here they call a firefly La belle.'

A large moth, so large that I thought it was a bird, blundered into one of the candles, put it out and fell to the floor. 'He's a big fellow,' I said.

'Is it badly burned?'

'More stunned than hurt.'

I took the beautiful creature up in my handkerchief and put it on the railing. For a moment it was still and by the dim candlelight I could see the soft brilliant colours, the intricate pattern on the wings. I shook the handkerchief gently and it flew away.

'I hope that gay gentleman will be safe,' I said.

'He will come back if we don't put the candles out. It's light enough by the stars.'

Indeed the starlight was so bright that shadows of the veranda posts and the trees outside lay on the floor . . .

I woke next morning in the green-yellow light, feeling uneasy as though someone were watching me. She must have been awake for some time. Her hair was plaited and she wore a fresh white chemise. I turned to take her in my arms, I meant to undo the careful plaits, but as I did so there was a soft discreet knock.

She said, 'I have sent Christophine away twice. We wake very early here. The morning is the best time.'

'Come in,' she called and Christophine came in with our coffee on a tray. She was dressed up and looking very imposing. The skirt of her flowered dress trailed after her making a rustling noise as she walked and her yellow silk turban was elaborately tied. Long heavy gold ear-rings pulled down the lobes of her ears. She wished us good morning smiling and put the tray of coffee, cassava cakes and guava jelly on the round table. I got out of bed and went into the dressing-room. Someone had laid my dressing-gown on the narrow bed. I looked out of the window. The cloudless sky was a paler blue than I'd imagined but as I looked I thought I saw the colour changing to a deeper blue. At noon I knew it would be gold, then brassy in the heat. Now it was fresh and cool and the air itself was blue. At last I turned away from the light and space and went back into the bedroom, which was still in the half dark. Antoinette was leaning back against the pillows with her eyes closed. She opened them and smiled when I came in. It was the black woman hovering over her who said, 'Taste my bull's blood, master.' The coffee she handed me was delicious and she had long-fingered hands, thin and beautiful I suppose.

'Not horse piss like the English madams drink,' she said. 'I know them. Drink their yellow horse piss, talk, talk their lying talk.' Her dress trailed and rustled as she walked to the door. There she turned. 'I send the girl to clear up the mess you make with the frangipani, it bring cockroach in the house. Take care not to slip on the flowers, young master.' She slid through the door.

'Her coffee is delicious but her language is horrible and she might hold her dress up. It must get very dirty, yards of it trailing on the floor.'

'When they don't hold their dress up it's for respect,' said Antoinette. 'Or for feast days or going to Mass.'

'And is this a feast day?'

'She wanted it to be a feast day.'

'Whatever the reason it is not a clean habit.'

'It is. You don't understand at all. They don't care about getting a dress dirty because it shows it isn't the only dress they have. Don't you like Christophine?'

'She is a very worthy person no doubt. I can't say I like her language.'

'It doesn't mean anything,' said Antoinette.

'And she looks so lazy. She dawdles about.'

'Again you are mistaken. She seems slow, but every move she makes is right so it's quick in the end.'

I drank another cup of bull's blood. (Bull's blood, I thought. The Young Bull.)

'How did you get that dressing-table up here?'

'I don't know. It's always been here ever since I can remember. A lot of the furniture was stolen, but not that.'

There were two pink roses on the tray, each in a small brown jug. One was full blown and as I touched it the petals dropped.

'Rose elle a vécu,' I said and laughed. 'Is that poem true? Have all beautiful things sad destinies?'

'No, of course not.'

Her little fan was on the table, she took it up laughing, lay back and shut her eyes. 'I think I won't get up this morning.'

'Not get up. Not get up at all?'

'I'll get up when I wish to. I'm very lazy you know. Like Christophine. I often stay in bed all day.' She flourished her fan. 'The bathing pool is quite near. Go before it gets hot, Baptiste will show you. There are two pools, one we call the champagne pool because it has a waterfall, not a big one you understand, but it's good to feel it on your shoulders. Underneath is the nutmeg pool, that's brown and shaded by a big nutmeg tree. It's just big enough to swim in. But be careful. Remember to put your clothes on a rock and before you dress again shake them very well. Look for the red ant, that is the worst. It is very small but bright red so you will be able to see it easily if you look. Be careful,' she said and waved her little fan.

One morning soon after we arrived, the row of tall trees outside my window were covered with small pale flowers too fragile to resist the wind. They fell in a day, and looked like snow on the rough grass—snow with a faint sweet scent. Then they were blown away.

The fine weather lasted longer. It lasted all that week and the next and the next and the next. No sign of a break. My fever weakness left me, so did all misgiving.

I went very early to the bathing pool and stayed there for hours, unwilling to leave the river, the trees shading it, the flowers that opened at night. They were tightly shut, drooping, sheltering from the sun under their thick leaves.

It was a beautiful place—wild, untouched, above all untouched, with an alien, disturbing, secret loveliness. And it kept its secret. I'd find myself thinking, 'What I see is nothing—I want what it hides— that is not nothing.'

In the late afternoon when the water was warmer she bathed with me. She'd spend some time throwing pebbles at a flat stone in the middle of the pool. 'I've seen him. He hasn't died or gone to any other river. He's still there. The land crabs are harmless. People say they are harmless. I wouldn't like to—'

'Nor would I. Horrible looking creatures.'

She was undecided, uncertain about facts—any fact. When I asked her if the snakes we sometimes saw were poisonous, she said, 'Not those. The fer de lance of course, but there are none here,' and added, 'but how can they be sure? Do you think they know?' Then, 'Our snakes are not poisonous. Of course not.'

However, she was certain about the monster crab and one afternoon when I was watching her, hardly able to believe she was the pale silent creature I had married, watching her in her blue chemise, blue with white spots hitched up far above her knees, she stopped laughing called a warning and threw a large pebble. She threw like a boy, with a sure graceful movement, and I looked down at very long pincer claws, jagged-edged and sharp vanishing.

'He won't come after you if you keep away from that stone. He lives there. Oh it's another sort of crab. I don't know the name in English. Very big, very old.'

As we were walking home I asked her who had taught her to aim so well. 'Oh, Sandi taught me, a boy you never met.' . . .

The kitchen and the swarming kitchen life were some way off. As for the money which she handed out so carelessly, not counting it, not knowing how much she gave, or the unfamiliar faces that appeared then disappeared, though never without a large meal eaten and a shot of rum I discovered—sisters, cousins, aunts and uncles—if she asked no questions how could I?

The house was swept and dusted very early, usually before I woke. Hilda brought coffee and there were always two roses on the tray. Sometimes she'd smile a sweet childish smile, sometimes she would giggle very loudly and rudely, bang the tray down and run away.

'Stupid little girl,' I'd say.

'No, no. She is shy. The girls here are very shy.'

After breakfast at noon there'd be silence till the evening meal which was served much later than in England. Christophine's whims and fancies, I was sure. Then we were left alone. Sometimes a sidelong look or a sly knowing glance disturbed me, but it was never for long. 'Not now,' I would think. 'Not yet.'

It was often raining when I woke during the night, a light capricious shower, dancing playful rain, or hushed muted, growing louder, more persistent, more powerful, an inexorable sound. But always music, a music I had never heard before.

Then I would look at her for long minutes by candle-light, wonder why she seemed sad asleep, and curse the fever or the caution that had made me so blind, so feeble, so hesitating . . .

'Suppose you took this happiness away when I wasn't looking . . .'

'And lose my own? Who'd be so foolish?'

'I am not used to happiness,' she said. 'It makes me afraid.'

'Never be afraid. Or if you are tell no one.'

'I understand. But trying does not help me.'

'What would?' She did not answer that, then one night whispered, 'If I could die. Now, when I am happy. Would you do that? You wouldn't have to kill me. Say die and I will die. You don't believe me? Then try, try, say die and watch me die.'

'Die then! Die!' I watched her die many times. In my way, not in hers. In sunlight, in shadow, by moon-light, by candlelight. In the long afternoons when the house was empty. Only the sun was there to keep us company. We shut him out. And why not? Very soon she was as eager for what's called loving as I was—more lost and drowned afterwards.

She said, 'Here I can do as I like,' not I, and then I said it too. It seemed right in that lonely place. 'Here I can do as I like.'

We seldom met anyone when we left the house. If we did they'd greet us and go on their way.

I grew to like these mountain people, silent, reserved, never servile, never curious (or so I thought), not knowing that their quick sideways looks saw everything they wished to see.

It was at night that I felt danger and would try to forget it and push it away.

'You are safe,' I'd say. She'd liked that—to be told 'you are safe.' Or I'd touch her face gently and touch tears. Tears—nothing! Words—less than nothing. As for the happiness I gave her, that was worse than nothing. I did not love her. I was thirsty for her, but that is not love. I felt very little tenderness for her, she was a stranger to me, a stranger who did not think or feel as I did.

One afternoon the sight of a dress which she'd left lying on her bedroom floor made me breathless and savage with desire. When I was exhausted I turned away from her and slept, still without a word or a caress. I woke and she was kissing me—soft light kisses. 'It is late,' she said and smiled. 'You must let me cover you up—the land breeze can be cold.'

'And you, aren't you cold?'

'Oh I will be ready quickly. I'll wear the dress you like tonight.'

'Yes, do wear it.' . . .

Die then. Sleep. It is all that I can give you. . . . wonder if she ever guessed how near she came to dying. In her way, not in mine. It was not a safe game to play—in that place. Desire, Hatred, Life, Death came very close in the darkness. Better not know how close. Better not think, never for a moment. Not close. The same . . . 'You are safe,' I'd say to her and to myself. 'Shut your eyes. Rest.'

Then I'd listen to the rain, a sleepy tune that seemed as if it would go on for ever . . . Rain, for ever raining. Drown me in sleep. And soon.

Next morning there would be very little sign of these showers. If some of the flowers were battered, the others smelt sweeter, the air was bluer and sparkling fresh. Only the clay path outside my window was muddy. Little shallow pools of water glinted in the hot sun, red earth does not dry quickly.

The idyll is ended when Rochester receives a letter warning him that Antoinette's mother was mad and had to be shut away when she tried to kill her husband. It is enough to poison his feelings for her, and thus to drive her insane too, so she becomes the madwoman in the attic in Charlotte Bronte's novel Jane Eyre.

From *Middlemarch*

George Eliot

TWO HOURS LATER, Dorothea was seated in an inner room or boudoir of a handsome apartment in the Via Sistina.

I am sorry to add that she was sobbing bitterly, with such abandonment to this relief of an oppressed heart as a woman habitually controlled by pride on her own account and thoughtfulness for others will sometimes allow herself when she feels securely alone. And Mr Casaubon was certain to remain away for some time at the Vatican.

Yet Dorothea had no distinctly shapen grievance that she could state even to herself; and in the midst of her confused thought and passion, the mental act that was struggling forth into clearness was a self-accusing cry that her feeling of desolation was the fault of her own spiritual poverty. She had married the man of her choice, and with the advantage over most girls that she had contemplated her marriage chiefly as the beginning of new duties: from the very first she had thought of Mr Casaubon as having a mind so much above her own, that he must often be claimed by studies which she could not entirely share; moreover, after the brief narrow experience of her girlhood she was beholding Rome, the city of visible history, where the past of a whole hemisphere seems moving in funeral procession with strange ancestral images and trophies gathered from afar.

But this stupendous fragmentariness heightened the dream-like strangeness of her bridal life. Dorothea had now been five weeks in Rome, and in the kindly mornings when autumn and winter seemed to go hand in hand like a happy aged couple one of whom would presently survive in chiller loneliness, she had driven about at first with Mr Casaubon, but of late chiefly with Tantripp and their experienced courier. She had been led through the best galleries, had been taken to the chief points of view, had been shown the grandest ruins and the most glorious churches, and she had ended by oftenest choosing to drive out to the Campagna where she could feel alone with the earth and sky, away from the oppressive masquerade of ages, in which her own life too seemed to become a masque with enigmatical costumes.

To those who have looked at Rome with the quickening power of a knowledge which breathes a growing soul into all historic shapes, and traces out the suppressed traditions which unite all contrasts, Rome may still be the spiritual centre and interpreter of the world. But let them conceive one more historical contrast: the gigantic broken revelations of that Imperial and Papal city thrust abruptly on the notions of a girl who had been brought up in English and Swiss Puritanism, fed on meagre Protestant histories and on art chiefly of the hand-screen sort; a girl whose ardent nature turned all her small allowance of knowledge into principles, fusing her actions into their mould, and whose quick emotions gave the most abstract things the quality of a pleasure or a pain; a girl who had lately become a wife, and from the enthusiastic acceptance of untried duty found herself plunged in tumultuous preoccupation with her personal lot. The weight of unintelligible Rome might lie easily on bright nymphs to whom it formed a background for the brilliant picnic of Anglo-foreign society; but Dorothea had no such defence against deep impressions. Ruins and basilicas, palaces and colossi, set in the midst of a sordid present, where all that was living and warm-blooded seemed sunk in the deep degeneracy of a superstition divorced from reverence; the dimmer but yet eager Titanic life gazing and struggling on walls and ceilings; the long vistas of white forms whose marble eyes seemed to hold the monotonous light of an alien world: all this vast wreck of ambitious ideals, sensuous and spiritual, mixed confusedly with the signs of breathing forgetfulness and degradation, at first jarred her as with an electric shock, and then urged themselves on her with that ache belonging to a glut of confused ideas which check the flow of emotion. Forms both pale and glowing took possession of her young sense, and fixed themselves in her memory even when she was not thinking of them, preparing strange associations which remained through her after-years. Our moods are apt to bring with them images which succeed each other like the magic-lantern pictures of a doze; and in certain states of dull forlornness Dorothea all her life continued to see the vastness of St. Peter's, the huge bronze canopy, the excited intention in the attitudes and garments of the prophets and evangelists in the mosaics above, and the red drapery which was being hung for Christmas spreading itself everywhere like a disease of the retina.

Not that this inward amazement of Dorothea's was anything very exceptional: many souls in their young nudity are tumbled out among incongruities and left to 'find their feet' among them, while their elders go about their business. Nor can I suppose that when Mrs Casaubon is discovered in a fit of weeping six weeks after her wedding, the situation will be regarded as tragic. Some discouragement, some faintness of heart at the new real future which replaces the imaginary, is not unusual, and we do not expect people to be deeply moved by what is not unusual. That element of tragedy which lies in the very fact of frequency, has not yet wrought itself into the coarse emotion of mankind; and perhaps our frames could hardly bear much of it. If we had a keen vision and feeling of all ordinary human life, it would be like hearing the grass grow or a squirrel's heart beat, and we should die of that roar which lies on the other side of silence. As it is, the quickest of us walk about well wadded with stupidity.

From *Mr and Mrs Elliot*

Ernest Hemingway

MR AND MRS ELLIOT tried very hard to have a baby. They tried as often as Mrs Elliot could stand it. They tried in Boston after they were married and they tried coming over on the boat. They did not try very often on the boat because Mrs Elliot was quite sick. She was sick and when she was sick she was sick as Southern women are sick. That is women from the southern part of the United States. Like all Southern women Mrs Elliot disintegrated very quickly under sea sickness, travelling at night, and getting up too early in the morning. Many of the people on the boat took her for Elliot's mother. Other people who knew they were married believed she was going to have a baby. In reality she was forty years old. Her years had been precipitated suddenly when she started travelling.

She had seemed younger, in fact she had seemed not to have any age at all, when Elliot married her after several weeks of making love to her after knowing her for a long time in her tea shop before he had kissed her one evening.

Hubert Elliot was taking postgraduate work in law at Harvard when he married. He was a poet with an income of nearly ten thousand dollars a year. He wrote very long poems rapidly. He was twenty-five years old and had never gone to bed with a woman until he married Mrs Elliot. He wanted to keep himself pure so that he could bring to his wife the same purity of mind and body that he expected of her. He called it to himself living straight. He had been in love with various girls before he kissed Mrs Elliot and always told them sooner or later that he had led a clean life. Nearly all the girls lost interest in him. He was shocked and really horrified at the way girls would become engaged to and marry men whom they must know had dragged themselves through the gutter. He once tried to warn a girl he knew against a man of whom he had almost proof that he had been a rotter at college and a very unpleasant incident had resulted.

Mrs Elliot's name was Cornelia. She had taught him to call her Calutina, which was her family nickname in the South. His mother cried when he brought Cornelia home after their marriage but brightened very much when she learned they were going to live abroad.

Cornelia had said, 'You dear sweet boy,' and held him closer than ever when he had told her how he had kept himself clean for her. Cornelia was pure too. 'Kiss me again like that,' she said.

Hubert explained to her that he had learned that way of kissing from hearing a fellow tell a story once. He was delighted with his experiment and they developed it as far as possible. Sometimes when they had been kissing together a long time, Cornelia would ask him to tell her again that he had kept himself really straight for her. The declaration always set her off again.

At first Hubert had no idea of marrying Cornelia. He had never thought of her that way. She had been such a good friend of his, and then one day in the little back room of the shop they had been dancing to the gramophone while her girl friend was in the front of the shop and she looked up into his eyes and he had kissed her. He could never remember just when it was decided that they were to be married. But they were married.

They spent the night of the day they were married in a Boston hotel. They were both disappointed but finally Cornelia went to sleep. Hubert could not sleep and several times went out and walked up and down the corridor of the hotel in his new Jaeger bathrobe that he had bought for his wedding trip. As he walked he saw all the pairs of shoes, small shoes and big shoes, outside the doors of the hotel rooms. This set his heart to pounding and he hurried back to his own room but Cornelia was asleep. He did not like to waken her and soon everything was quite all right and he slept peacefully.

The next day they called on his mother and the next day they sailed for Europe. It was possible to try to have a baby but Cornelia could not attempt it very often although they wanted a baby more than anything else in the world. They landed at Cherbourg and came to Paris. They tried to have a baby in Paris. Then they decided to go to Dijon where there was summer school and where a number of people who crossed on the boat with them had gone. They found there was nothing to do in Dijon. Hubert, however, was writing a great number of poems and Cornelia typed them for him. They were all very long poems. He was very severe about mistakes and would make her re-do an entire page if there was one mistake. She cried a good deal and they tried several times to have a baby before they left Dijon.

They came to Paris and most of their friends from the boat came back too. They were tired of Dijon and anyway would now be able to say that after leaving Harvard or Columbia or Wabash they had studied at the University of Dijon down in the Côte d'Or. Many of them would have preferred to go to Languedoc, Montpellier, or Perpignan if there are universities there. But all those places are too far away. Dijon is only four and a half hours from Paris and there is a diner on the train.

So they all sat around the Café du Dome, avoiding the Rotonde across the street because it is always so full of foreigners for a few days and then the Elliots rented a château in Touraine through an advertisement in the *New York Herald*. Elliot had a number of friends by now all of whom admired his poetry and Mrs Elliot had prevailed upon him to send over to Boston for her girl friend who had been in the tea shop. Mrs Elliot had became much brighter after her girl friend came and they had many good cries together. The girl friend was several years older than Cornelia and called her Honey. She too came from a very old Southern family.

The three of them, with several of Elliot's friends who called him Hubie, went down to the château in Touraine. They found Touraine to be a very flat hot country very much like Kansas. Elliot had nearly enough poems for a book now. He was going to bring it out in Boston and had already sent his cheque to, and made a contract with, a publisher.

In a short time the friends began to drift back to Paris. Touraine had not turned out the way it looked when it was started. Soon all the friends had gone off with a rich young and unmarried poet to a seaside resort near Trouville. There they were all very happy.

Elliot kept on at the château in Touraine because he had taken it for all summer. He and Mrs Elliot tried very hard to have a baby in the big bedroom on the big, hard bed. Mrs Elliot was learning the touch system on the typewriter, but she found that while it increased the speed it made more mistakes. The girl friend was now typing practically all of the manuscripts. She was very neat and efficient and seemed to enjoy it.

Elliot had taken to drinking white wine and lived apart in his own room. He wrote a great deal of poetry during the night and in the morning looked very exhausted. Mrs Elliot and the girl friend now slept together in the big medieval bed. They had many a good cry together. In the evening they all sat at dinner together in the garden under a plane tree and the evening wind blew and Elliot drank white wine and Mrs Elliot and the girl friend made conversation and they were all quite happy.

From *May We Borrow Your Husband?*

Graham Greene

IT WAS TWO DAYS after that, just at sunset, that Poopy arrived with her husband. I was back at work on Rochester, sitting in an overcoat on my balcony, when a taxi drove up – I recognized the driver as someone who plied regularly from Nice airport. What I noticed first, because the passengers were still hidden, was the luggage, which was bright blue and of an astonishing newness. Even the initials – rather absurdly PT – shone like newly-minted coins. There were a large suitcase and a small suitcase and a hat-box, all of the same cerulean hue, and after that a respectable old leather case totally unsuited to air travel, the kind one inherits from a father, with half a label still left from Shepheard's Hotel or the Valley of the Kings. Then the passenger emerged and I saw Poopy for the first time. Down below, the interior-decorators were watching too, and drinking Dubonnet.

She was a very tall girl, perhaps five feet nine, very slim, very young, with hair the colour of conkers, and her costume was as new as the luggage. She said, '*Finalmente*,' looking at the undistinguished façade with an air of rapture – or perhaps it was only the shape of her eyes. When I saw the young man I felt certain they were just married; it wouldn't have surprised me if confetti had fallen out from the seams of their clothes. They were like a photograph in the *Tatler*; they had camera smiles for each other and an underlying nervousness. I was sure they had come straight from the reception, and that it had been a smart one, after a proper church wedding.

They made a very handsome couple as they hesitated a moment before going up the steps to the reception. The long beam of the Phare de la Garoupe brushed the water behind them, and the floodlighting went suddenly on outside the hotel as if the manager had been waiting for their arrival to turn it up. The two decorators sat there without drinking, and I noticed that the elder one had covered the contusion on his cheek with a very clean white handkerchief. They were not, of course, looking at the girl but at the boy. He was over six feet tall and as slim as the girl, with a face that might have been cut on a coin, completely handsome and completely dead – but perhaps that was only an effect of his nerves. His clothes, too, I thought, had been bought for the occasion, the sports-jacket with a double slit and the grey trousers cut a little narrowly to show off the long legs. It seemed to me that they were both too young to marry – I doubt if they had accumulated forty-five years between them – and I had a wild impulse to lean over the balcony and warn them away – 'Not this hotel. Any hotel but this.' Perhaps I could have told them that the heating was insufficient or the hot water erratic or the food terrible, not that the English care much about food, but of course they would have paid me no attention – they were so obviously 'booked', and what an ageing lunatic I should have appeared in their eyes. ('One of those eccentric English types one finds abroad' – I could imagine the letter home.) This was the first time I wanted to interfere, and I didn't know them at all. The second time it was already too late, but I think I shall always regret that I did not give way to that madness ...

It had been the silence and attentiveness of those two down

below which had frightened me, and the patch of white handkerchief hiding the shameful contusion. For the first time I heard the hated name: 'Shall we see the room, Poopy, or have a drink first?'

They decided to see the room, and the two glasses of Dubonnet clicked again into action.

I think she had more idea of how a honeymoon should be conducted than he had, because they were not seen again that night.

I was late for breakfast on the terrace, but I noticed that Stephen and Tony were lingering longer than usual. Perhaps they had decided at last that it was too cold for a bathe; I had the impression, however, that they were lying in wait. They had never been so friendly to me before, and I wondered whether perhaps they regarded me as a kind of cover, with my distressingly normal appearance. My table for some reason that day had been shifted and was out of the sun, so Stephen suggested that I should join theirs: they would be off in a moment, after one more cup ... The contusion was much less noticeable today, but I think he had been applying powder.

'You staying here long?' I asked them, conscious of how clumsily I constructed a conversation compared with their easy prattle.

'We had meant to leave tomorrow,' Stephen said, 'but last night we changed our minds.'

'Last night?'

'It was such a beautiful day, wasn't it? "Oh", I said to Tony, "surely we can leave poor dreary old London a little longer?" It has an awful staying power – like a railway sandwich.'

'Are your clients so patient?'

'My dear, the clients? You never in your life saw such atrocities as we get from Brompton Square. It's always the same. People who pay others to decorate for them have ghastly taste themselves.'

'You do the world a service then. Think what we might suffer without you. In Brompton Square.'

Tony giggled, 'I don't know how we'd stand it if we had not our private jokes. For example, in Mrs Clarenty's case, we've installed what we call the Loo of Lucullus.'

'She was enchanted,' Stephen said.

'The most obscene vegetable forms. It reminded me of a harvest festival.'

They suddenly became very silent and attentive, watching somebody over my shoulder. I looked back. It was Poopy, all by herself. She stood there, waiting for the boy to show her which table she could take, like a new girl at school who doesn't know the rules. She even seemed to be wearing a school uniform: very tight trousers, slit at the ankle – but she hadn't realized that the summer term was over. She had dressed up like that, I felt certain, so as not to be noticed, in order to hide herself, but there were only two other women on the terrace and they were both wearing sensible tweed skirts. She looked at them nostalgically as the waiter led her past our table to one nearer the sea. Her long legs moved awkwardly in the pants as though they felt exposed.

'The young bride,' Tony said.

'Deserted already,' Stephen said with satisfaction.

'Her name is Poopy Travis, you know.'

'It's an extraordinary name to choose. She couldn't have been *christened* that way, unless they found a very liberal vicar.'

'He is called Peter. Of an undefined occupation. Not Army, I think, do you?'

'Oh no, not Army. Something to do with land perhaps – there's an agreeable *herbal* smell about him.'

'You seem to know nearly all there is to know,' I said.

'We looked at their police *carnet* before dinner.'

'I have an idea,' Tony said, 'that PT hardly represents their activities last night.' He looked across the tables at the girl with an expression extraordinarily like hatred.

'We were both taken,' Stephen said, 'by the air of innocence. One felt he was more used to horses.'

'He mistook the yearnings of the rider's crotch for something quite different.'

Perhaps they hoped to shock me, but I don't think it was that. I really believe they were in a state of extreme sexual excitement; they had received a *coup de foudre* last night on the terrace and were quite incapable of disguising their feelings. I was an excuse to talk, to speculate about the desired object. The sailor had been a stop-gap: this was the real thing. I was inclined to be amused, for what could this absurd pair hope to gain from a young man newly married to the girl who now sat there patiently waiting, wearing her beauty like an old sweater she had forgotten to change? But that was a bad simile to use: she would have been afraid to wear an old sweater, except secretly, by herself, in the playroom. She had no idea that she was one of those who can afford to disregard the fashion of their clothes. She caught my eye and, because I was so obviously English, I suppose, gave me half a timid smile. Perhaps I too would have received the *coup de foudre* if I had not been thirty years older and twice married.

Tony detected the smile. 'A regular body-snatcher,' he said. My breakfast and the young man arrived at the same moment before I had time to reply. As he passed the table I could feel the tension.

'*Cuir de Russie*,' Stephen said, quivering a nostril. 'A mistake of inexperience.'

The youth caught the words as he went past and turned with an astonished look to see who had spoken, and they both smiled insolently back at him as though they really believed they had the power to take him over …

For the first time I felt disquiet.

Something was not going well; that was sadly obvious. The girl nearly always came down to breakfast ahead of her husband – I have an idea he spent a long time bathing and shaving and applying his *Cuir de Russie*. When he joined her he would give her a courteous brotherly kiss as though they had not spent the night together in the same bed. She began to have those shadows under the eyes which come from lack of sleep – for I couldn't believe that they were 'the lineaments of gratified desire'. Sometimes from my balcony I saw them returning from a walk – nothing, except perhaps a pair of horses, could have been more handsome. His gentleness towards her might have reassured her mother, but it made a man impatient to see him squiring her across the undangerous road, holding open doors, following a pace behind her like the husband of a princess. I longed to see some outbreak of irritation caused by the sense of satiety, but they never seemed to be in conversation when they returned from their walk, and at table I caught only the kind of phrases people use who are dining together for the sake of politeness. And yet I could swear that she loved him, even by the way she avoided watching him. There was nothing avid or starved about her; she stole her quick glances when she was quite certain that his attention was absorbed elsewhere – they were tender, anxious perhaps, quite undemanding. If one inquired after him when he wasn't there, she glowed with the pleasure of using his name. 'Oh, Peter overslept this morning.' 'Peter cut himself. He's staunching the blood now.' 'Peter's mislaid his tie. He thinks the floor-waiter has purloined it.' Certainly she loved him; I was far less certain of what his feelings were.

And you must imagine how all the time those other two were closing in. It was like a medieval siege: they dug their trenches and threw up their earthworks. The difference was that the besieged didn't notice what they were at – at any rate, the girl didn't; I don't know about him. I longed to warn her, but what could I have said that wouldn't have shocked her or angered her? I believe the two would have changed their floor if that would have helped to bring them closer to the fortress; they probably discussed the move together and decided against it as too overt.

Because they knew that I could do nothing against them, they regarded me almost in the role of an ally. After all, I might be useful one day in distracting the girl's attention – and I suppose they were not quite mistaken in that; they could tell from the way I looked at her how interested I was, and they probably calculated that my interests might in the long run coincide with theirs. It didn't occur to them that, perhaps, I was a man with scruples. If one really wanted a thing scruples were obviously, in their eyes, out of place. There was a tortoiseshell star mirror at St Paul they were plotting to obtain for half the price demanded (I think there was an old mother who looked after the shop when her daughter was away at a *boîte* for women of a certain taste); naturally, therefore, when I looked at the girl, as they saw me so often do, they considered I would be ready to join in any 'reasonable' scheme.

'When I looked at the girl' – realize that I have made no real attempt to describe her. In writing a biography one can, of course, just insert a portrait and the affair is done: I have the prints of Lady Rochester and Mrs Barry in front of me now. But speaking as a professional novelist (for biography and reminiscence are both new forms to me), one describes a woman not so much that the reader should see her in all the cramping detail of colour and shape (how often Dickens's elaborate portraits seem like directions to the illustrator which might well have been left out of the finished book), but to convey an emotion. Let the reader make his own image of a wife, a mistress, some passer-by 'sweet and kind' (the poet required no other descriptive words), if he has a fancy to. If I were to describe the girl (I can't bring myself at this moment to write her hateful name), it would be not to convey the colour of her hair, the shape of her mouth, but to express the pleasure and the pain with which I recall her – I, the writer, the observer, the subsidiary character, what you will. But if I didn't bother to convey them to her, why should I bother to convey them to you, *hypocrite lecteur*?

How quickly those two tunnelled. I don't think it was more than four mornings after the arrival that, when I came down to breakfast, I found they had moved their table next to the girl's and were entertaining her in her husband's absence. They did it very well; it was the first time I had seen her relaxed and happy – and she was happy because she was talking about Peter. Peter was agent for his father, somewhere in Hampshire – there were three thousand acres to manage. Yes, he was fond of riding and so was she. It all tumbled out – the kind of life she dreamed of having when she returned home. Stephen just dropped in a word now and then, of a rather old-fashioned courteous interest, to keep her going. Apparently he had once decorated some hall in their neighbourhood and knew the names of some people Peter knew – Winstanley, I think – and that gave her immense confidence.

'He's one of Peter's best friends,' she said, and the two flickered their eyes at each other like lizards' tongues.

'Come and join us, William,' Stephen said, but only when he had noticed that I was within earshot. 'You know Mrs Travis?'

How could I refuse to sit at their table? And yet in doing so I seemed to become an ally.

'Not *the* William Harris?' the girl asked. It was a phrase which I hated, and yet she transformed even that, with her air of innocence. For she had a capacity to make everything new: Antibes became a discovery and we were the first foreigners to have made it. When she said, 'Of course, I'm afraid I haven't actually *read* any of your books,' I heard the over-familiar remark for the first time; it even seemed to me a proof of her honesty – I nearly wrote her virginal honesty. 'You must know an awful lot about people,' she said, and again I read into the banality of the remark an appeal – for help against whom, those two or the husband who at that moment appeared on the terrace? He had the same nervous air as she, even the same shadows under the lids, so that they might have been taken by a stranger, as I wrote before, for brother and sister. He hesitated a moment when he saw all of us there and she called across to him, 'Come and meet these nice people, darling.' He didn't look any too pleased, but he sat glumly down and asked whether the coffee was still hot.

'I'll order some more, darling. They know the Winstanleys, and this is *the* William Harris.'

He looked at me blankly; I think he was wondering if I had anything to do with tweeds.

'I hear you like horses,' Stephen said, 'and I was wondering whether you and your wife would come to lunch with us at Cagnes on Saturday. That's tomorrow, isn't it? There's a very good racecourse at Cagnes …'

'I don't know,' he said dubiously, looking to his wife for a clue.

'But, darling, of course we must go. You'd love it.'

His face cleared instantly. I really believe he had been troubled by a social scruple: the question whether one accepts invitations on a honeymoon. 'It's very good of you,' he said, 'Mr …'

'Let's start as we mean to go on. I'm Stephen and this is Tony.'

'I'm Peter.' He added a trifle gloomily, 'And this is Poopy.'

'Tony, you take Poopy in the Sprite, and Peter and I will go by *autobus*.' (I had the impression, and I think Tony had too, that Stephen had gained a point.)

'You'll come too, Mr Harris?' the girl asked, using my surname as though she wished to emphasize the difference between me and them.

'I'm afraid I can't. I'm working against time.'

I watched them that evening from my balcony as they returned from Cagnes and, hearing the way they all laughed together, I thought, 'The enemy are within the citadel: it's only a question of time.' A lot of time, because they proceeded very carefully, those two. There was no question of a quick grab which I suspect had caused the contusion in Corsica.

It became a regular habit with the two of them to entertain the girl during her solitary breakfast before her husband arrived. I never sat at their table again, but scraps of the conversation would come over to me, and it seemed to me that she was never quite so cheerful again. Even the sense of novelty had gone. I heard her say once, 'There's so little to do here,' and it struck me as an odd observation for a honeymooner to make.

Then one evening I found her in tears outside the Musée Grimaldi. I had been fetching my papers, and, as my habit was, I made a round by the Place Nationale with the pillar erected in 1819 to celebrate – a remarkable paradox – the loyalty of Antibes to the monarchy and her resistance to *les Troupes Etrangères*, who were seeking to re-establish the monarchy. Then, according to rule, I went on by the market and the old port and Lou-Lou's restaurant up the ramp towards the cathedral and the Musée, and there in the grey evening light, before the street-lamps came on, I found her crying under the cliff of the château.

I noticed too late what she was at or I wouldn't have said, 'Good evening, Mrs Travis.' She jumped a little as she turned and dropped her handkerchief, and when I picked it up I found it soaked with tears – it was like holding a small drowned animal in my hand. I said, 'I'm sorry,' meaning that I was sorry to have startled her, but she took it in quite another sense. She said, 'Oh, I'm being silly, that's all. It's just a mood. Everybody has moods, don't they?'

'Where's Peter?'

'He's in the museum with Stephen and Tony looking at the Picassos. I don't understand them a bit.'

'That's nothing to be ashamed of. Lots of people don't.'

'But Peter doesn't understand them either. I know he doesn't.

213

He's just pretending to be interested.'

'Oh well …'

'And it's not that either. I pretended for a time too, to please Stephen. But he's pretending just to get away from me.'

'You are imagining things.'

Punctually at five o'clock the *phare* lit up, but it was still too light to see the beam.

I said, 'The museum will be closing now.'

'Walk back with me to the hotel.'

'Wouldn't you like to wait for Peter?'

'I don't smell, do I?' she asked miserably.

'Well, there's a trace of Arpège. I've always liked Arpège.'

'How terribly experienced you sound.'

'Not really. It's just that my first wife used to buy Arpège.'

We began walking back, and the mistral bit our ears and gave her an excuse when the time came for the reddened eyes.

She said, 'I think Antibes so sad and grey.'

'I thought you enjoyed it here.'

'Oh, for a day or two.'

'Why not go home?'

'It would look odd, wouldn't it, returning early from a honeymoon?'

'Or go on to Rome – or somewhere. You can get a plane to most places from Nice.'

'It wouldn't make any difference,' she said. 'It's not the place that's wrong, it's me.'

'I don't understand.'

'He's not happy with me. It's as simple as that.'

She stopped opposite one of the little rock houses by the ramparts. Washing hung down over the street below and there was a cold-looking canary in a cage.

'You said yourself … a mood …'

'It's not his fault,' she said. 'It's me. I expect it seems very stupid to you, but I never slept with anyone before I married.' She gulped miserably at the canary.

'And Peter?'

'He's terribly sensitive,' she said, and added quickly, 'That's a good quality. I wouldn't have fallen in love with him if he hadn't been.'

'If I were you, I'd take him home – as quickly as possible.' I couldn't help the words sounding sinister, but she hardly heard them. She was listening to the voices that came nearer down the ramparts – to Stephen's gay laugh. 'They're very sweet,' she said. 'I'm glad he's found friends.'

How could I say that they were seducing Peter before her eyes?

From *The Pearls*

Isak Dinesen

Isak Dinesen, the pen name of the Danish writer Karen Blixen, is best known for her autobiographical account of her life in Kenya, Out of Africa, *which was made into a film starring Meryl Streep and Robert Redford. Her literary reputation also rests on her short stories, which hark back to an era when people were resigned to their fate and faced it with courage and determination – she was born in 1885.*

ABOUT EIGHTY YEARS ago a young officer in the guards, the younger son of an old country family, married in Copenhagen the daughter of a rich wool merchant, whose father had been a pedlar and had come to town from Jutland. In those days, such a marriage was an unusual thing, there was much talk of it, and a song was made about it, and sung in the streets.

The bride was twenty years old, and a beauty – a big girl with black hair and a high colour, and a distinction about her as if she were made from whole timber. She had two old unmarried aunts, sisters of her grandfather the pedlar, whom the growing fortune of the family had stopped short in a career of hard work and thrift, and made to sit in state in a parlour. When the elder of them first heard rumours of her niece's engagement, she went and paid her a visit, and in the course of their conversation told her a story.

'When I was a child, my dear,' she said, 'young Baron Rosenkrantz became engaged to a wealthy goldsmith's daughter, have you heard such a thing? Your great-grandmother knew her. The bridegroom had a twin sister, who was a lady at Court, she drove to the goldsmith's house to see the bride. When she had left again, the girl said to her lover: "Your sister laughed at my frock, and because, when she spoke French, I could not answer. She has a hard heart, I saw that. If we are to be happy you must never see her again, I could not bear it." The young man, to comfort her, promised that he would never see his sister again. Soon afterwards, on a Sunday, he took the girl to dine with his mother. As he drove her home she said to him: "Your mother had tears in her eyes when she looked at me. She has hoped for another wife for you. If you love me, you must break with your mother." Again the enamoured young man promised to do as she wished, although it cost him much, for his mother was a widow, and he was her only son. The same week he sent his valet with a bouquet to his bride. Next day, she said to him: "I cannot stand the mien your valet has when he looks at me. You must send him away at the first of the month." "Mademoiselle," said Baron Rosenkrantz, "I cannot have a wife who lets herself be affected by my valet's mien; Here is your ring; farewell forever."'

While the old woman spoke she kept her little glittering eyes upon her niece's face. She had an energetic nature, and had long ago made up her mind to live for others, and she had established herself as the conscience of the family. But in reality she was, with no hopes or fears of her own, a vigorous old moral parasite on the whole clan and particularly on the younger members of it. Jensine, the bride, was a full-blooded young person and a gratifying object to a parasite, moreover the young and the old maid had many qualities in common. Now the girl went on pouring out coffee with a quiet face, but behind it she was furious, and said to herself: 'Aunt Maren shall be paid back for this.' All the same, as was often the case, the aunt's admonitions went deep into her, and she pondered them in her heart.

After the wedding, in the Cathedral of Copenhagen, on a fine June day, the newly married couple went away to Norway for their wedding trip; they sailed as far north as Hardanger. At that time, a journey to Norway was a romantic undertaking, and Jensine's friends asked her why they did not go to Paris, but she herself was pleased to start her married life in the wilderness, and to be alone with her husband. She did not, she thought, want or need any further impressions or experiences. And in her heart she added: 'God help me.'

The gossips of Copenhagen would have it that the bridegroom had married for money, and the bride for a name, but they were all wrong. The match was a love-affair, and the honeymoon, technically, an idyll. Jensine would never have married a man whom she did not love, she held the God of love in great respect, and had already for some years sent a little daily prayer to him: 'Why dost thou tarry?' But now she reflected that he had perhaps granted her her prayer with a vengeance, and that her books had given her but little information as to the real nature of love.

The scenery of Norway, amongst which she made her first experience of the passion, contributed to the overpowering impression of it. The country was at its loveliest, the sky was blue, the bird-cherry flowered everywhere and filled the air with sweet and bitter fragrance, and the nights were so light that you could see to read at midnight. Jensine, in a crinoline and with an alpenstock, climbed many steep paths on her husband's arm – or alone, for she was strong and light-footed. She stood upon the summits, her clothes blown about her, and wondered and wondered. She had lived in Denmark, and for a year in a pension in Lubeck, and her idea of the earth was that it must spread out horizontally, flat or undulating, before her feet. But in these mountains, everything seemed strangely to stand up vertically, like some great animal that rises on its hindlegs, and you know not whether it is to play, or to crush you. She was higher than she had ever been, and the air went to her head like wine. Also wherever she looked there was running water, rushing from the sky-high mountains into the lakes, in silvery rivulets or in roaring falls, rainbow-adorned. It was as if Nature itself was weeping, or laughing, aloud.

At first all this was so new to her that she felt her old ideas of the world blown about in all directions, like her skirts and her shawl. But soon the impressions converged into a sensation of the deepest alarm, a panic such as she had never experienced.

She had been brought up in an atmosphere of prudence and foresight. Her father was an honest tradesman, afraid both to lose his own money, and to let down his customers; sometimes this double risk had thrown him into melancholia. Her mother had been a God-fearing young woman, a member of a pietistic sect, her two old aunts were persons of strict moral principle, with an eye to the opinions of the world. At home Jensine had at times believed herself a daring spirit, and had longed for adventure. But in this wildly romantic landscape, and taken by surprise and overwhelmed by wild, unknown, formidable forces within her own heart, she looked round for support, and where was she to find it? Her young husband, who had brought her there, and with whom she was all alone, could not help her. He was, on the contrary, the cause of the turbulence in her, and he was also, in her eyes, preeminently exposed to the dangers of the outward world. For very soon after her marriage, Jensine realized – as she had perhaps dimly known from their first meeting – that he was a human being entirely devoid and incapable of fear.

She had read in books of heroes and had admired them with all her heart. But Alexander was not like the heroes of her books. He was not braving or conquering the dangers of this world, but he was unaware of their existence. To him, the mountains were a playground, and all the phenomena of life, love itself included, were his playmates within it.

'In a hundred years, my darling,' he said to her, 'it will all be one.'

She could not imagine how he had managed to live till now, but then she knew that his life had been in every way different from hers. Now she felt, with horror, that here she was, within a world of undreamt-of heights and depths, delivered into the hands of a person totally ignorant of the law of gravitation. Under the circumstances, her feelings for him intensified into both a deep moral indignation, as if he had deliberately betrayed her, and into an extreme tenderness, such as she would have felt towards an exposed, helpless child. These two passions were the strongest of which her nature was capable; they took speed with her, and developed into a possession. She recalled the fairytale of the boy who is sent out into the world to learn to be afraid, and it seemed to her that for her own sake and his, in self-defence, as well as in order to protect and save him, she must teach her husband to fear.

He knew nothing of what went on in her. He was in love with her, and he admired and respected her. She was innocent and pure, she sprang from a stock of people capable of making a fortune by their wits, she could speak French and German, and knew history and geography. For all these qualities he had a religious reverence. He was prepared for surprises in her, for their acquaintance was but slight, and they had not been alone together in a room more than three or four times before their wedding. Besides he did not pretend to understand women, but held their incalculableness to be part of their grace. The moods and caprices of his young wife all confirmed in him the assurance, with which she had inspired him at their first meeting, that she was what he needed in life. But he wanted to make her his friend, and reflected that he had never had a real friend in his life.

He did not talk to her of his love affairs of the past, indeed he could not have spoken of them to her if he had wanted to, but in other ways he told her as much as he could remember of himself and his life. One day he recounted how he had gambled in Baden-Baden, risked his last cent, and then won. He did not know that she thought, by his side: 'He is really a thief, or if not that, a receiver of stolen goods, and no better than a thief.'

At other times he made fun of the debts he had had, and the trouble he had had to take to avoid meeting his tailor. This talk sounded really uncanny to Jensine's ears. For to her, debts were an abomination, and that he should have lived on in the midst of them without anxiety, trusting to fortune to pay up for him, seemed against nature. Still, she reflected, she herself, the rich girl he had married, had come along in time, as the willing tool of fortune, to justify his trust in the eyes of his tailor himself.

He told her of a duel that he had fought with a German officer, and showed her a scar from it.

As, at the end of it all, he took her in his arms, on the high hilltops, for all the skies to see them, in her heart she cried: 'If it be possible, let this cup pass from me.'

When Jensine set out to teach her husband to fear, she had the tale of Aunt Maren in her mind, and she made the vow that she would never cry quarter, but that this must be his part. As the relation between herself and him was to her the central factor of existence, it was natural that she should first try to scare him with the possibility of losing her herself. She was an unsophisticated girl and resorted to simple measures.

From now on she became more reckless than he in their climbs. She would stand on the edge of a precipice, leaning on her parasol, and ask him how deep it was to the bottom. She balanced across narrow, brittle bridges, high above foaming streams and chattered to him the while. She went out rowing in a small boat, on the lake, in a thunderstorm. At nights she dreamed about the perils of the days, and woke up with a shriek, so that he took her in his arms to comfort her. But her daring did her no good. Her husband was surprised and enchanted at the change of the demure maiden into a Walkyrie; he put it down to the influence of married life, and felt not a little proud. She herself, in the end, wondered whether she was not driven on in her exploits by his pride and praise, as much as by her resolution to conquer him; then she was angry with herself, and with all women, and she pitied him, and all men.

Sometimes Alexander would go out fishing. These were welcome opportunities to Jensine to be alone and collect her thoughts. So the young bride would wander about alone, in a tartan frock, a small figure in the hills. Once or twice, in these walks, she thought of her father, and the memory of his anxious concern for her, brought tears to her eyes. But she sent him away again; she must be left alone to settle matters of which he could know nothing.

One day, when she sat and rested on a stone, a group of children, who were herding goats, approached and stared at her.

She called them up, and gave them sweets from her reticule. Jensine had adored her dolls, and as much as a modest girl of the period dared, she had longed for children of her own. Now she thought with sudden dismay: 'I shall never have children! As long as I must strain myself against him in this way, we will never have a child.' The idea distressed her so deeply that she got up and walked away.

On another of her lonely walks she came to think of a young man in her father's office, who had loved her. His name was Peter Skov, he was a brilliant young man of business, and she had known him all her life. She now recalled how, when she had had the measles, he had sat and read to her every day, and how he had accompanied her when she went out skating, and had been distressed lest she should catch cold, or fall, or go through the ice. From where she stood, she could see her husband's small figure in the distance. 'Yes,' she thought, 'this is the best thing I can do. When I get back to Copenhagen, then by my honour, which is still my own,' although she had doubts about this point, 'Peter Skov shall be my lover.'

On their wedding day Alexander had given his bride a string of pearls. It had belonged to his Grandmother, who had come from Germany, and who was a beauty and a *belesprit*; she had left it to him to give to his future wife. Alexander had talked much to her of his Grandmother; he said he first fell in love with her, because she was a little like his Grandmamma. He asked her to wear the pearls always. Jensine had never had a string of pearls before, and she was proud of it.

Lately, when she had so often been in need of support, she had got into the habit of twisting the string, and pulling it with her lips.

'If you go on doing that,' Alexander said one day, 'you will break the string.'

She looked at him. It was the first time that she had known him to foresee disaster. 'He loved his Grandmother,' she thought, 'or is it that you must be dead to carry weight with this man?'

Since then she often thought of the old woman. She, too, had come from her own milieu and had been a stranger in her husband's family and circle of friends. She had at last managed to get this string of pearls from Alexander's Grandfather, and it was remembered of her. Were the pearls, she wondered, a token of victory, or of submission? Jensine came to look upon Grandmamma as her best friend in the family, she would have liked to pay her a grand-daughterly visit, and to consult her on her own troubles.

The honeymoon was nearing its end, and that strange warfare, the existence of which was known to one of the belligerents only, had come to no decision. Both the young people were sad to go away. Only now did Jensine fully realize the beauty of the landscape round her, for after all, in the end she had made it her ally. Up here, she reflected, the dangers of the world were obvious, always in sight. In Copenhagen, life looked secure, but might prove to be even more redoubtable. She thought of her pretty house, waiting for her there, with lace curtains, chandeliers and linen cupboards; she could not tell what life within it would be like.

The day before they were to sail they were staying in a small village, from where it was six hours' drive in a carriole down to the landing-place of the coast steamer. They had been out before breakfast, and when Jensine sat down and loosened her bonnet, the string of pearls caught in her bracelet, and the pearls sprang all over the floor, as if she had burst into a rain of tears. Alexander got down on his hands and knees, and as he picked them up one by one, he placed them in her lap.

She sat in a kind of mild panic. She had broken the one thing in the world that she had been afraid of breaking, what omen did that make to them? 'Do you know how many there were?' she asked him.

'Yes,' he said from the floor, 'Grandpapa gave Grandmamma the string on their golden wedding, with a pearl for each of their fifty years. But afterwards he began to add one every year, on her birthday. There are fifty-two, it is easy to remember, it is the number of cards in a pack.'

At last they got them all collected, and folded them up in his silk handkerchief.

'Now I cannot put them on till I get to Copenhagen,' she said.

At that moment their landlady came in with the coffee; she

observed the catastrophe and at once offered to assist them. The shoemaker in the village, she said could do up the pearls for them. Two years ago an English lord and his lady, with a party, had travelled in the mountains, and when the young lady broke her string of pearls, in the same way, he had strung them for her to her perfect satisfaction. He was an honest old man, although very poor, and a cripple. As a young man he had got lost in a snowstorm in the hills, and been found only two days later, and they had had to take off both his feet. Jensine said that she would take her pearls to the shoemaker, and the landlady showed her the way to his house.

She walked down alone, while her husband was strapping their boxes, and found the shoemaker in his little dark workshop. He was a small, thin, old man in a leather apron, with a shy, sly smile in a face harassed by long suffering. She counted the pearls up to him, and gravely confided them into his hands, he looked at them, and promised to have them ready by next midday. After she had settled with him, she kept sitting on a small chair, with her hands in her lap. To say something, she asked him the name of the English lady who had broken her string of pearls, but he did not remember it.

She looked round at the room; it was poor and bare, with a couple of religious pictures nailed on the wall. In a strange way it seemed to her that here she had come home. An honest man, hard tried by destiny, had passed his long years in this little room, it was a place where people worked, and bore troubles patiently, in anxiety for their daily bread. She was still so near to her school books that she remembered them all, now she began to think of what she had read about deep-water fish, which have been so much used to bear the weight of many thousand fathoms of water, that if they are raised to the surface, they will burst. Was she herself, she wondered, such a deep-water fish, that felt at home only under the pressure of existence? Was her father? Had her grandfather and his people before him, been the same? What was a deep-water fish to do, she thought on, if she were married to one of those salmon which here she had seen springing in the water-falls? Or to a flying-fish? She said goodbye to the old shoemaker, and walked off.

As she was going home she caught sight, on the path before her, of a small corpulent man in a black hat and coat, who walked on briskly. She remembered that she had seen him before, she even believed that he was staying in the same house as she. There was a seat by the path, from where one had a magnificent view, the man in black sat down, and Jensine, whose last day in the mountains it was, sat down on the other end of the seat. The stranger lifted his hat a little to her, she had believed him to be an elderly man, but now saw that he could not be much over thirty, he had an energetic face, and clear, penetrating eyes.

After a moment he spoke to her, with a little smile. 'I saw you coming out from the shoemaker,' he said, 'you have not lost your sole in the mountains?'

'No, I took him some pearls,' said Jensine.

'You took him pearls?' said the stranger humorously, 'that is what I go to collect from him.'

She wondered if he were a bit deranged.

'That old man,' said he, 'has got in his hut, a big store of our old national treasures – pearls, if you like – which I happen to be collecting just now. In case you want children's tales, there is not a man in Norway who can give you a better lot than our shoemaker. He once dreamed of becoming a student, and a poet, do you know that? But he was hard hit by destiny, and had to take to a shoemaker's trade.'

After a pause he said: 'I have been told that you and your husband come from Denmark, on your wedding trip. That is an unusual thing to do, these mountains are high and dangerous. Which of you two was it who desired to come here? Was it you?'

'Yes,' said she.

'Yes,' said the stranger, 'I thought so, that he might be the bird, which upwards soars, and you the breeze, which carries him along. Do you know that quotation? Does it tell you anything?'

'Yes,' said she, somewhat bewildered.

'Upwards,' said he, and sat back, silent, with his hands upon his walking-stick.

After a little while he went on: 'The summit! Who knows? We two are pitying the shoemaker for his bad luck, that he had to give up his dreams of being a poet, of fame and a great name. How do we know but that he has had the best of luck? Greatness, the applause of the masses! Indeed, my young lady, perhaps they are better left alone. Perhaps in common trade they can not reasonably purchase a shoemaker's sign-board, and the knowledge of cobbling. One may do well in getting rid of them at cost price. What do you think, Madam?'

'I think that you are right,' she said slowly.

He gave her a sharp glance from a pair of ice-blue eyes. 'Indeed,' said he, 'is that your advice, on this fair summer day? Cobbler, stick to your last. One should do better, you think, in making up pills and draughts for the sick human beings, and cattle, of this world?' He chuckled a little. 'It is a very good jest. In a hundred years it will be written in a book: A little lady from Denmark gave him the advice to stick to his last. Unfortunately he did not follow it. Goodbye, Madam, goodbye.' With these words he got up, and walked on, she saw his black figure grow smaller amongst the hills.

The landlady had come out to hear if she had found the shoemaker. Jensine looked after the stranger. 'Who was that gentleman?' she asked.

The woman shaded her eyes with her hand. 'Oh, indeed,' said she, 'he is a learned man, a great man, he is here to collect old stories and songs. He was an apothecary once. But he has had a theatre in Bergen, and written plays for it, too. His name is Herr Ibsen.'

In the morning, news came up from the landing-place that the boat would be in sooner than expected, and they had to start in haste. The landlady sent her small son to the shoemaker to fetch Jensine's pearls. When the travellers were already seated in the carriole he brought them, wrapped in a leaf from a book, with a tarred string round them. Jensine undid them, and was about to count them, but thought better of it, and instead clasped the string round her throat.

'Ought you not to count them?' Alexander asked her.

She gave him a great glance. 'No,' she said.

She was silent on the drive; his words rang in her ears: 'Ought you not to count them?' She sat by his side, a triumpher, now she knew what a triumpher felt like.

Alexander and Jensine came back to Copenhagen at a time when most people were out of town, and there were no great social functions. But she had many visits from the wives of his young military friends, and the young people went together to the Tivoli of Copenhagen in the summer evenings. Jensine was made much of by all of them.

Her house lay by one of the old canals of the town, and looked over to the Thorwaldsen Museum; sometimes she would stand by the window, gaze at the boats and think of Hardanger. During all this time she had not taken off her pearls or counted them. She was sure that there would at least be one pearl missing, she imagined that she felt the weight on her throat different from before. What would it be, she thought, which she had sacrificed for her victory over her husband? A year, or two years of their married life, before their golden wedding? This golden wedding seemed a long way off, but still each year was precious, and how was she to part with one of them?

In the last months of this summer, people began to discuss the possibility of war. The Schleswig-Holstein question had become imminent. A Danish Royal Proclamation of March had repudiated all German claims upon Schleswig. Now in July, a German ultimatum demanded that it be withdrawn.

Jensine was an ardent patriot and loyal to the King, who had granted them a free Constitution; the rumours put her into the highest agitation. She thought the young officers, Alexander's friends, frivolous in their light, boastful talk of the country's danger—if she wanted to debate it seriously she had to go to her own people. With her husband she could not talk of it at all, but in her heart she knew that he was as convinced of Denmark's invincibility as of his own immortality.

She read the newspapers from beginning to end. One day in the *Berlingske Tidende*, she came upon the following phrase: 'The moment is grave for the nation. But we have trust in our just cause, and we are without fear.'

It was, perhaps, the words of 'without fear' which now made her collect her courage, she sat down in her chair by the window, took off her pearls and put them in her lap. She sat for a moment with her hands folded upon them, as in prayer. Then she counted them. There were fifty-three pearls on her string. She could not believe her own eyes, and counted them over again, but there was no mistake, there were fifty-three pearls and the one in the middle was the biggest.

Jensine sat for a long time in her chair, quite giddy. Her mother, she knew, had believed in the Devil; at this moment the daughter did the same, she would not have been surprised had she heard a laughter from behind the sofa. Had the powers of the Universe, she thought, combined here to make fun of a poor girl?

When she could again collect her thoughts, she remembered that before she had been given the necklace, the old goldsmith of her husband's family had repaired the clasp of it, he would therefore know the pearls and might tell her what to believe. But she was so thoroughly scared that she dared not go to him herself, and only a few days later she asked Peter Skov, who came to pay her a visit, to take the string to him.

Peter returned and told her that the goldsmith had put on his spectacles to examine the pearls, and then in amazement had declared that there was one more than when he had last seen them.

'Yes, Alexander gave me that,' Jensine interrupted him, blushing deeply at her own lie.

Peter reflected, as the goldsmith had done, that it was a cheap generosity in a lieutenant to make the heiress he married a rich present. But he repeated to her the old man's words.

'Mr. Alexander,' he had declared, 'shows himself a rare judge of pearls. I do not hesitate to pronounce this one pearl worth as much as all the others put together.' Jensine, terrified but smiling, thanked Peter, but he went away sadly, for he felt as if he had annoyed or frightened her.

She had not been feeling well for some time and when, in September, they had a spell of heavy, sultry weather in Copenhagen, it rendered her pale and sleepless. Her father and her two old aunts were upset about her, and tried to make her come and stay at his Villa on the Strandvej, outside town. But she would not leave her own house or her husband, nor would she, she thought, ever get well, until she had got to the bottom of the mystery of the pearls. After a week, she made up her mind to write to the shoemaker at Odda. If, as Herr Ibsen had told her, he had been a student and a poet, he would be able to read, and would answer her letter. It seemed to her that in her present situation she had no friend in the world but this crippled old man. She wished that she could go back to his workshop, to the bare walls and the little three-legged chair; she dreamed at night that she was there. He had smiled kindly at her, he knew many children's tales. He might know how to comfort her. Only for a moment she trembled at the idea that he might be dead, and that then she would never know.

With the following weeks the shadow of the war grew deeper. Her father was worrying over the prospects, and about King Frederik's health. Under these new circumstances, the old merchant began to take pride in the fact that he had a daughter married to a soldier; any such connection would have been miles away from him before. He and her old aunts showed Alexander and Jensine great respect.

One day, half against her own will, Jensine asked Alexander straight out if he thought there would be war. Yes, he answered quickly and confidently, there would be war. It could not be avoided.

He went on to whistle a bit of a soldier's song. The sight of her face made him stop. 'Are you frightened of it?' he asked. She considered it hopeless and even unseemly to explain to him her feelings about the war.

'Are you frightened for my sake?' he asked her again. She turned her head away.

'To be a hero's widow,' he said, 'would be just the part for you, my dear.' Her eyes filled with tears, as much of anger as of woe.

Alexander came and took her hand. 'If I fall,' he said, 'it will be a consolation to me to remember that I have kissed you as often as you would let me.' He did so now once more and added: 'Will it be a consolation to you?'

Jensine was an honest girl; when she was questioned she endeavoured to find the truthful answer. Now she thought: Would it be a consolation to me? But she could not, in her heart, find the reply.

With all this Jensine had much to think of, so that she half forgot about the shoemaker, and, when one morning she found his letter on the breakfast table, she for a minute took it to be a mendicant's letter, of which she received many. The next moment she grew very pale. Her husband, opposite her, asked her what was the matter. She gave him no reply, but got up, went into her own small sitting-room, and opened the letter by the fire-place. The characters of it, carefully printed, recalled to her the old man's face as if he had sent her his portrait.

'Dear young Danish Missus,' the letter went, 'Yes, I put the pearl on to your necklace. I meant to give you a small surprise. You made such a fuss about your pearls, when you brought them to me, as if you were afraid that I should steal one of them from you. Old people, as well as young, must have a little fun at times. If I have frightened you, I beg that you will forgive me all the same. This pearl I got two years ago, when I strung the English lady's necklace, I forgot to put the one in, and only found it afterwards. It has been with me for two years, but I have no use for it, it is better that it should be with a young lady. I remember that you sat in my chair, quite young and pretty. I wish you good luck, and that something pleasant may happen to you upon the very same day as you get this letter. And may you wear the pearl long, with a humble heart, a firm trust in the Lord God, and a friendly thought of me, who am old, here up at Odda. Goodbye. Your friend, Peiter Viken.'

Jensine had been reading the letter with her elbows on the mantelpiece, to steady herself. As she looked up, she met the grave eyes of her own image in the looking-glass above it. They were severe, they might be saying: 'You are really a thief, or if not that, a receiver of stolen goods, and no better than a thief.' She stood for a long time, nailed to the spot. At last she thought: 'It is all over. Now I know that I shall never conquer these people, who know neither care nor fear. It is as in the Bible: I shall bruise their heel, but they shall bruise my head. And Alexander, as far as he is concerned, ought to have married the English lady.'

To her own deep surprise, she found that she did not mind. Alexander, himself, had become a very small figure in the background of life, what he did or thought mattered not in the least. That she herself had been made a fool of did not matter. 'In a hundred years,' she thought, 'it will all be one.'

What mattered then? She tried to think of the war, but found that the war did not matter either. She felt a strange giddiness, as if the room was sinking away round her, but not unpleasantly. 'Was there,' she thought, 'nothing left remarkable under the visiting moon?' At the word of the visiting moon, the eyes of the image in the looking-glass opened wide, the two young women stared at one another intensely. Something, she decided, was of great importance, which had come into the world now, and in a hundred years would still remain. The pearls. In a hundred years, she saw, a young man would hand them over to his wife and tell the young woman her own story about them, just as Alexander had given them to her and had told her of his grandmother.

The thought of these two young people, in a hundred years' time, moved her to such tenderness that her eyes filled with tears and made her happy, as if they had been old friends of hers, whom she had found again.

'Not cry quarter?' she thought, 'Why not? Yes, I shall cry as loud as I can. I can not, now, remember the reason why I would not cry.'

The very small figure of Alexander, by the window in the other room, said to her: 'Here is the eldest of your Aunts coming down the street with a big bouquet.'

Slowly, slowly, Jensine took her eyes off the looking-glass, and came back to the world of the present. She went to the window. 'Yes,' she said, 'they are from Bella Vista,' which was the name of her father's villa.

Each from their window, the husband and wife, looked down into the street.

VIII Marrying for Money
or Convenience

From *The Small House at Allington*

Anthony Trollope

In Anthony Trollope's The Small House at Allington, *Adolphus Crosbie, something of a swell, proposed to the lovely, innocent Lily Dale, expecting that her uncle, Christopher Dale, the Squire of Allington, would give her a dowry. But he did not, so when Crosbie went to stay at Courcy Castle with the Earl de Courcy and his family, he proposed to his daughter Lady Alexandrina and threw over Lily. He soon began to have regrets.*

HE AND HIS BRIDE were in the post-chaise, being carried away to the Folkestone railway station; for that place had been chosen as the scene of their honeymoon. It had been at one time intended that the journey to Folkestone should be made simply as the first stage to Paris, but Paris and all foreign travelling had been given up by degrees.

'I don't care a bit about France—we have been there so often,' Alexandrina said.

She had wished to be taken to Naples, but Crosbie had made her understand at the first whispering of the word, that Naples was quite out of the question. He must look now in all things to money. From the very first outset of his career he must save a shilling wherever a shilling could be saved. To this view of life no opposition was made by the De Courcy interest. Lady Amelia had explained to her sister that they ought so to do their honeymooning that it should not cost more than if they began keeping house at once. Certain things must be done which, no doubt, were costly in their nature. The bride must take with her a well-dressed lady's-maid. The rooms at the Folkestone hotel must be large, and on the first

233

floor. A carriage must be hired for her use while she remained; but every shilling must be saved the spending of which would not make itself apparent to the outer world. Oh, deliver us from the poverty of those who, with small means, affect a show of wealth! There is no whitening equal to that of sepulchres whited as they are whited!

By the proper administration of a slight bribe Crosbie secured for himself and his wife a compartment in the railway carriage to themselves. And as he seated himself opposite to Alexandrina, having properly tucked her up with all her bright-coloured trappings, he remembered that he had never in truth been alone with her before. He had danced with her frequently, and been left with her for a few minutes between the figures. He had flirted with her in crowded drawing-rooms, and had once found a moment at Courcy Castle to tell her that he was willing to marry her, in spite of his engagement with Lilian Dale. But he had never walked with her for hours together as he had walked with Lily. He had never talked to her about government, and politics, and books, nor had she talked to him of poetry, of religion, and of the little duties and comforts of life. He had known the Lady Alexandrina for the last six or seven years; but he had never known her—perhaps never would know her—as he had learned to know Lily Dale within the space of two months.

And now that she was his wife, what was he to say to her? They two had commenced a partnership which was to make of them for the remaining term of their lives one body and one flesh. They were to be all-in-all to each other. But how was he to begin this all-in-all partnership? Had the priest, with his blessing, done it so sufficiently that no other doing on Crosbie's own part was necessary? There she was, opposite to him, his very actual wife—bone of his bone; and what was he to say to her? As he settled himself on his seat, taking over his own knees a part of a fine fur rug trimmed with scarlet, with which he had covered her other mufflings, he bethought himself how much easier it would have been to talk to Lily. And Lily would have been ready with all her ears, and all her mind, and all her wit, to enter quickly upon whatever thoughts had occurred to him. In that respect Lily would have been a wife indeed—a wife that would have transferred herself with quick mental activity into her husband's mental sphere. Had he begun about his office Lily would have been ready for him, but Alexandrina had never yet asked him a single question about his official life. Had he been prepared with a plan for to-morrow's happiness Lily would have taken it up eagerly, but Alexandrina never cared for such trifles.

'Are you quite comfortable?' he said, at last.

'Oh, yes, quite, thank you. By-the-by, what did you do with my dressing-case?'

And that question she did ask with some energy.

'It is under you. You can have it as foot-stool if you like it.'

'Oh, no; I should scratch it. I was afraid that if Hannah had it, it might be lost.' Then again there was silence, and Crosbie again considered as to what he would next say to his wife.

We all know the advice given us of old as to what we should do under such circumstances; and who can be so thoroughly justified in following that advice as a newly-married husband? So he put out his hand for hers and drew her closer to him.

'Take care of my bonnet,' she said, as she felt the motion of the railway carriage when he kissed her. I don't think he kissed her again till he had landed her and her bonnet safely at Folkestone. How often would he have kissed Lily, and how pretty would her bonnet have been when she reached the end of her journey, and how delightfully happy would she have looked when she scolded him for bending it! But Alexandrina was quite in earnest about her bonnet; by far too much in earnest for any appearance of happiness.

So he sat without speaking, till the train came to the tunnel.

'I do so hate tunnels,' said Alexandrina.

He had half intended to put out his hand again, under some mistaken idea that the tunnel afforded him an opportunity. The whole journey was one long opportunity, had he desired it; but his wife hated tunnels, so he drew his hand back again. Lily's little fingers would have been ready for his touch. He thought of this, and could not help thinking of it.

He had *The Times* newspaper in his dressing-bag. She also had a novel with her. Would she be offended if he took out the paper and read it? The miles seemed to pass by very slowly, and there was still another hour down to Folkestone. He longed for his *Times*, but resolved at last that he would not read unless she read first. She also had remembered her novel; but by nature she was more patient than he, and she thought that on such a journey any reading might perhaps be almost improper. So she sat tranquilly, with her eyes fixed on the netting over her husband's head.

At last he could stand it no longer, and he dashed off into a conversation, intended to be most affectionate and serious.

'Alexandrina,' he said, and his voice was well-tuned for the tender serious manner, had her ears been alive to such tuning. 'Alexandrina, this is a very important step that you and I have taken today.'

'Yes; it is, indeed,' said she.

'I trust we shall succeed in making each other happy.'

'Yes; I hope we shall.'

'If we both think seriously of it, and remember that that is our chief duty, we shall do so.'

'Yes, I suppose we shall. I only hope we shan't find the house very cold. It is so new, and I am so subject to colds in my head. Amelia says we shall find it very cold; but then she was always against our going there.'

'The house will do very well,' said Crosbie. And Alexandrina could perceive that there was something of the master in his tone as he spoke.

'I am only telling you what Amelia said,' she replied.

Had Lily been his bride, and had he spoken to her of their future life and mutual duties, how she would have kindled to the theme! She would have knelt at his feet on the floor of the carriage, and, looking up into his face, would have promised him to do her best— her best—her very best. And with what an eagerness of inward resolution would she have determined to keep her promise. He thought of all this now, but he knew that he ought not to think of it. Then, for some quarter of an hour, he did take out his newspaper, and she, when she saw him do so, did take out her novel.

He took out his newspaper, but he could not fix his mind upon the politics of the day. Had he not made a terrible mistake? Of what use to him in life would be that thing of a woman that sat opposite to him? Had not a great punishment come upon him and had he not deserved the punishment? In truth, a great punishment had come upon him. It was not only that he had married a woman incapable of understanding the higher duties of married life, but that he himself would have been capable of appreciating the value of a woman who did understand them. He would have been happy with Lily Dale; and therefore we may surmise that his unhappiness with Lady Alexandrina would be greater…

During that week at Courcy Castle—the week which he passed there immediately after his visit to Allington—he had deliberately made up his mind that he was more fit for the bad course than for the good one. The course was now before him, and he had no choice but to walk in it.

It was very cold when they got to Folkestone, and Lady Alexandrina shivered as she stepped into the private-looking carriage which had been sent to the station for her use.

'We shall find a good fire in the parlour at the hotel,' said Crosbie.

'Oh, I hope so,' said Alexandrina, 'and in the bedroom too.'

The young husband felt himself to be offended, but he hardly knew why. He felt himself to be offended, and with difficulty induced himself to go through all those little ceremonies the absence of which would have been remarked by everybody. He did his work, however, seeing to all her shawls and wrappings, speaking with good-nature to Hannah, and paying special attention to the dressing-case.

'What time would you like to dine?' he asked, as he prepared to leave her alone with Hannah in the bedroom.

'Whenever you please; only I should like some tea and bread-and-butter presently.'

Crosbie went into the sitting-room, ordered the tea and bread-and-butter, ordered also the dinner, and then stood himself up with his back to the fire, in order that he might think a little of his future career.

He was a man who had long since resolved that his life should be a success. It would seem that all men would so resolve, if the matter were simply one of resolution. But the majority of men, as I take it, make no such resolution, and very many men resolve that they will be unsuccessful. Crosbie, however, had resolved on success, and had done much towards carrying out his purpose. He had made a name for himself, and had acquired a certain fame. That, however, was, as he acknowledged to himself, departing from him. He looked the matter straight in the face, and told himself that his fashion must be abandoned; but the office remained to him. He might still rule over Mr. Optimist, and make a subservient slave of Butterwell. That must be his line in life now, and to that line he would endeavour to be true. As to his wife, and his home—he would look to them for his breakfast, and perhaps his dinner. He would have a comfortable arm-chair, and if Alexandrina should become a mother, he would endeavour to love his children; but above all things he would never think of Lily. After that he stood and thought of her for half an hour.

'If you please, sir, my lady wants to know at what time you have ordered dinner.'

'At seven, Hannah.'

'My lady says she is very tired, and will lie down till dinner time.'

'Very well, Hannah. I will go into her room when it is time to dress. I hope they are making you comfortable downstairs?'

Then Crosbie strolled out on the pier in the dusk of the cold winter evening.

Mr. Crosbie and his wife went upon their honeymoon tour to Folkestone in the middle of February, and returned to London about the end of March. Nothing of special moment to the interests of our story occurred during those six weeks, unless the proceedings of the young married couple by the sea-side may be thought to have any special interest. With regard to those proceedings I can only say that Crosbie was very glad when they were brought to a close. All holiday-making is hard work, but holiday-making with nothing to do is the hardest work of all. At the end of March they went into their new house, and we will hope that Lady Alexandrina did not find it very cold.

From *Vanity Fair*

William Makepeace Thackeray

*The calculating adventuress Becky Sharp has married the impecunious
cavalry officer Rawdon Crawley, who has financial expectations of his
aunt. Shortly after, George Osborne, also in the army, marries Amelia
Sedley, who is given away at the wedding by her brother Jos, recently
back from India. Amelia and Becky were at school together. All these
characters subsequently meet up at Brighton. The time is Spring 1815.*

GEORGE OSBORNE gave a yawn. 'It's rather slow work,' said he,
'down here; what *shall* we do?'

'Shall we go and look at some horses that Snaffler's just brought
from Lewes Fair?' Crawley said.

'Suppose we go and have some jellies at Dutton's,' said the rogue
Jos, willing to kill two birds with one stone. 'Devilish fine gal at
Dutton's.'

'Suppose we go and see the Lightning come in, it's just about
time?' George said. This advice prevailing over the stables and the
jelly, they turned towards the coach-office to witness the Lightning's
arrival.

As they passed, they met the carriage—Jos Sedley's open
carriage, with its magnificent armorial bearings—that splendid
conveyance in which he used to drive about at Cheltenham majestic
and solitary, with his arms folded, and his hat cocked or, more
happy, with ladies by his side.

Two were in the carriage now; one a little person, with light hair,
and dressed in the height of the fashion; the other in a brown silk
pelisse, and a straw bonnet with pink ribbons, with a rosy, round,
happy face, that did you good to behold. She checked the carriage as
it neared the three gentlemen, after which exercise of authority she
looked rather nervous, and then began to blush most absurdly. 'We
have had a delightful drive, George,' she said, 'and—and we're so
glad to come back and, Joseph, don't let him be late.'

'Don't be leading our husbands into mischief, Mr. Sedley, you wicked, wicked man, you,' Rebecca said, shaking at Jos a pretty little finger covered with the neatest French kid glove. 'No billiards, no smoking, no naughtiness!'

'My dear Mrs. Crawley—Ah now! upon my honour!' was all Jos could ejaculate by way of reply; but he managed to fall into a tolerable attitude, with his head lying on his shoulder, grinning upwards at his victim, with one hand at his back which he supported on his cane, and the other hand (the one with the diamond ring) fumbling in his shirt-frill and among his under waistcoats. As the carriage drove off he kissed the diamond hand to the fair ladies within. He wished all Cheltenham, all Chowringhee, all Calcutta, could see him in that position, waving his hand to such a beauty, and in company with such a famous buck as Rawdon Crawley of the Guards.

Our young bride and bridegroom had chosen Brighton as the place where they would pass the first few days after their marriage; and having engaged apartments at the Ship Inn, enjoyed themselves there in great comfort and quietude, until Jos presently joined them. Nor was he the only companion they found there. As they were coming into the hotel from a seaside walk one afternoon, on whom should they light but Rebecca and her husband. The recognition was immediate. Rebecca flew into the arms of her dearest friend . . .

These two young couples had plenty of tales to relate to each other. The marriages of either were discussed; and their prospects in life canvassed with the greatest frankness and interest on both sides. George's marriage was to be made known to his father by his friend Captain Dobbin; and young Osborne trembled rather for the result of that communication. Miss Crawley, on whom all Rawdon's hopes depended, still held out. Unable to make an entry into her house in Park Lane, her affectionate nephew and niece had followed her to Brighton, where they had emissaries continually planted at her door.

'I wish you could see some of Rawdon's friends who are always about *our* door,' Rebecca said, laughing. 'Did you ever see a dun, my dear; or a bailiff and his man? Two of the abominable wretches watched all last week at the greengrocer's opposite, and we could not get away until Sunday. If aunty does not relent, what *shall* we do?'

Rawdon, with roars of laughter, related a dozen amusing anecdotes of his duns, and Rebecca's adroit treatment of them. He vowed with a great oath, that there was no woman in Europe who could talk a creditor over as she could. Almost immediately after their marriage, her practice had begun, and her husband found the immense value of such a wife. They had credit in plenty, but they had bills also in abundance, and laboured under a scarcity of ready-money. Did these debt-difficulties affect Rawdon's good spirits? No. Everybody in Vanity Fair must have remarked how well those live who are comfortably and thoroughly in debt: how they deny themselves nothing; how jolly and easy they are in their minds. Rawdon and his wife had the very best apartments at the inn at Brighton; the land-lord, as he brought in the first dish, bowed before them as to his greatest customers; and Rawdon abused the dinners and wine with an audacity which no grandee in the land could surpass. Long custom, a manly appearance, faultless boots and clothes, and a happy fierceness of manner, will often help a man as much as a great balance at the banker's.

The two wedding parties met constantly in each other's apartments. After two or three nights the gentlemen of an evening had a little piquet, as their wives sat and chatted apart. This pastime, and the arrival of Jos Sedley, who made his appearance in his grand open carriage, and who played a few games at billiards with Captain Crawley, replenished Rawdon's purse somewhat, and gave him the benefit of that ready-money for which the greatest spirits are sometimes at a standstill.

So the three gentlemen walked down to see the Lightning coach come in. Punctual to the minute, the coach crowded inside and out, the guard blowing his accustomed tune on the horn—the Lightning came tearing down the street, and pulled up at the coach-office.

'Hullo! there's old Dobbin,' George cried, quite delighted to see his old friend perched on the roof; and whose promised visit to Brighton had been delayed until now. 'How are you old fellow? Glad you're come down. Emmy'll be delighted to see you,' Osborne said, shaking his comrade warmly by the hand as soon as his descent from the vehicle was effected—and then he added, in a lower and agitated voice, 'What's the news? Have you been in Russell Square? What does the governor say? Tell me everything.'

Dobbin looked very pale and grave. 'I've seen your father,' said he. 'How's Amelia—Mrs. George? I'll tell you all the news presently: but I've brought the great news of all: and that is'——

'Out with it, old fellow,' George said.

'We're ordered to Belgium. All the army goes—Guards and all. Heavytop's got the gout, and is mad at not being able to move. O'Dowd goes in command, and we embark from Chatham next week.' This news of war could not but come with a shock upon our lovers, and caused all these gentlemen to look very serious.

Anna on the Neck

Anton Chekhov

A FTER THE WEDDING they had not even light refreshments; the happy pair simply drank a glass of champagne, changed into their travelling things, and drove to the station. Instead of a gay wedding ball and supper, instead of music and dancing, they went on a journey to pray at a shrine a hundred and fifty miles away. Many people commended this, saying that Modest Alexeitch was a man high up in the service and no longer young, and that a noisy wedding might not have seemed quite suitable; and music is apt to sound dreary when a government official of fifty-two marries a girl who is only just eighteen. People said, too, that Modest Alexeitch, being a man of principle, had arranged this visit to the monastery expressly in order to make his young bride realize that even in marriage he put religion and morality above everything.

The happy pair were seen off at the station. The crowd of relations and colleagues in the service stood, with glasses in their hands, waiting for the train to start to shout 'Hurrah!' and the bride's father, Pyotr Leontyitch, wearing a top-hat and the uniform of a teacher, already drunk and very pale, kept craning towards the window, glass in hand and saying in an imploring voice:

'Anyuta! Anya, Anya! one word!'

Anna bent out of the window to him, and he whispered something to her, enveloping her in a stale smell of alcohol, blew into her ear – she could make out nothing – and made the sign of the cross over her face, her bosom, and her hands; meanwhile he was breathing in gasps and tears were shining in his eyes. And the schoolboys, Anna's brothers, Petya and Andrusha, pulled at his coat from behind, whispering in confusion:

'Father, hush! … Father, that's enough. …'

When the train started, Anna saw her father run a little way after the train, staggering and spilling his wine, and what a kind, guilty, pitiful face he had:

'Hurra–ah!' he shouted.

The happy pair were left alone. Modest Alexeitch looked about the compartment, arranged their things on the shelves, and sat down, smiling, opposite his young wife. He was an official of medium height, rather stout and puffy, who looked exceedingly well nourished, with long whiskers and no moustache. His clean-shaven, round, sharply defined chin looked like the heel of a foot. The most characteristic point in his face was the absence of moustache, the bare, freshly shaven place, which gradually passed into the fat cheeks, quivering like jelly. His deportment was dignified, his movements were deliberate, his manner was soft.

'I cannot help remembering now one circumstance,' he said, smiling. 'When, five years ago, Kosorotov received the order of St. Anna of the second grade, and went to thank His Excellency, His Excellency expressed himself as follows: "So now you have three Annas: one in your buttonhole and two on your neck." And it must be explained that at that time Kosorotov's wife, a quarrelsome and frivolous person, had just returned to him, and that her name was Anna. I trust that when I receive the Anna of the second grade His Excellency will not have occasion to say the same thing to me.'

He smiled with his little eyes. And she, too, smiled, troubled at the thought that at any moment this man might kiss her with his thick damp lips, and that she had no right to prevent his doing so.

The soft movements of his fat person frightened her; she felt both fear and disgust. He got up, without haste took off the order from his neck, took off his coat and waistcoat, and put on his dressing-gown.

'That's better,' he said, sitting down beside Anna.

Anna remembered what agony the wedding had been, when it had seemed to her that the priest, and the guests, and every one in church had been looking at her sorrowfully and asking why, why was she, such a sweet, nice girl, marrying such an elderly, uninteresting gentleman. Only that morning she was delighted that everything had been satisfactorily arranged, but at the time of the wedding, and now in the railway carriage, she felt cheated, guilty, and ridiculous. Here she had married a rich man and yet she had no money, her wedding-dress had been bought on credit, and when her father and brothers had been saying good-bye, she could see from their faces that they had not a farthing. Would they have any supper that day? And tomorrow? And for some reason it seemed to her that her father and the boys were sitting tonight hungry without her, and feeling the same misery as they had the day after their mother's funeral.

'Oh, how unhappy I am!' she thought. 'Why am I so unhappy?'

With the awkwardness of a man with settled habits, unaccustomed to deal with women, Modest Alexeitch touched her on the waist and patted her on the shoulder, while she went on thinking about money, about her mother and her mother's death. When her mother died, her father, Pyotr Leontyitch, a teacher of drawing and writing in the high school, had taken to drink, impoverishment had followed, the boys had not had boots or goloshes, their father had been hauled up before the magistrate, the warrant officer had come and made an inventory of the furniture. ... What a disgrace! Anna had had to look after her drunken father, darn her brothers' stockings, go to market, and when she was complimented on her youth, her beauty, and her elegant manners, it seemed to her that every one was looking at her cheap hat and the holes in her boots that were inked over. And at night there had been tears and a haunting dread that her father would soon, very soon, be dismissed from the school for his weakness, and that he would not survive it, but would die, too, like their mother. But ladies of their acquaintance had taken the matter in hand and looked about for a good match for Anna. This Modest Alexevitch, who was neither young nor good-looking but had money, was soon found. He had a hundred thousand in the bank and the family estate, which he had let on lease. He was a man of principle and stood well with His Excellency; it would be nothing to him, so they told Anna, to get a note from His Excellency to the directors of the high school, or even to the Education Commissioner, to prevent Pyotr Leontyitch from being dismissed.

While she was recalling these details, she suddenly heard strains of music which floated in at the window, together with the sound of voices. The train was stopping at a station. In the crowd beyond the platform an accordion and a cheap squeaky fiddle were being briskly played, and the sound of a military band came from beyond the villas and the tall birches and poplars that lay bathed in the moonlight; there must have been a dance in the place. Summer visitors and townspeople, who used to come out here by train in fine weather for a breath of fresh air, were parading up and down on the platform. Among them was the wealthy owner of all the summer villas – a tall, stout, dark man called Artynov. He had prominent eyes and looked like an Armenian. He wore a strange costume; his shirt was unbuttoned, showing his chest; he wore high boots with spurs, and a black cloak hung from his shoulders and dragged on the ground like a train. Two boar-hounds followed him with their sharp noses to the ground.

Tears were still shining in Anna's eyes, but she was not thinking now of her mother, nor of money, nor of her marriage; but shaking hands with schoolboys and officers she knew, she laughed gaily and said quickly:

'How do you do? How are you?'

She went out on to the platform between the carriages into the moonlight, and stood so that they could all see her in her new splendid dress and hat.

'Why are we stopping here?' she asked.

'This is a junction. They are waiting for the mail train to pass.'

Seeing that Artynov was looking at her, she screwed up her eyes coquettishly and began talking aloud in French; and because her voice sounded so pleasant, and because she heard music and the moon was reflected in the pond, and because Artynov, the notorious Don Juan and spoiled child of fortune, was looking at her eagerly and with curiosity, and because every one was in good spirits – she suddenly felt joyful, and when the train started and the officers of her acquaintance saluted her, she was humming the polka the strains of which reached her from the military band playing beyond the trees; and she returned to her compartment feeling as though it had been proved to her at the station that she would certainly be happy in spite of everything.

The happy pair spent two days at the monastery, then went back to town.

From *Is He Popenjoy?*

Anthony Trollope

In Anthony Trollope's memorably titled novel Is He Popenjoy? *Mary Lovelace, the daughter of the Dean of Brotherton, marries Lord George Germain, the brother of the unmarried Marquis of Brotherton. Her father has been rather keener than she about this match for, as he says, 'You ought to remember, my dear, that marquises do not grow on every hedge.' Mary's attractions for the impecunious Lord George are her beauty and her wealth, which overcome the fact that one of her grandfathers had been a candlemaker in Southwark while the other had kept livery stables in Bath. During their three-month engagement, 'She strove very hard to be in love, and sometimes she thought that she had succeeded.'*

THE MARRIED COUPLE passed their honeymoon in Ireland, Lady Brotherton having a brother, an Irish peer, who lent them for a few months his house on the Blackwater. . . Perhaps a sojourn in

Ireland did as well as anything could towards assisting the young wife in her object of falling in love with her husband. He would hardly have been a sympathetic companion in Switzerland or Italy, as he did not care for lakes or mountains. But Ireland was new to him and new to her, and he was glad to have an opportunity of seeing something of a people as to whom so little is really known in England. And at Ballycondra, on the Blackwater, they were justified in feeling a certain interest in the welfare of the tenants around them. There was something to be done, and something of which they could talk. Lord George, who couldn't hunt, and wouldn't dance, and didn't care for mountains, could inquire with some zeal how much wages a peasant might earn, and what he would do with it when earned. It interested him to learn that whereas an English labourer will certainly eat and drink his wages from week to week—so that he could not be trusted to pay any sum half-yearly—an Irish peasant, though he be half starving, will save his money for the rent. And Mary, at his instance, also cared for these things. It was her gift, as with many women, to be able to care for everything. It was, perhaps, her misfortune that she was apt to care too much for many things. The honeymoon in Ireland answered its purpose, and Lady George, when she came back to Manor Cross, almost thought that she had succeeded. She was at any rate able to assure her father that she had been as happy as the day was long, and that he was absolutely—'perfect'.

This assurance of perfection the Dean no doubt took at its proper value. He patted his daughter's cheek as she made it, and kissed her, and told her that he did not doubt but that with a little care she might make herself a happy woman.

In due course Lord George and Mary do become devoted to one another, and Trollope makes his point about the varied routes that can lead to a happy marriage.

From *Our Mutual Friend*

Charles Dickens

MR. AND MRS. LAMMLE have walked for some time on the Shanklin sands, and one may see by their footprints that they have not walked arm in arm, and that they have not walked in a straight track, and that they have walked in a moody humour; for the lady has prodded little spirting holes in the damp sand before her with her parasol, and the gentleman has trailed his stick after him. As if he were of the Mephistopheles family indeed, and had walked with a drooping tail.

'Do you mean to tell me, then, Sophronia——'

Thus he begins after a long silence, when Sophronia flashes fiercely, and turns upon him.

'Don't put it upon me, sir. I ask you, do you mean to tell me?'

Mr. Lammle falls silent again, and they walk as before. Mrs. Lammle opens her nostrils and bites her under-lip. Mr. Lammle takes his gingerous whiskers in his left hand and bringing them together, frowns furtively at his beloved out of a thick gingerous bush.

'Do I mean to say!' Mrs. Lammle after a time repeats with indignation. 'Putting it on me! The unmanly disingenuousness!'

Mr. Lammle stops, releases his whiskers, and looks at her. 'The what?'

Mrs. Lammle haughtily replies, without stopping, and without looking back. 'The meanness.'

He is at her side again in a pace or two, and he retorts, 'That is not what you said. You said disingenuousness.'

'What if I did?'

'There is no "if" in the case. You did.'

'I did, then. And what of it?'

'What of it?' says Mr. Lammle. 'Have you the face to utter the word to me?'

'The face, too!' replied Mrs. Lammle, staring at him with cold scorn. 'Pray, how dare you, sir, utter the word to me?'

'I never did.'

As this happens to be true, Mrs. Lammle is thrown on the feminine resource of saying, 'I don't care what you uttered or did not utter.'

Mr. Lammle breaks the latter.

'You shall proceed in your own way. You claim a right to ask me do I mean to tell you. Do I mean to tell you what?'

'That you are a man of property?'

'No.'

'Then you married me on false pretences?'

'So be it. Next comes what you mean to say. Do you mean to say you are a woman of property?'

'No.'

'Then you married me on false pretences.'

'If you were so dull a fortune-hunter that you deceived yourself, or if you were so greedy and grasping that you were over-willing to be deceived by appearances, is it my fault, you adventurer?' the lady demands, with great asperity.

'I asked Veneering, and he told me you were rich.'

'Veneering!' with great contempt. 'And what does Veneering know about me?'

'Was he not your trustee?'

'No. I have no trustee but the one you saw on the day when you fraudulently married me. And his trust is not a very difficult one, for it is only an annuity of a hundred and fifteen pounds. I think there are some odd shillings or pence if you are very particular.'

Mr. Lammle bestows a by no means loving look upon the partner of his joys and sorrows, and he mutters something; but checks himself.

'Question for question. It is my turn again, Mrs. Lammle. What made you suppose me a man of property?'

'You made me suppose you so. Perhaps you will deny that you always presented yourself to me in that character?'

'But you asked somebody, too. Come, Mrs. Lammle, admission for admission. You asked somebody?'

'I asked Veneering.'

'And Veneering knew as much of me as he knew of you, or as anybody knows of him.'

After more silent walking, the bride stops short, to say in a passionate manner:

'I never will forgive the Veneerings for this!'

'Neither will I,' returns the bridegroom.

With that they walk again; she, making those angry spirts in the sand; he, dragging that dejected tail. The tide is low, and seems to have thrown them together high on the bare shore. A gull comes sweeping by their heads, and flouts them. There was a golden surface on the brown cliffs but now, and behold they are only damp earth. A taunting roar comes from the sea, and the far-out rollers mount upon one another, to look at the entrapped impostors, and to join in impish and exultant gambols.

'Do you pretend to believe,' Mrs. Lammle resumes, sternly, 'when you talk of my marrying you for worldly advantages, that it was within the bounds of reasonable probability that I would have married you for yourself?'

'Again there are two sides to the question, Mrs. Lammle. What do you pretend to believe?'

'So you first deceive me and then insult me!' cries the lady, with a heaving bosom.

'Not at all. I have originated nothing. The double edged question was yours.'

'Was mine!' the bride repeats, and her parasol breaks in her angry hand.

His colour has turned to a livid white, and ominous marks have come to light about his nose, as if the finger of the very devil himself had, within the last few moments, touched it here and there. But he has repressive power, and she has none.

'Throw it away,' he coolly recommends as to the parasol; 'you have made it useless; you look ridiculous with it.'

Whereupon she calls him in her rage, 'a deliberate villain', and so casts the broken thing from her as that it strikes him in falling. The finger-marks are something whiter for the instant, but he walks on at her side.

She bursts into tears, declaring herself the wretchedest, the most deceived, the worst-used of women. Then she says that if she had the courage to kill herself, she would do it. Then she calls him vile impostor. Then she asks him why in the disappointment of his base speculation, he does not take her life with his own hand, under the present favourable circumstances. Then she cries again. Then she is enraged again, and makes some mention of swindlers. Finally, she sits down crying on a block of stone, and is in all the known and unknown humours of her sex at once. Pending her changes, those aforesaid marks in his face have come and gone, now here now there, like white stops of a pipe on which the diabolical performer has played a tune. Also his livid lips are parted at last, as if he were breathless with running. Yet he is not.

'Now, get up, Mrs. Lammle, and let us speak reasonably.' She sits upon her stone, and takes no heed of him.

'Get up, I tell you.'

Raising her head, she looks contemptuously in his face, and repeats, 'You tell me! Tell me, forsooth!'

She affects not to know that his eyes are fastened on her as she droops her head again; but her whole figure reveals that she knows it uneasily.

'Enough of this. Come! Do you hear? Get up!'

Yielding to his hand, she rises, and they walk again; but this time with their faces turned towards their place of residence.

'Mrs. Lammle, we have both been deceiving, and we have both been deceived. We have both been biting, and we have both been bitten. In a nut-shell, there's the state of the case.'

'You sought me out——'

'Tut! Let us have done with that. We know very well how it was. Why should you and I talk about it, when you and I can't disguise it? To proceed. I am disappointed and cut a poor figure.'

'Am I no one?'

'Some one—and I was coming to you, if you had waited a moment. You, too, are disappointed and cut a poor figure.'

'An injured figure!'

'You are now cool enough, Sophronia, to see that you can't be injured without my being equally injured; and that therefore the mere word is not to the purpose. When I look back I wonder how I can have been such a fool as to take you to so great an extent upon trust.'

'And when I look back——' the bride cries, interrupting.

'And when you look back, you wonder how you can have been—you'll excuse the word?'

'Most certainly, with so much reason.'

'—Such a fool as to take me to so great an extent upon trust. But the folly is committed on both sides. I cannot get rid of you; you cannot get rid of me. What follows?'

'Shame and misery,' the bride bitterly replies.

'I don't know. A mutual understanding follows, and I think it may carry us through. Here I split my discourse (give your arm, Sophronia) into three heads, to make it shorter and plainer. Firstly, it's enough to have been done, without the mortification of being known to have been done. So we agree to keep the fact to ourselves. You agree?'

'If it is possible, I do.'

'Possible! We have pretended well enough to one another. Can't we, united, pretend to the world? Agreed. Secondly, we owe the Veneerings a grudge, and we owe all other people the grudge of wishing them to be taken in, as we ourselves have been taken in. Agreed?'

'Yes. Agreed.'

'We come smoothly to thirdly. You have called me an adventurer, Sophronia. So I am. In plain uncomplimentary English, so I am. So are you, my dear. So are many people. We agree to keep our own secret, and to work together in furtherance of our own schemes.'

'What schemes?'

'Any scheme that will bring us money. By our own schemes, I mean our joint interest. Agreed?'

She answers, after a little hesitation, 'I suppose so. Agreed.'

'Carried at once, you see! Now Sophronia, only half-a-dozen words more. We know one another perfectly. Don't be tempted into twitting me with the past knowledge that you have of me, because it is identical with the past knowledge that I have of you, and in twitting me, you twit yourself, and I don't want to hear you do it. With this good understanding established between us, it is better never done. To wind up all:—You have shown temper to-day, Sophronia. Don't be betrayed into doing so again, because I have a Devil of a temper myself.'

So the happy pair, with this hopeful marriage contract thus signed, sealed, and delivered, repair homeward. If, when those infernal finger-marks were on the white and breathless countenance of Alfred Lammle, Esquire, they denoted that he conceived the purpose of subduing his dear wife Mrs. Alfred Lammle, by at once divesting her of any lingering reality or pretence of self-respect, the purpose would seem to have been presently executed. The mature young lady has mighty little need of powder now for her downcast face, as he escorts her in the light of the setting sun to their abode of bliss.

From *Une Vie*

Guy de Maupassant

FOUR DAYS LATER the travelling coach arrived which was to convey them to Marseilles.

After her first distress, Jeanne had already grown accustomed to Julian's proximity, to his kisses and caresses, though she still felt the same repugnance for their more intimate relations. She admired and loved him, and she soon recovered her natural gaiety. She bade her parents a brief and cheerful farewell. The Baroness alone displayed emotion. Just as the carriage was starting, she placed a purse, well filled and heavy as lead, in her daughter's hands.

'That's for pocket-money,' she said.

Jeanne put it away, and the horses set off. Towards evening Julian asked, 'How much money did your mother give you?'

She had forgotten about the purse, but now she emptied it into her lap. From it issued a stream of gold, amounting to two thousand francs. She clapped her hands. 'How extravagant I shall be!' and she put the money away again.

After a week's appalling heat, they arrived at Marseilles. On the following day they sailed for Corsica on a little packet-boat, the *Roi-Louis*, that touched at Ajaccio on its way to Naples.

Corsica! The bush! Bandits! Mountains! Napoleon's birth-place! Jeanne felt that she was leaving prosaic reality and entering, wide awake, a land of dreams. Side by side on the deck of the ship, they watched the cliffs of Provence glide past. The sea, intensely azure, lay like a painted ocean. It had an appearance of solidity in the blazing sunshine, beneath the infinite and almost unnaturally blue sky.

'Do you remember our sail with old Lastique?' asked Jeanne.

For answer he lightly kissed her ear.

The paddles of the steamer churned up the water, disturbing its deep repose, and in their wake a long straight furrow, foamy and white, like the froth of champagne, stretched away out of sight. Suddenly in front of the bows, only a few fathoms away, a dolphin leaped out of the water, then dived head first and disappeared. With a cry of alarm, Jeanne threw herself into Julian's arms. Then she laughed at her fears, and watched eagerly for the dolphin's re-appearance. In a few moments it bobbed up again, like a huge mechanical toy. Then it dived, and rose again to the surface. Soon there were two, then three, then six dolphins gambolling around the clumsy ship, as if they were escorting a gigantic brother, a wooden fish with iron fins. They appeared now on the port, now on the starboard side, sometimes all together, sometimes singly, chasing one another as if in merry sport. They described great curves as they leapt into the air, then they plunged again into the sea one after the other. Quivering with delight, Jeanne clapped her hands in ecstasy at each appearance of these great creatures which swam so gracefully. Her heart leaped with them in simple and childlike joy. All at once they vanished. She caught one more glimpse of them in the far distance, out to sea. Then they were lost to sight, and Jeanne had a momentary sensation of sadness at their departure.

Evening came, tranquil, radiant, full of light and quiet

happiness. There was no motion either in the air or in the sea. And the infinite calm of ocean and sky communicated itself to the spellbound souls that seemed no less untroubled. The great sun was sinking slowly towards invisible Africa, that burning land of Africa which seemed already to project something of its heat. But, when the sun had set, the lovers felt upon their faces a cool caress, too slight to be called a breeze.

They did not go down to their cabin, which reeked of all the vile odours that are characteristic of packet-boats. Wrapped in their cloaks, they lay side by side on the deck. Julian fell asleep at once. But Jeanne, thrilled by the wonder of the voyage, remained open-eyed. The monotonous sound of the paddles lulled her, and she gazed at the myriad stars shining overhead, piercingly bright, sparkling as with liquid fire in the clear southern sky. But towards morning she dropped off to sleep. Sounds and voices awakened her. The sailors were singing as they washed down the decks. She roused her husband, who was fast asleep, and they both rose. She drew in rapturously the salt air, tingling with it to her finger-tips. There was sea all round them. On the bow, however, something that looked grey and blurred in the early dawn—something that resembled a bank of curious, pointed, jagged clouds—loomed above the waves.

Presently it grew more distinct, and as the sky brightened the outlines were more sharply defined, and a long chain of peaked, fantastic mountains stood forth. Corsica lay before them, veiled in a thin haze. Behind the mountains the sun was rising, throwing into relief the jutting peaks. Then all the heights were flooded with light, while the rest of the island remained enveloped in mist.

The captain, a little wizened old man, tanned, wrinkled, and shrivelled by salt gales, came on deck. He addressed Jeanne in a voice grown hoarse under the strain of thirty years of shouting orders above the din of storms. 'Do you catch the scent of her, the witch?' he asked.

Jeanne became aware of a strong, strange odour of wild, aromatic plants.

'That is the scent of Corsica, madam. She is a pretty woman, and that is her perfume. If I had been away for twenty years, I should know it again from five miles off. Corsica is my home. And our

Emperor away over there on St. Helena, they say he is always talking about this perfume of his country. He is a kinsman of mine.'

Taking off his hat, the captain saluted Corsica, and saluted too, far away across the ocean, the captive, the great Emperor, his kinsman. Jeanne was moved almost to tears. The seaman pointed with his arm towards the horizon. 'There are the Sanguinaires,' he said.

Julian was standing by his wife, with his arm round her waist, and both tried to make out the islands he had indicated. At last they caught sight of some pyramidical rocks which the ship presently skirted, entering into a large sheltered bay, surrounded by high mountains, whose lower slopes looked as if covered with moss.

The captain pointed to this expanse of verdure. 'The bush,' he exclaimed.

As the ship proceeded, sailing slowly on an azure lake of such transparency that sometimes the bottom was visible, the ring of mountains seemed to close in behind it. Presently at the end of the bay, close to the water's edge, at the foot of the mountains, the dazzlingly white town came in sight. A few small Italian vessels lay at anchor in the harbour. Four or five boats circled around the Roi-Louis to take off passengers. Julian, who was putting the baggage together, said to his wife in an undertone, 'I suppose it will be enough if I give the steward a franc?'

For the last week he had continually vexed his wife by asking her this sort of question. She replied, with a shade of impatience, 'It's better to give too much than too little.'

He had endless disputes with waiters, cabmen, and shop-keepers, and when by some quibble he had succeeded in obtaining a reduction, he would rub his hands and say to Jeanne, 'I hate being done.'

She shuddered when she saw a bill presented, foreseeing that Julian would raise objections to every item. Humiliated by his haggling, she blushed to the roots of her hair under the contemptuous glances of the servants, whose eyes followed her husband, while they held in their open hands his inadequate tips. He had another altercation with the boatman who put them ashore.

The first tree she saw was a palm.

They went to a great empty hotel at the corner of a large square and had luncheon. Just as Jeanne was preparing to go for a stroll round the town, Julian took her arm, and murmured tenderly, 'Let's go and rest for a little, puss.'

They stayed three days in that little town, which lies hidden away at the far end of its blue bay, and is as hot as a furnace behind its screen of mountains, which intercept every breath of wind. Then they made out an itinerary for their journey. To avoid being held up by any difficult part of the road, they decided to hire saddle-horses, and chose two small, fiery-eyed Corsican stallions, lean and untiring. They set out one morning at daybreak. Their guide rode a mule, and carried provisions, for that wild country boasted of no hostelries.

At first the road followed the line of the coast. Then it plunged into a shallow valley leading towards the high mountains. It was continually crossing dried-up beds of torrents, where, like a lurking animal, a thread of water still trickled and gurgled faintly beneath the rocks. Destitute of cultivation, the country had an utterly barren aspect. The hillsides were covered with a growth of tall grass, burnt brown by the scorching heat. Sometimes the travellers met a mountaineer, either on foot, or riding a small pony, or astride a donkey no bigger than a dog. Each of these wayfarers carried on his back a loaded gun, old and rusty, but a formidable weapon in such hands. The air was heavy with the pungent perfume of the aromatic plants which cover the island. The road wound its way upward gradually, following the long flanks of the mountain sides. Peaks of pink or blue granite lent fairy hues to the wide landscape, and the undulations of the ground were on so mighty a scale that the immense forests of chestnut trees on the lower slopes dwindled to thickets.

Now and then the guide pointed towards the jagged peaks and mentioned a name. Jeanne and Julian gazed, but could see nothing. At last they would distinguish a grey object, resembling a pile of stones which had slipped down from the summit. This was a village, a small hamlet of granite, clinging there, perched like a bird's nest, and almost invisible on the vast mountain-side. Presently Jeanne grew weary of riding at a pace which never exceeded a walk.

'Let us go a little faster,' she said, and urged on her horse. As she did not hear her husband galloping behind her, she turned round, and burst out laughing when she saw him, pale, clutching his horse's mane, and bumping ludicrously in the saddle. His lack of skill and his terror were rendered more absurd by their contrast with his handsome person and his air of a dashing cavalier.

After that they trotted gently. On either side of the road lay a never-ending growth of bushes and trees, which covered the hillsides like a cloak. This was the bush, the impenetrable bush. It consisted of holm oak, juniper, arbutus mastic, buckthorn, heather, laurustinus, myrtle and box, interlaced, like a tangled head of hair, with twining clematis, bracken of enormous size, honeysuckle, cistus, rosemary, lavender, briar—a tangled fleece flung upon the backs of the mountains.

They felt hungry. The guide joined them, and led them to one of those delightful springs common in craggy country. A slender jet of icy water issued from a crevice in the rock and trickled over the edge of a chestnut leaf, placed there by some passer-by to guide the slender stream to his lips.

Jeanne felt such keen delight that she could scarcely suppress her cries of joy. They set out again, and began to go downhill, skirting the gulf of Sagone. Towards evening they passed through Cargèse, a Greek village founded in bygone times by refugees exiled from their country. Tall, handsome girls of singularly graceful bearing, with finely moulded hips, long hands and slender wrists, were grouped around a fountain. Julian called out good evening to them, and they replied in musical tones and in the harmonious language of the country from which they had fled.

At Piana they had to beg for hospitality, as in ancient days and in uncivilised countries. Trembling with joy, Jeanne awaited the opening of the door at which Julian had knocked. Oh, this was real travelling, with all the unforeseen incidents that arise far from the beaten track. It so happened that they had come to the house of a young married couple, who welcomed them as the patriarchs of old must have welcomed the guests sent by God. They slept on a maize paillasse, in an old worm-eaten house. Its woodwork, full of worm-holes, infested by the long teredo which eats away rafters, creaked and sighed like a living thing.

They left at sunrise, and shortly afterwards halted in full view of a forest—a veritable forest—of purple granite, with peaks, columns, steeples, all moulded into weird shapes by the age-long erosion of winds and mists. Rising to the height of a thousand feet, slender, rounded, twisted, crooked, contorted, startling and fantastic, these amazing rocks had the appearance of trees, plants, beasts, monuments, men, robed monks, horned devils, giant birds, an assemblage of prodigies, a nightmare menagerie, petrified at the will of some eccentric deity.

Jeanne's heart was too full for speech. She took Julian's hand and pressed it; the sight of so much beauty inspired in her a yearning for love. Suddenly emerging from that scene of chaos, they came upon another bay, girt with a glowing wall of red granite. The flaming rocks were reflected in the blue water.

'O Julian!' gasped Jeanne, too deeply moved to utter another word. She had a lump in her throat, and the tear-drops welled from her eyes. Julian looked at her in amazement.

'What is the matter, puss?'

Smiling, she dried her eyes, and said in a somewhat tremulous voice, 'It's nothing. Simply nerves. I don't know why, but I was a little upset. I am so happy that the least thing moves me to the heart.'

Julian could make nothing of these womanish vapours, of these tremors that thrill those sensitive beings who are transported by a trifle, moved to the depths alike by an ecstasy or by a catastrophe, convulsed by incomprehensible emotions, thrown off their balance with equal readiness by joy and by despair. Her tears seemed to him absurd. The roughness of the road completely engrossed his own attention.

'It would be better,' he said, 'if you were to look after your horse.'

By an almost impracticable track they reached the level of the bay, and then turned to the right in order to ascend the gloomy vale of Ota. The path proved appalling.

'Suppose we walk up on foot?' suggested Julian.

Jeanne asked nothing better. She was delighted to walk and to be alone with him after her recent emotion. While the guide went on ahead with the mule and the horses, they followed slowly. The mountain was cleft from summit to base with a deep fissure, and the path plunged into this breach. It lay far down between two mighty walls, and down this crevasse foamed a raging torrent. The air was glacial, and against the black granite a glimpse of blue sky high above dizzied and startled the eye. Jeanne was alarmed by a sudden noise. Raising her eyes, she saw a great bird fly out of a cleft. It was an eagle. It seemed as if his outstretched wings would span the two walls of the chasm. He soared towards the blue ether, and vanished from sight. After a while the fault in the mountain divided into two branches. The path climbed upwards in sharp zig-zags, with a ravine on either side. Light of foot and light of heart, Jeanne went first. Pebbles rolled away under her step, and she leaned boldly over the precipices. Her husband followed her. He was a little out of breath, and kept his eyes on the ground for fear of dizziness.

The next moment they were bathed in sunlight, and they felt as if they had emerged from an inferno. They were thirsty. They followed a trail of moisture, which led them over chaotic heaps of stones to a tiny spring, trained to flow through a hollow stick for the convenience of the goat-herds. The ground all around was carpeted with moss. Jeanne knelt down to drink, and Julian followed her example. As she tasted the cool water, he seized her by the waist and tried to usurp her place at the end of the wooden pipe. She resisted. Their lips brushed together, met, and repulsed each other. In the varying fortunes of the struggle both in turn caught the thin end of the pipe, seizing it in their teeth, and held it fast. And the thread of cold water, continually recaptured only to be abandoned, broke and joined again, and splashed their faces, necks, hands and clothes. Little pearly drops glistened in their hair, and their kisses were mingled with the stream.

Suddenly Jeanne had an amorous fancy. She filled her mouth with the crystal fluid, until her cheeks were swollen like goatskin water-bottles. Then she signed to Julian that with her lips on his she wished to quench his thirst. Smiling and with outstretched arms, he threw back his head and leaned towards her with open mouth. And as he drank at one draught from this living fountain, his veins were filled with feverish desire. Jeanne leaned against him with unwonted tenderness. Her heart was beating and her bosom heaved. With languorous, glistening eyes, she murmured in a low voice, 'Julian, I love you,' and this time it was she who wooed. She threw herself down on the moss, hiding her blushing face in her hands. He caught her in his arms and embraced her passionately.

It was long before they reached the top of the ascent. They did not arrive at Evisa till the evening. They put up at the house of Paoli Palabretti, a relation of their guide. He was a tall man, somewhat bent, with the melancholy air of a consumptive. He showed them their room, a dreary chamber of bare stone, but good accommodation by the standards of Corsica, where luxury is unknown. In his Corsican dialect, a hotch-potch of French and Italian, he expressed his pleasure at their arrival. He was interrupted by a clear voice. A small dark woman, with large black eyes, sun-browned skin and slender waist, her teeth flashing in a continual smile, darted into the room. She kissed Jeanne and shook hands with Julian, exclaiming, 'Good-evening, madam; good-evening, sir. How are you?'

She took their hats and wraps, using one arm only, for the other she carried in a sling. Then she sent everyone out, bidding her husband take the guests for a walk till dinner-time.

Monsieur Palabretti hastened to obey. Walking between the young couple, he showed them round the village. He moved and talked with a languid air, coughing frequently, and observing after each paroxysm, 'It's the cold air of the valley; it has gone to my chest.'

He led them along an out-of-the-way path shaded by gigantic chestnut trees. Suddenly he stopped short.

'Just here,' he said in his monotonous voice, 'my cousin Jean Rinaldi was killed by Mathieu Lori. Look. I was standing there, quite close to Jean, when Mathieu appeared, ten paces away from us. 'Jean,' he cried, 'don't you go to Albertacce. If you do I'll kill you, I swear I will.' I took Jean by the arm. 'Don't go, Jean. He'll kill you.' It was all because of a girl called Paulina Sinacoupi, whom they were both courting. But Jean began shouting, 'I'm going, Mathieu; I shan't stay away for you.' Then, before I could take aim, Mathieu lowered his gun and fired. Jean jumped up in the air with both feet together, like a child skipping, and then fell right back on top of me, so that I dropped my gun and it rolled away down to that big chestnut tree over there. Jean's mouth was wide open. But he never said another word. He was quite dead.'

The young people stared aghast at the tranquil witness of this crime.

'And the murderer?' asked Jeanne.

Paoll Palabretti had a prolonged fit of coughing. Then he replied, 'He got away to the mountains. But my brother killed him the following year—my brother Philippi Palabretti, you know, the bandit.'

Jeanne shuddered. 'Your brother a bandit?'

The eyes of the placid Corsican flashed proudly.

'Yes, madam, and a famous one he was. He accounted for six gendarmes. He and Nicolas Morali were surrounded in the Niolo and fell after six days' fighting, when they were dying of hunger.'

Then he added in tones of resignation, 'It's the way of the country'; just as he would have said, 'It's the cold air of the valley.'

They went home to dinner, and the little Corsican woman treated them as if she had known them twenty years.

Jeanne was haunted by an uneasy doubt. Would she recapture in Julian's arms those strange and violent emotions which she had experienced as she lay on the moss by the fountain? When they were alone in their room, she dreaded lest his kisses should once more leave her cold. But her fears were soon allayed. It was her first night of love.

The next day, at the hour of departure, she could hardly tear herself away from the lonely cottage where, it seemed, a new bliss had come into her life. She drew her little hostess into her room, and, while she declared that she had no intention of offering her a present, she insisted with vehemence on sending her a souvenir from Paris, an idea to which she attached an almost superstitious importance. The young Corsican woman was unwilling to accept it, and held out for a long time. In the end she yielded. 'Very well,' she said, 'send me a small pistol, quite a little one.'

Jeanne opened her eyes wide. The other woman added softly in her ear, as if communicating some exquisite and intimate secret, 'It's to kill my brother-in-law.'

Smiling, she briskly unwound the bandages from her disabled arm, and showed the round white flesh. Right across it ran a stiletto wound, now almost healed.

'If I had not been as strong as he, he would have killed me,' she said. 'My husband is not jealous, because he knows me, and he is ill, you see, and that calms his blood. Besides, I am an honest woman, madam. But my brother-in-law always believes everything he is told. He is jealous on my husband's behalf, and he will certainly be at it again. But if I had a small pistol, I should have an easy mind and could depend on revenging myself.'

Jeanne promised to send the weapon, kissed her new friend tenderly, and went her way.

The rest of the journey passed like a dream, composed of endless embraces and intoxicating caresses. Jeanne noticed nothing, neither landscapes, people, nor places where she stayed. She had eyes only for Julian. There sprang up between them a childish and charming intimacy, made up of all the absurdities of love, of fond, foolish prattle, of pet names for all the curves and corners of their bodies.

When they arrived at Bastia, the guide had to be paid. Julian fumbled in his pockets, unable to find what he wanted. He said to Jeanne, 'As you are not using your mother's two thousand francs, give them to me to keep. They will be safer in my belt, and it will save me the trouble of getting change.'

She handed over her purse.

They went to Leghorn, Florence, Genoa, and drove the whole length of the Corniche. One morning they arrived at Marseilles in a mistral.

Two months had elapsed since their departure from *Les Peuples*, and it was now the fifteenth of October. Jeanne's spirits were affected by the high, cold wind which seemed to come from far-away Normandy, and she felt depressed. Of late, Julian had seemed changed, as if weary and indifferent, and she had a fear that she could not define. She delayed their return journey for four more days, reluctant to leave that pleasant land of sunshine. It seemed to her that she had accomplished the whole circuit of happiness. At last they resumed their journey.

In Paris they were to make all the purchases necessary for their permanent installation at *Les Peuples*. On the strength of her mother's present, Jeanne was looking forward to bringing home many treasures. But her first thought was for the pistol she had promised the young Corsican woman at Evisa. The day after their arrival, she said to Julian, 'Please, dear, will you give me Mamma's money? I want to do my shopping.'

He turned a frowning face towards her. 'How much do you want?'

She was taken aback. 'Why, whatever you like,' she faltered.

'I'll give you a hundred francs,' he replied; 'but be careful not to waste it.'

Disconcerted and bewildered, she hardly knew what to say. At last she began hesitatingly, 'But I gave you that money to . . .'

He interrupted her. 'Exactly. From the moment that we share a common purse, what does it matter whether it's in your pocket or mine? I'm not refusing it to you, am I, as I'm giving you a hundred francs?'

Without another word, she took the five gold coins, but she did not venture to ask for more, and she bought nothing but the pistol.

IX Honeymoon Disasters

From *Frankenstein*

Mary Shelley

Frankenstein, a young scientist, constructs a living creature. He soon regrets his action and flees, but the creature pursues him and extracts a promise that he will make it a mate. Frankenstein embarks on this task but then thinks better of it and destroys the woman on which he has been working. The creature vows revenge. We join the story on Frankenstein's wedding day.

AFTER THE CEREMONY was performed a large party assembled at my father's, but it as agreed that Elizabeth and I should commence our journey by water, sleeping that night at Evian and continuing our journey on the following day. The day was fair, the wind favourable; all smiled on our nuptial embarkation.

Those were the last moments of my life during which I enjoyed the feeling of happiness. We passed rapidly along; the sun was hot, but we were sheltered from its rays by a kind of canopy while we enjoyed the beauty of the scene, sometimes on one side of the lake, where we saw Mont Saleve, the pleasant banks of Montalegre, and at a distance surmounting all, the beautiful Mont Blanc and the assemblage of snowy mountains that in vain endeavour to emulate her; sometimes coasting the opposite banks, we saw the mighty Jura opposing its dark side to the ambition that would quit its native country, and an almost insurmountable barrier to the invader who should wish to enslave it.

I took the hand of Elizabeth. 'You are sorrowful, my love. Ah! If you knew what I have suffered and what I may yet endure, you would endeavour to let me taste the quiet and freedom from despair that this one day at least permits me to enjoy.'

'Be happy, my dear Victor,' replied Elizabeth; 'there is, I hope, nothing to distress you; and be assured that if a lively joy is not painted in my face, my heart is contented. Something whispers to me not to depend too much on the prospect that is opened before us, but I will not listen to such a sinister voice. Observe how fast we move along and how the clouds, which sometimes obscure and sometimes rise above the dome of Mont Blanc, render this scene of beauty still more interesting. Look also at the innumerable fish that are swimming in the clear waters, where we can distinguish every pebble that lies at the bottom. What a divine day! How happy and serene all nature appears!'

Thus Elizabeth endeavoured to divert her thoughts and mine from all reflection upon melancholy subjects. But her temper was fluctuating; joy for a few instants shone in her eyes, but it continually gave place to distraction and reverie.

The sun sank lower in the heavens; we passed the river Drance and observed its path through the chasms of the higher and the glens of the lower hills. The Alps here come closer to the lake, and we approached the amphitheatre of mountains which forms its eastern boundary. The spire of Evian shone under the woods that surrounded it and the range of mountain above mountain by which it was overhung.

The wind, which had hitherto carried us along with amazing rapidity, sank at sunset to a light breeze; the soft air just ruffled the water and caused a pleasant motion among the trees as we approached the shore, from which it wafted the most delightful scent of flowers and hay. The sun sank beneath the horizon as we landed, and as I touched the shore I felt those cares and fears revive which soon were to clasp me and cling to me forever.

It was eight o'clock when we landed; we walked for a short time on the shore, enjoying the transitory light, and then retired to the inn and contemplated the lovely scene of waters, woods, and mountains, obscured in darkness, yet still displaying their black outlines.

The wind, which had fallen in the south, now rose with great violence in the west. The moon had reached her summit in the heavens and was beginning to descend; the clouds swept across it swifter than the flight of the vulture and dimmed her rays, while the lake reflected the scene of the busy heavens, rendered still busier by the restless waves that were beginning to rise. Suddenly a heavy storm of rain descended.

I had been calm during the day, but so soon as night obscured the shapes of objects, a thousand fears arose in my mind. I was anxious and watchful, while my right hand grasped a pistol which was hidden in my bosom; every sound terrified me, but I resolved that I would sell my life dearly and not shrink from the conflict until my own life or that of my adversary was extinguished.

Elizabeth observed my agitation for some time in timid and fearful silence, but there was something in my glance which communicated terror to her, and trembling, she asked, 'What is it that agitates you, my dear Victor? What is it you fear?'

'Oh! Peace, peace, my love!' replied I; 'this night over, and all will be safe; but this night is dreadful, very dreadful.'

I passed an hour in this state of mind, when suddenly I reflected how fearful the combat which I momentarily expected would be to my wife, and I earnestly entreated her to retire, resolving not to join her until I had obtained some knowledge as to the situation of my enemy.

She left me, and I continued some time walking up and down the passages of the house and inspecting every corner that might afford a retreat to my adversary. But I discovered no trace of him and was beginning to conjecture that some fortunate chance had intervened to prevent the execution of his menaces when suddenly I heard a shrill and dreadful scream. It came from the room into which Elizabeth had retired. As I heard it, the whole truth rushed into my mind, my arms dropped, the motion of every muscle and fibre was suspended; I could feel the blood trickling in my veins and tingling in the extremities of my limbs. This state lasted but for an instant; the scream was repeated, and I rushed into the room.

Great God! Why did I not then expire! Why am I here to relate the destruction of the best hope and the purest creature of earth? She was there, lifeless and inanimate, thrown across the bed, her head hanging down and her pale and distorted features half covered by her hair. Every where I turn I see the same figure, her bloodless arms and relaxed form flung by the murderer on its bridal bier. Could I behold this and live? Alas! Life is obstinate and clings closest where it is most hated. For a moment only did I lose recollection; I feel senseless on the ground.

John Ruskin

Unlike Frankenstein's, most honeymoon disaster stories cannot be attributed to an external character, but rather discover the monstrous within the relationship. John Ruskin was the only child of elderly parents who did not send him to school. Even when he went to Oxford he was accompanied by his mother. Of the greatest sensibility in his reactions to nature, mountains, art and architecture, he failed dismally when it came to the opposite sex. As Kenneth Clark put it, he could only treat them as a mixture of pet kitten and fairy. In April 1848 he married the lovely Euphemia Gray from Perth, whom he had known since she was a child. Her father had run badly into debt and so was anxious to get her off his hands. They spent their wedding night at Blair Athol and, in the statement that he made at the time of the annulment of his marriage to Effie in 1854, Ruskin gave his reasons for not having consummated his marriage then.

M ISS GRAY APPEARED in a very weak and nervous state in consequence of this distress [her father's debts] and I was at first afraid of subjecting her system to any new trials. My own passion was also much subdued by anxiety; and I had no difficulty in abstaining on the first night ... It may be thought strange that I could abstain from a woman who to most people was so attractive. But though her face was beautiful, her person was not formed to excite passion. On the contrary there were certain circumstances in her person which completely checked it.

In a letter to her father written in 1854 Effie expanded on how matters proceeded.

For days John talked about his relation to me but avowed no intention of making me his wife. He alleged various reasons, hatred to children, religious motives, a desire to preserve my beauty, and finally this last year told me his true reason (and that to me is as villainous as all the rest) that he had imagined women were quite different to what he saw I was and that the reason why he did not make me his wife was because he was disgusted with my person the first evening 10th April. After I began to see things better I argued with him and took the Bible but he soon silenced me and I was not sufficiently awake to what position I was in – and then he said that after six years he would marry me when I was 25.

Ruskin made plain in his statement how he 'soon silenced' Effie.

She sometimes expressed doubts about it being right to live as we were living; but always continuing to express her wish to live so. I gravely charged her to tell me if she thought she would be happier in consummating marriage or healthier, I, being willing at any time to consummate it; but I answered to her doubts of it being right, that many of the best characters in Church history had preserved virginity in marriage, and that it could not be wrong to do for a time what they had done through life.

Ruskin's conceptions of the female body seem to have been based solely on what he had seen in the art galleries of Europe, where the conventions of painting and sculpture excluded the depiction of pubic hair. When confronted with Effie's he must have thought she was a freak. Matters were not helped by her own total ignorance of matters sexual – 'I had never been told the duties of married persons to each other and knew little or nothing about their relations in the closest union on earth.' Luckily Effie fell in love with the painter John Everett Millais. Ruskin seems almost to have connived in this, seizing on his protégé as the ideal man to bring matters to a head and take Effie off his hands. They married in 1855 and had a large family. Ruskin's love life remained disastrous since he persisted in becoming infatuated with very young girls.

Tchaikovsky

The composer Tchaikovsky's marriage is as sad a case as John Ruskin's. In 1877 he wedded Antonina Ivanovna Milyukova in Moscow: 'She is poor, but a good and honest girl who loves me very much.' On the wedding night, which was spent on the train from Moscow to St Petersburg, Tchaikovsky said, 'I slept like a log.' On the second night matters came to a head and, as he told his brother Anatoly:

WE HAD CONVERSATIONS that further clarified our mutual relations. *She has agreed with absolutely everything and will never be displeased. She needs only to cherish and care for me.* I have reserved for myself complete freedom of action. After taking a good dose of valerian [a sedative] and prevailing upon my discomfited wife not to be discomfited, I again fell asleep like a log. Such sleep is a great benefactor. I feel the time is not far off when I shall calm down *completely*.

What seems most remarkable about this is not so much Tchaikovsky's expectation of a sexless mariage blanche *as that it was only now that he thought he made himself clear on this point. He was soon telling his brother that, 'in the physical respect, my wife has become absolutely repulsive to me.' He went on to say, 'she is very limited, but even that is good. I should be afraid of an intelligent woman. But I stand so far above this one, I dominate her to such a degree, that at least I have no fear of her at all.' But he was wrong about her compliance, or else it was only some days later that she finally realized that her husband's proclivities lay elsewhere. In any event, they were to separate after eleven weeks.*

From *The Dowry*

Guy de Maupassant

N O ONE WAS surprised at the marriage of Maître Simon Lebrument and Mademoiselle Jeanne Cordier. Maître Lebrument had just acquired the practice of Maître Papillon, the notary. Money had, of course, to be found for the purchase, and Mademoiselle Jeanne Cordier had three hundred thousand francs in portable form, in bank notes and in bonds payable to bearer.

Lebrument was a good-looking young fellow with an air about him. It smacked, no doubt, of the provincial lawyer, but still, it was certainly an air, and that was a rare quality in Boutigny-le-Rebours.

Mademoiselle Cordier was graceful and blooming, but her grace had a certain awkwardness; her bloom was not quite fresh. On the whole, however, she was an attractive and presentable girl.

The wedding turned the whole of Boutigny topsy turvy. Congratulations were lavished upon the newly-wedded pair, who presently retired to enjoy their bliss in the privacy of their own house. Their honeymoon was to consist of a few days at home, followed by a little trip to Paris.

The tête à tête was all that was delightful. Maître Lebrument wooed his bride with infinite tact and delicacy. He had taken as his motto: 'Everything comes to him who waits.' He was at once patient and ardent, and his methods were speedily crowned with success. After a few days Madame Lebrument worshipped her husband. She could not do without him; she wanted him near her all day long, while she caressed and embraced him and played with his hands, his beard, his nose. She would perch herself upon his knees, seize him by the ears and say:

'Now open your mouth and shut your eyes.'

Confidingly he would open his mouth, half close his eyes, and be rewarded with a long and tender kiss which sent a thrill all down his spine. For his part, it seemed as if his two hands, his two lips, and his whole person, were quite inadequate for all the caresses he desired to lavish on his wife from dawn to dusk, and from dusk to dawn.

At the end of the week, he said to his young wife:

'If you like, we will go to Paris next Tuesday. We will play at being a pair of unmarried lovers and go to all the restaurants, theatres, music-halls, and everywhere.'

She jumped for joy.

'Yes, yes! do let's go as soon as possible.'

'Very well,' he replied, 'And there's one thing we mustn't forget. Mind you ask your father to have your dowry ready. I will take it along and seize the opportunity to pay Maître Papillon.'

'I will tell him to-morrow morning,' she said.

He caught her in his arms, and the playful love-making, in which she had learnt to revel during the past week, began again.

On the following Tuesday, her parents went to see their daughter and son-in-law off on their journey to the capital.

His father-in-law said to Maître Lebrument:

'Upon my word, it is scarcely prudent to carry so much money in your despatch case.'

But the young notary smiled.

'Don't be alarmed, my dear sir; I am used to that sort of thing. You must know that in my profession I sometimes have a million or so on me. In this way, we shall avoid all sorts of tedious formalities and delays. Don't be in the least anxious.'

The porter called out:

'Take your seats for Paris.'

They jumped into a carriage where there were two old ladies. Lebrument murmured in his wife's ear:

'What a bore; I shan't be able to smoke.'

She whispered back:

'I think it a bore, too, but not because of your cigar.'

The engine whistled and the train started. The journey lasted an hour, during which they did not talk much, because the two old ladies remained wide awake.

In the station yard at Saint Lazare, Lebrument said to his wife:

'If you like, we will first go and have luncheon on the Boulevard, and then come back and quietly pick up our luggage and take it to the hotel.'

She agreed with alacrity:

'O yes, let us lunch at a restaurant. Is it far?'

'Yes, some little way off, but we can take an omnibus.'

'Why not a cab?' she asked in surprise.

He smiled and pretended to scold her.

'Is that your idea of economy? A cab for a five minutes' run, at six sous a minute. I see you don't mean to stint yourself.'

'O, very well,' she said, a little crestfallen.

A three-horse omnibus came lumbering along. Lebrument hailed it. The clumsy vehicle stopped. The young notary urged his wife forward and said hastily:

'You go inside; I'm going outside. I must have just one cigarette before luncheon.'

There was no time to reply. The conductor had caught her by the arm to help her on to the step and had pushed her into the omnibus. She collapsed on to the seat, in utter bewilderment and watched the feet of her husband, as he ascended to the roof. She was jammed in between a fat man, who reeked of stale tobacco, and an old woman who smelt of dog. All the other passengers sat in a silent row; a grocer's boy; a working girl; an infantry sergeant; a gentleman with gold-rimmed spectacles and a silk hat with an enormous brim, turned up on either side like the gutter on a roof; two ladies with a proud and peevish expression, whose pose seemed to say: 'Here we are, but we are above this sort of thing'; two nuns; a bareheaded girl, and an undertaker's man. They looked like a set of caricatures, a collection of freaks, a series of comic studies of the human face, like those rows of grotesque dummies, which are set up as targets at fairs. The jolting of the omnibus tossed and jerked their heads and shook their flaccid cheeks. Stupefied by the rattle of the wheels, they looked like somnolent idiots.

Madame Lebrument sat motionless, and a vague sense of depression stole over her.

'Why didn't he come inside with me?' she wondered. 'He could so easily have sacrificed his cigarette.'

The nuns stopped the omnibus and followed each other out,

diffusing a stale odour of old clothes. The omnibus moved on, but was stopped again. A cook got in, red-faced and out of breath. She sat down with her basket of provisions on her lap. A strong smell of dishwater filled the omnibus.

'It is further than I expected,' thought Jeanne.

The undertaker's man got out; his place was taken by a coachman, smelling of the stable. The bare-headed girl was succeeded by a porter from whom emanated a strong odour of perspiration. Jeanne felt uneasy and downhearted, ready to burst into tears, she hardly knew why.

Other passengers came and went. The omnibus jolted on through endless streets, stopped at all its halting places and went on again.

'What a long way it is!' said Jeanne to herself.

'I do hope he hasn't forgotten or fallen asleep. The last few days have been very tiring.'

By degrees all the other passengers had left the omnibus. She remained alone, absolutely alone. The conductor called out:

'Vaugirard!'

As she did not move, he repeated:

'Vaugirard!'

She stared at him, realizing that his remark was addressed to her, as there was no one else in the omnibus. The man repeated for the third time:

'Vaugirard!'

'Where are we?' she asked.

'At Vaugirard, of course,' he replied in a surly voice, 'I have called it out a dozen times.'

'Is it far from the Boulevard?'

'Which Boulevard?'

'The Boulevard des Italiens.'

'We passed it long ago.'

'O, really? Then will you please tell my husband?'

'Your husband? Where is he?'

'On the roof, of course.'

'On the roof? There hasn't been anyone up there for ever so long.'

'What!' she exclaimed with a gesture of horror. 'It's impossible. He got on to the omnibus with me. Please look again. He must be there.'

The conductor began to make insinuations:

'Come, come, young woman, enough said. If you have lost one man, you'll find plenty more. Clear out. Nothing doing. You'll pick up another in the street.'

Tears rose to her eyes.

'You are mistaken,' she exclaimed, 'I assure you, you are mistaken. He had a large despatch case under his arm.'

The conductor burst out laughing.

'A large despatch case? Yes, I remember. He got down at the Madeleine. It's all one. He has given you the slip. Ha! ha.'

The omnibus was standing still. She got down and, in spite of herself, instinctively glanced at the roof of the omnibus. There was not a soul on it. At that she burst into a loud passion of weeping, without caring who saw or heard her.

'What is to become of me?' she sobbed.

An inspector came up to her:

'What is the matter?'

'Here's a lady, whose husband has deserted her on the way,' the conductor replied jeeringly.

'Is that all? Then get on with your work,' said the inspector, turning on his heel.

She walked straight on, too utterly bewildered and distressed to realize what had befallen her. Where was she to go? What was she to do? What had become of him? What could be the cause of such a mistake, such an oversight, such forgetfulness, such incredible absentmindedness?

She had two francs in her pocket. To whom could she turn? Suddenly she thought of her cousin Barral, branch clerk at the Admiralty. She had just enough money for her cab and she drove straight to his house. She met him on the doorstep, just as he was leaving for office. Like Lebrument he carried a large despatch case under his arm.

'Henry!' she cried, jumping out of the cab.

He stood still in amazement.

'Jeanne! You here? All alone? What are you doing? Where have you come from?'

With her eyes full of tears she faltered:

'I have just lost my husband.'

'Lost him? Where?'

'On an omnibus.'

'On an omnibus? My dear!'

Through her tears she poured out her story, and he listened, his mind working busily.

'Did he seem quite himself this morning?' he asked.

'Yes.'

'That's good. Had he much money on him?'

'Yes, he had my dowry.'

'Your dowry? All of it?'

'Every penny. He meant to pay for the practice he has just bought.'

'Well, my dear little cousin, at this very moment your husband is probably scuttling across the frontier into Belgium.'

Even then she did not grasp his meaning. She stammered:

'My husband—what do you mean?'

'I mean that he has made a clean sweep of all your money—just that.'

She stood rooted to the spot. Then, half-strangled with emotion, she gasped:

'Then he must . . . he must be . . . a scoundrel.'

The strain was too much for her; she threw herself sobbing into her cousin's arms. A little crowd began to collect, so he gently pushed her inside the house, and with his arm round her waist, supported her up the stairs.

When the door was opened, he said to the astonished maid:

'Sophie, run over to the restaurant and bring luncheon for two. I'm not going to office to-day.'

From *The Kreutzer Sonata*
Leo Tolstoy

The profound uncertainty that Tolstoy felt over the place of lust in marriage (see page 71) appears only to have been exacerbated by marriage itself. Here, from a novella written over twenty years after Tolstoy's wedding, the main character, Poznyshev, describes his honeymoon to a group of fellow travellers on a train across Russia.

'THUS IT IS EVERYBODY marries, thus it was I married. Then commenced the much be-lauded phase called the honeymoon. What bathos there is in the name itself!'

'Wandering about Paris one day,' he said, 'looking at the various shows and spectacles, I saw a sign-board with the effigy of a bearded woman and a walrus. I went in to look and discovered the bearded woman was only a man in a low-cut woman's dress and the sea-monster an ordinary dog covered with a walrus' skin swimming about in a bath full of water. The whole affair was highly boring. As I left, the showman deferentially escorted me, and addressing the public who were outside the door, he pointed to me and spoke, "You can ask this gentleman whether the show is worth looking at. Walk in, walk in! One franc a head." I was ashamed to say it was not worth looking at and the showman certainly relied on my feeling so. It is probably the same with those who have gone through all the inanities of the honeymoon and refuse to disabuse others. I did not myself disabuse anybody, but I don't see why I shouldn't tell the truth now. I feel it indeed urgent to announce the truth about it.

'The truth is, it was tiresome, wretched, and above all boring, inconceivably boring.'

'All my endeavours to make the honeymoon a success were destined to fail. It was a period of shame, irksomeness, and it quickly became an unendurable torture.

'Things took this turn very soon. Finding one day my wife was bored—I think it was the third or fourth day after the marriage—I inquired the cause and began embracing her, this being to my mind, all she could possibly expect or wish from me. But she put my arms away and began crying. "What's the matter?" She was unable to say, but she was clearly extremely sad and depressed. Her nerves probably revealed to her the true nature of our relations, but she could not formulate what she instinctively felt. I went on questioning her and she murmured something about being lonely without her mother. I felt this was not true and I set about comforting her without referring at all to her mother. I didn't realise she was only depressed in mind and her mother was only a pretext. Yet she at once took offence at my not mentioning her mother, as if I did not credit what she had told me. She could now see, she said, that I didn't love her. Whereupon I blamed her for being capricious and suddenly a change came over her face. The melancholy that had settled on it gave place to an expression of irritation and she started reproaching me in the most spiteful language with being selfish and cruel. I looked intently at her. All her features combined to express utter coldness and enmity—I might almost say hatred—for me.

'I remember the horror which then seized me. What did it mean? How could it be? Love, the union of souls! And instead of that, this was what it had come to! "Can it be so?" I asked myself. "Surely this is not she."

'I tried to soothe and quiet her, but soon found myself opposed by such an impregnable wall of icy, venomous hostility, that before I knew what I was doing I was maddened into a state of violent irritation, with the result that we addressed a number of nasty remarks to each other.

'The impression left by that first quarrel of ours was unspeakable, horrible. I have termed it a quarrel, but it was in truth nothing of the sort. It was simply the discovery of the abyss that yawned between us. What we called love had been exhausted and we stood face to face in our real mutual relation, two egoists, perfect strangers to one another.

'I have given the name of "quarrel" to what happened. But it wasn't a quarrel. It was simply a glimpse of our true relations to each other. I did not then notice that the coldness and hostility was our usual relation to each other, because during the first period of married life those feelings were soon concealed again from our observation by the vapours of "love"' and I assumed we had only quarrelled and grown reconciled and that no such misunderstanding would ever take place again.

'But in the first month of the honeymoon it was not long before another period commenced, during which we again for a time ceased to be necessary to one another, and in consequence another quarrel occurred. That second misunderstanding impressed me more deeply than the first. "So the first was not a mere accident," I thought to myself; "it was the outcome of a necessity and will occur as a result of the same necessity." Another reason why I was struck more deeply by the second quarrel was its ridiculously trivial pretext. It was something about money which I never grudged and could not dream of grudging my wife. I only recall that she put such an interpretation on the affair as to make a remark of mine appear to be the expression of a desire on my part to gain an undue ascendency over her by means of money to which she feigned that I claimed an exclusive right. The charge was baseless, stupid, mean, unnatural.

'I lost my temper and rebuked her for want of delicacy. She accused me in turn and in the expression of her face and eyes I read the same cruel, callous hostility which had caused a chill in my heart before.

'With my father, with my brother, I had quarrelled, I remember, now and then; but there never had arisen that especially venomous hatred which had sprung up between my wife and me. It was not long, however, before our mutual hatred was once more disguised by so-called love, and I once more tried to console myself that our two quarrels were mistakes, simple misunderstandings which could easily be cleared up. But the occurrence of the third and fourth quarrels dispelled my delusion. I saw clearly that this was no accident, no misunderstanding, but the upshot of necessity, that it could not be otherwise, that it would again and again recur.

'My heart froze within me at the prospect. My suffering was yet further intensified by the notion that I alone was living with my wife in such continual discord, so different from the way in which I used to flatter myself we should live, that others were more lucky than we. I did not then know this is the ordinary lot, that others believe their misery (as I believed mine) to be exceptional, that they not only conceal it from outsiders, but try to disguise it to themselves.

'In our case it began at once after the marriage, and went on gradually gaining in intensity and fierceness. From the very first weeks of our wedded existence I knew at the bottom of my heart I was caught in a trap, that what I had experienced was not what I had had in my mind and confidently hoped for, that my marriage, so far from being a fount of happiness, was a burden very heavy to bear. But like everyone else, I refused to admit it, not only to others (I wouldn't own to it now if it were not ended for ever), but even to myself.

'Whenever I reflect on it now, it is a mystery to me how I could have remained blind to my actual condition. One sure token by which we might readily have recognised it was the fact that all our quarrels turned upon wretched trifles; indeed their cause was so ridiculously trivial that, once over, we could not remember how they had come about. The reasoning power was not quick enough to forge specious pretexts sufficiently quick for the outbursts of heartfelt hostility which continued to occur between us without interruption or change. Still more remarkable, however, was the inadequacy of the excuses for reconciliation. They assumed occasionally the shape of words, explanations, even tears, but at times—and the remembrance of it fills me even now with disgust—while hurling the most injurious and venomous abuse at each other, a period of silence would presently begin, filled up with smiles, kisses, embraces.'

From *Journey by Moonlight*
Antal Szerb

O N THE TRAIN everything seemed fine. The trouble began in Venice, with the back-alleys.

Mihály first noticed the back-alleys when the motor-ferry turned off the Grand Canal for a short cut and they began appearing to right and left. But at the time he paid them no attention, being caught up from the outset with the essential Veniceness of Venice: the water between the houses, the gondolas, the lagoon, and the pink-brick serenity of the city. For it was Mihály's first visit to Italy, at the age of thirty-six, on his honeymoon.

During his protracted years of wandering he had travelled in many lands, and spent long periods in France and England. But Italy he had always avoided, feeling the time had not yet come, that he was not yet ready for it. Italy he associated with grown-up matters, such as the fathering of children, and he secretly feared it, with the same instinctive fear he had of strong sunlight, the scent of flowers, and extremely beautiful women.

The trip to Italy might well have been postponed forever, but for the fact that he was now married and they had decided on the conventional Italian holiday for their start to married life. Mihály had now come, not to Italy as such, but on his honeymoon, a different matter entirely. Indeed, it was his marriage that made the trip possible. Now, he reasoned, there was nothing to fear from the danger Italy represented.

Their first days were spent quietly enough, between the pleasures of honeymooning and the gentler, less strenuous forms of sightseeing. Like all highly intelligent and self-critical people, Mihály and Erzsi strove to find the correct middle way between snobbery and its reverse. They did not weary themselves to death 'doing' everything prescribed by Baedeker; still less did they wish to be bracketed with those who return home to boast, 'The museums? Never went near them,' and gaze triumphantly at one another.

One evening, returning to their hotel after the theatre, Mihály felt he somehow needed another drink. Quite what of he wasn't yet sure, but he rather hankered after some sort of sweet wine and, remembering the somewhat special, classical, taste of Samian, and the many times he had tried it in Paris, in the little wine merchant's at number 7 rue des Petits Champs, he reasoned that, Venice being effectively Greece, here surely he might find some Samian, or perhaps Mavrodaphne, since he wasn't yet quite *au fait* with the wines of Italy. He begged Erzsi to go up without him. He would follow straightaway. It would be just a quick drink, 'really, just a glass' he solemnly insisted as she, with the same mock-seriousness, made a gesture urging moderation, as befits the young bride.

Moving away from the Grand Canal, where their hotel stood, he arrived in the streets around the Frezzeria. Here at this time of night the Venetians promenade in large numbers, with the peculiar ant-like quality typical of the denizens of that city. They proceed only along certain routes, as ants do when setting out on their journeyings across a garden path, the adjacent streets remaining empty. Mihály too stuck to the ant-route, reckoning that the bars and *fiaschetterie* would surely lie along the trodden ways, rather than in the uncertain darkness of empty side-streets. He found several places where drinks were sold, but somehow none was exactly what he had in mind. There was something wrong with each. In one the clientèle were too elegant, in another they were too drab; another he did not really associate with the sort of thing he was after, which would have a somehow more *recherché* taste. Gradually he came to feel that surely only one place in Venice would have it, and that he would have to discover on the basis of pure instinct. Thus he arrived among the back-alleys.

Narrow little streets branched into narrow little alleyways, and the further he went the darker and narrower they became. By stretching his arms out wide he could have simultaneously touched the opposing rows of houses, with their large, silent windows, behind which, he imagined, mysteriously intense Italian lives lay in slumber. The sense of intimacy made it feel almost an intrusion to have entered these streets at night.

What was the strange attraction, the peculiar ecstasy, that seized him among the back-alleys? Why did it feel like finally coming home? Perhaps a child dreams of such places, the child raised in a gardened cottage who fears the open plain. Perhaps there is an adolescent longing to live in such a closed world, where every square foot has a private significance, ten paces infringe a boundary, decades are spent around a shabby table, whole lives in an armchair . . . But this is speculation.

He was still wandering among the alleys when it occurred to him that day was already breaking and he was on the far side of Venice, on the Fondamenta Nuova, within sight of the burial island and, beyond that, the mysterious islands which include San Francesco Deserto, the former leper colony, and, in the far distance, the houses of Murano. This was where the poor of Venice lived, too remote and obscure to profit from the tourist traffic. Here was the hospital, and from here the gondolas of the dead began their journey. Already people were up and on their way to work, and the world had assumed that utter bleakness as after a night without sleep. He found a gondolier, who took him home.

Erzsi had long been sick with worry and exhaustion. Only at one-thirty had it occurred to her that, appearances notwithstanding, even in Venice one could doubtless telephone the police, which she did, with the help of the night porter, naturally to no avail.

Mihály was still like a man walking in his sleep. He was abominably tired, and quite incapable of providing rational answers to Erzsi's questions.

'The back-alleys,' he said. 'I had to see them by night, just once . . . it's all part of . . . it's what everyone does.'

'But why didn't you tell me? Or rather, why didn't you take me with you?'

Mihály was unable to reply, but with an offended look climbed into bed and drifted towards sleep, full of bitter resentment.

'So this is marriage,' he thought. 'What does it amount to, when every attempt to explain is so hopeless? Mind you, I don't fully understand all this myself.'

285

When they reach Florence Mihály gets a letter from Zoltán Pataki, Erzsi's first husband, containing a list of pointers as to how he should look after her.

'Perhaps it's true what Pataki says,' he thought. 'I am so abstracted and introverted by nature. Of course that's a simplification—no one can ever be so neatly categorised—but this much is certain, that I am singularly useless and incompetent in all practical matters, and generally not the man in whose calm superiority a woman can trust. And Erzsi is precisely the sort of woman who loves to entrust herself to someone, who likes to know that she belongs completely to someone. She isn't one of those motherly types (perhaps that's why she has no children) but one of those who really want to be their lover's child. My God, how deceived she is going to be in me, sooner or later. I could more easily become a Major-General than play the role of father. That's one human quality I completely lack, amongst others. I can't bear it when people depend on me, not even servants. That's why I did everything on my own, as a boy. I hate responsibility and I always come to despise people who expect things from me.

'The whole thing's crazy: crazy from Erzsi's point of view. She would have been better off with ninety-nine men out of a hundred than she is with me. Any average, normal fellow would have made a better husband than me. Now I can see it not from my own point of view, but purely from hers. Why didn't I think of all this before I got married? Or rather: why didn't Erzsi, who is so wise, think it through more carefully?'

But of course Erzsi couldn't have thought it through, because she was in love with Mihály, and, when it came to him, was not wise, had not recognised his shortcomings, and still, it seems, did not recognise them. It was just a game of feelings. Erzsi with raw, uninhibited appetite was seeking the happiness in love she had never found with Pataki. But perhaps once she had had her fill, because such passionate feeling does not usually last very long. . .

By the time he got back to the hotel, after a long rambling walk, it seemed inevitable to him that she would, one day, leave him, and do so after horrible crises and sufferings, after squalid affairs with other men, her name 'dragged through the mud', as the saying goes. To a certain extent he took comfort in the inevitable, and when they sat down to dinner he could already, a little, look upon her as a lovely fragment of his past, and he was filled with solemn emotion. Past and present always played special games inside Mihály, lending each other colour and flavour. He loved to relocate himself in his past, at one precise point, and from that perspective re-assemble his present life: for example, 'What would I have made of Florence if I had come here at sixteen?' and this re-ordering would always give the present moment a richer charge of feeling. But it could also be done the other way round, converting the present into a past: 'What fine memories will I have, ten years from now, of once having been in Florence with Erzsi . . . what will such memories hold, what associations of feeling, which I cannot guess at at this moment?'

This sense of occasion he expressed by ordering a huge festive meal and calling for the most expensive wine. Erzsi knew Mihály. She knew that the fine meal signified a special mood, and she did her best to rise to the occasion. She skilfully directed the conversation, putting one or two questions bearing on the history of Florence, prodding him to think about such matters, because she knew that historical associations, together with wine, drew him out of his solemnity, and were in fact the only thing that could overcome his apathy. Mihály poured out enthusiastic, colourful, factually unreliable explanations, then with shining eyes tried to analyse the meaning for him, the wonder, the ecstasy of the mere word: Tuscany. 'Because there is no part of this land that hasn't been trodden by the armies of history. The Caesars, the gorgeously apparelled troops of the French kings, all passed this way. Here every pathway leads to some important site and one street in Florence holds more history than seven counties back home.'

Erzsi listened with delight. The actual history of Tuscany did not for one minute interest her, but she adored him when he came alive like this. She loved the way that at these moments, in his historical day-dreams, precisely when he reached the furthest point from actual living people and the present world, his remoteness left him and he became a normal person. Her sympathy soon merged with more powerful feelings, and she thought with pleasure of the expected sequel later that night, all the more because the night before he had been in a bad mood, and fell asleep, or pretended to, the moment he lay down.

She knew that Mihály's exalted mood could easily be diverted from history towards herself. It was enough to put her hand in his and gaze deep into his eyes. He forgot Tuscany, and his face, flushed as it was with wine, grew pale with sudden desire. Then he began to woo and flatter her, as if trying to win her love for the very first time.

'How strange,' Erzsi thought. 'After a year of intimacy he still woos me with that voice, with that diffidence, as if totally unsure of success. In fact the more he wants me, the more distant and fastidious his manner becomes, as if to embellish his desire, to give it the proper respect—and the greatest intimacy, physical intimacy, doesn't bring him any closer. He can only feel passion when he senses a distance between us.'

So it was. Mihály's desire spoke to her across a distance, in the knowledge that she would leave him. Already she had become for him a sort of beautiful memory. He drank heavily to sustain this mood, to make himself believe that he wasn't with Erzsi but with the memory of Erzsi. With Erzsi as history.

But meanwhile Erzsi drank too, and on her wine always had a strong effect. She became loud, jolly and extremely impatient. This Erzsi was rather new to him. Before their marriage she had had little opportunity for unguarded behaviour when with him in public. He found this new Erzsi extremely attractive, and they went up to the bedroom with equal haste.

That night, when she was at once the new Erzsi and the Erzsi of history, Erzsi-as-memory, when Zoltán Pataki's letter, with its implicit reminder of the Ulpius days, had so deeply shaken him, Mihály forgot his long-standing resolution and admitted elements into his married life which he had always wanted to keep away from Erzsi. There is a kind of lovemaking fashionable among certain adolescent boys and still-virgin girls, which lets them seek pleasure in a roundabout way, avoiding all responsibility. And there are people, like Mihály, who actually prefer this irresponsible form of pleasure to the serious, adult, and, as it were, officially approved variety. But Mihály, in his heart, would have been thoroughly ashamed to acknowledge this inclination, being fully aware of its adolescent nature, of its adolescent limitations. Once he had arrived at a truly serious adult relationship with Erzsi he had determined it would express itself only along the 'officially approved lines', as befitting two serious-minded adult lovers.

That night in Florence was the first and only derogation. Erzsi was filled with wonder, but she accepted him willingly and reciprocated his unaccustomed gentleness. She did not understand what was happening, nor did she understand afterwards his terrible depression and shame.

'Why?' she asked. 'It was so good that way, and anyhow I love you.'

And she fell asleep. Now he was the one who lay awake for hours. He felt that finally, definitively, he was facing the bankruptcy and collapse of his marriage. He had to acknowledge that here too he had failed as an adult, and, what was even worse, he had to concede that Erzsi had never before given him so much pleasure as now, when he made love to her not as a partner in adult passion but as an immature girl, a flirtation on a springtime outing.

He climbed out of bed. As soon as he was sure she was still asleep he went to the dressing table where her reticule lay. He rummaged in it for the cheques (Erzsi was their cashier). He found the two National Bank lira cheques, each for the same amount, one in his name, the other in hers. He withdrew his own, and in its place smuggled in a sheet of paper of similar size. Then, very carefully, he put it in his wallet, and went back to bed.

The next day, on the way to Rome, he alights from the train for a cup of coffee. It leaves without him. Whether he intended this is unclear, but thereafter he is content to be carried on, alone, by events.

From *The Stone Diaries*

Carol Shields

Daisy Goodwill's first marriage, which was alluded to on page 82, is to Harold Hoad, in 1927. Daisy is 22. A week before the marriage her mother-in-law-to-be gives her lunch, and much advice.

'WHEN YOU SET the table, be it breakfast, lunch or dinner, be sure the knife blade is turned in. In. Not out. Salad forks, of course, go outside the dinner fork. Harold always takes Grape-Nuts for breakfast. A question of digestion and general health. I feel I should make myself clear on this point. I'm speaking of b.m.'s. Bowel movements. He has been troubled in that particular department since he was a very young boy, and so Grape-Nuts are a necessity, also a very economical food. We must never be ashamed of economy, Daisy . . . Once Harold was eating a handful of popcorn and began to choke. I always keep a close eye on him when we have a popcorn evening. Finally, a word about your honeymoon. You have not been to Europe before, and so you may be surprised to find a rather curious device in your hotel rooms. I am speaking of France and Italy, not England, of course. This little porcelain bowl is not what it appears to be, but is used by continentals for reasons of personal hygiene. You must be careful not to touch these things, since they are covered with germs, completely and absolutely covered. Germs of the worst sort. The kind of germs that can bring you a lifetime of suffering, suffering that is passed from one person to another, and even to the next generation. When a woman marries, she must be constantly alert to the possibility of harm. She no longer thinks only of herself. From the moment the marriage vows are exchanged at the altar, a woman's husband becomes her sacred trust.'

And after the wedding:

He knows how much he needs her. He longs for correction, for love like a scalpel, a whip, something to curb his wild impulses and morbidity.

She honestly believes she can change him, take hold of him and make something noble of his wild nature. He is hungry, she knows, for repression. His soft male mouth tells her so, and his moist looks of abjection. This, in fact, is her whole reason for marrying him, this and the fact that it is 'time' to marry – she is, after all, twenty-two years old. She feels her life taking on a shape, gathering itself around an urge to be summoned. She wants to want something but doesn't know what she is allowed. She would like to be prepared, to be strong.

But she is unable to stop her young husband from drinking on their wedding night. He chugs gin straight from a bottle all night long as the train carries them to Montreal, drinks and sleeps and snores, and vomits into the little basin in their first-class sleeper. He stops drinking during the eight days of the Atlantic crossing, but only because he is seasick every minute of the time, as is she. It is late June, but the weather on the North Atlantic is abominable this year. The sea waves heave and sway, and the rain pours down. They arrive in Paris shaken. Her college French proves useless, but they manage somehow to find their hotel on rue Victor Hugo, and there on a wide stiff bed they sleep for thirty-six hours. When they wake up, sore of body and dry of mouth, he tells her that he hates goddamned Paris and loathes foreign wogs who jibber-jabber in French and pee on the street.

He manages in the space of an hour to rent an immense car, a Delage Torpedo, black as a hearse with square rear windows like wide startled eyes. Grasping the steering wheel, he seems momentarily revived, singing loudly and tunelessly, as if a great danger had passed, though his tongue whispers of gin: Daisy, Daisy, give me your answer true. I'm half crazy all for the love of you. He shoots out through the Paris suburbs and into the countryside, honking at people crossing the road, at cows and chickens, at the pale empty air of France. They hurtle down endless rural avenues of trees, past fields of ravishing poppies and golden gorse, and eventually, after hours and hours, they reach the mountains.

She keeps pleading with him to stop, whimpering then shouting that he oughtn't to be driving this wildly and drinking wine at the same time, that he is putting their lives in danger. He almost groans with the pleasure of what he is hearing, his darling scolding bride who is bent so sweetly on reform.

They stop, finally, at the sleepy Alpine town of Corps, their tires grinding to a halt on the packed gravel, and register at the Hotel de la Poste. A hunched-looking porter carries their valises up two flights of narrow stairs to an austere room with a sloping ceiling and a single window which is heavily curtained.

Daisy lies down, exhausted, on the rather lumpy bed. Her georgette dress, creased and stained, spreads out beneath her. She can't imagine what she's doing in this dim, musty room, and yet she feels she's been here before, that all the surfaces and crevasses are familiar, part of the scenery sketched into an apocryphal journal. Sleep beckons powerfully, but she resists, looking around at the walls for some hopeful sign. There is a kind of flower-patterned paper, she sees, that lends the room a shabby, rosy charm. This, too, seems familiar. It is seven o'clock in the evening. She is lying on her back in a hotel room in the middle of France. The world is rolling over her, over and over. Her young husband, this stranger, has flung open the window, then pushed back the shutters, and now the sun shines brightly into the room.

And there he is, perched on the window sill, balanced there, a big fleshy shadow blocking the sunlight. In one hand he grasps a wine bottle from which he takes occasional gulps; in his other is a handful of centimes which he is tossing out the window to a group of children who have gathered on the cobbled square. He is laughing, a crazy cackling one-note sound.

She can hear the musical ringing of the coins as they strike the stone, and the children's sharp singing cries. A part of her consciousness drifts toward sleep where she will be safe, but something else is pulling at her, a force she will later think of, rather grandly, as the obligation of tragedy and its insistence on moving in a forward direction. She stares sternly at the ceiling, the soiled plaster, waiting.

At that moment she feels a helpless sneeze coming on – her old allergy to feather pillows. The sneeze is loud, powerful, sudden, an explosion that closes her throat and forces her eyes shut for a fraction of a second. When she opens them again, Harold is no longer on the window sill. All she sees is an empty rectangle of glaring light. A splinter of time passes, too small and quiet to register in the brain; she blinks back her disbelief, and then hears a bang, a crashing sound like a melon splitting, a wet injurious noise followed by the screaming of children and the sound of people running in the street.

She remembers that she lay flat on the bed for at least a minute before she got up to investigate.

From *Private Lives*

Noel Coward

The beautifully symmetrical plot of Noel Coward's 1930 play Private Lives *centres round not one but two honeymoons. Elyot and Amanda were once married but are now divorced and just married, for the second time, to Sibyl and Victor. Both couples, it turns out, are staying in the same French hotel and in rooms with adjoining terraces separated only by a line of small trees in tubs. Elyot and Amanda, each out on their terraces alone, meet just as the hotel orchestra plays 'their tune'. Their first move is to infuriate their new spouses by demanding that each new couple leave the hotel at once. Elyot and Amanda soon realise that they have made a ghastly mistake, and that they still love each other much more than they do Sibyl and Victor, however much they may have quarrelled in the past – and will in the future.*

AMANDA (*controlling herself with an effort*): Please, Victor, please, for this last time I implore you. Let's go to Paris now, to-night. I mean it with all my heart—please——

VICTOR (*with gentle firmness*): No, Mandy!

AMANDA: I see quite clearly that I have been foolish enough to marry a fat old gentleman in a club armchair.

VICTOR: It's no use being cross.

AMANDA: You're a pompous ass.

VICTOR (*horrified*): Mandy!

AMANDA (*enraged*): Pompous ass, that's what I said, and that's what I meant. Blown out with your own importance.

VICTOR: Mandy, control yourself.

AMANDA: Get away from me. I can't bear to think I'm married to such rugged grandeur.

VICTOR (*with great dignity*): I shall be in the bar. When you are ready to come down and dine, let me know.

AMANDA (*flinging herself into a chair*): Go away, go away.

VICTOR *stalks off, at the same moment that* ELYOT *stamps on, on the other side, followed by* SIBYL *in tears.*

ELYOT: If you don't stop screaming, I'll murder you.

SIBYL: I wish to heaven I'd never seen you in my life, let alone married you. I don't wonder Amanda left you, if you behaved to her as you've behaved to me. I'm going down to have dinner by myself and you can just do what you like about it.

ELYOT: Do, and I hope it chokes you.

SIBYL: Oh Elli, Elli——

She goes wailing indoors. Elyot stamps down to the balustrade and lights a cigarette, obviously trying to control his nerves. Amanda sees him, and comes down too.

AMANDA: Give me one for God's sake.

ELYOT (*hands her his case laconically*): Here.

AMANDA (*taking a cigarette*): I'm in such a rage.

ELYOT (*lighting up*): So am I.

AMANDA: What are we to do?

ELYOT: I don't know.

AMANDA: Whose yacht is that?

ELYOT: The Duke of Westminster's I expect. It always is.

AMANDA: I wish I were on it.

ELYOT: I wish you were too.

AMANDA: There's no need to be nasty.

ELYOT: Yes there is, every need. I've never in my life felt a greater urge to be nasty.

AMANDA: And you've had some urges in your time, haven't you?

ELYOT: If you start bickering with me, Amanda, I swear I'll throw you over the edge.

AMANDA: Try it, that's all, just try it.

ELYOT: You've upset everything, as usual.

AMANDA: I've upset everything! What about you?

ELYOT: Ever since the first moment I was unlucky enough to set eyes on you, my life has been insupportable.

AMANDA: Oh do shut up, there's no sense in going on like that.

ELYOT: Nothing's any use. There's no escape, ever.

AMANDA: Don't be melodramatic.

ELYOT: Do you want a cocktail? There are two here.

AMANDA: There are two over here as well.

ELYOT: We'll have my two first. (AMANDA *crosses over into* ELYOT's *part of the terrace. He gives her one, and keeps one himself.*)

AMANDA: Shall we get roaring screaming drunk?

ELYOT: I don't think that would help, we did it once before and it was a dismal failure.

AMANDA: It was lovely at the beginning.

ELYOT: You have an immoral memory Amanda. Here's to you. (*They raise their glasses solemnly and drink.*)

AMANDA: I tried to get away the moment after I'd seen you, but he wouldn't budge.

ELYOT: What's his name.

AMANDA: Victor, Victor Prynne.

ELYOT (*toasting*): Mr. and Mrs. Victor Prynne. (*He drinks.*) Mine wouldn't budge either.

AMANDA: What's her name?

ELYOT: Sibyl.

AMANDA (*toasting*): Mr. and Mrs. Elyot Chase. (*She drinks.*) God pity the poor girl.

ELYOT: Are you in love with him?

AMANDA: Of course.

ELYOT: How funny.

AMANDA: I don't see anything particularly funny about it, you're in love with yours aren't you?

ELYOT: Certainly.

AMANDA: There you are then.

ELYOT: There we both are then.

AMANDA: What's she like?

ELYOT: Fair, very pretty, plays the piano beautifully.

AMANDA: Very comforting.

ELYOT: How's yours?

AMANDA: I don't want to discuss him.

ELYOT: Well, it doesn't matter, he'll probably come popping out in a minute and I shall see for myself. Does he know I'm here?

AMANDA: Yes, I told him.

ELYOT (*with sarcasm*): That's going to make things a whole lot easier.

AMANDA: You needn't be frightened, he won't hurt you.

ELYOT: If he comes near me I'll scream the place down.

AMANDA: Does Sibyl know I'm here?

ELYOT: No, I pretended I'd had a presentiment. I tried terribly hard to persuade her to leave for Paris.

AMANDA: I tried too, it's lucky we didn't both succeed, isn't it? Otherwise we should probably all have joined up in Rouen or somewhere.

ELYOT (*laughing*): In some frowsy little hotel.

AMANDA (*laughing too*): Oh dear, it would have been much, much worse.

ELYOT: I can see us all sailing down in the morning for an early start.

AMANDA (*weakly*): Lovely, oh lovely.

ELYOT: Glorious! (*They both laugh helplessly.*)

AMANDA: What's happened to yours?

ELYOT: Didn't you hear her screaming? She's downstairs in the dining-room I think.

AMANDA: Mine is being grand, in the bar.

ELYOT: It really is awfully difficult.

AMANDA: Have you known her long?

ELYOT: About four months, we met in a house party in Norfolk.

AMANDA: Very flat, Norfolk.

ELYOT: How old is dear Victor?

AMANDA: Thirty-four, or five; and Sibyl?

ELYOT: I blush to tell you, only twenty-three.

AMANDA: You've gone a mucker alright.

ELYOT: I shall reserve my opinion of your choice until I've met dear Victor.

AMANDA: I wish you wouldn't go on calling him 'Dear Victor'. It's extremely irritating.

ELYOT: That's how I see him. Dumpy, and fair, and very considerate, with glasses. Dear Victor.

AMANDA: As I said before I would rather not discuss him. At least I have good taste enough to refrain from making cheap gibes at Sibyl.

ELYOT: You said Norfolk was flat.

AMANDA: That was no reflection on her, unless she made it flatter.

ELYOT: Your voice takes on an acid quality whenever you mention her name.

AMANDA: I'll never mention it again.

ELYOT: Good, and I'll keep off Victor.

AMANDA (*with dignity*): Thank you.

There is silence for a moment. The orchestra starts playing the same tune that they were singing previously.

ELYOT: That orchestra has a remarkable small repertoire.

AMANDA: They don't seem to know anything but this, do they?

She sits down on the balustrade, and sings it, softly. Her eyes are looking out to sea, and her mind is far away. ELYOT *watches her while she sings. When she turns to him at the end, there are tears in her eyes. He looks away awkwardly and lights another cigarette.*

ELYOT: You always had a sweet voice, Amanda.

AMANDA (*a little huskily*): Thank you.

ELYOT: I'm awfully sorry about all this, really I am. I wouldn't have had it happen for the world.

AMANDA: I know. I'm sorry too. It's just rotten luck.

ELYOT: I'll go away to-morrow whatever happens, so don't you worry.

AMANDA: That's nice of you.

ELYOT: I hope everything turns out splendidly for you, and that you'll be very happy.

AMANDA: I hope the same for you, too.

The music, which has been playing continually through this little scene, returns persistently to the refrain. They both look at one another and laugh.

ELYOT: Nasty insistent little tune.

AMANDA: Strange how potent cheap music is.

Call at Corazón

Paul Bowles

'BUT WHY WOULD you want a little horror like that to go along with us? It doesn't make sense. You know what they're like.'

'I know what they're like,' said her husband. 'It's comforting to watch them. Whatever happens, if I had that to look at, I'd be reminded of how stupid I was ever to get upset.'

He leaned farther over the railing and looked intently down at the dock. There were baskets for sale, crude painted toys of hard natural rubber, reptile-hide wallets and belts, and a few whole snakeskins unrolled. And placed apart from these wares, out of the hot sunlight, in the shadow of a crate sat a tiny, furry monkey. The hands were folded, and the forehead was wrinkled in sad apprehensiveness.

'Isn't he wonderful?'

'I think you're impossible – and a little insulting,' she replied.

He turned to look at her. 'Are you serious?' He saw that she was.

She went on, studying her sandalled feet and the narrow deck-boards beneath them: 'You know I don't really mind all this nonsense, or your craziness. Just let me finish.' He nodded his head in agreement, looking back at the hot dock and the wretched tin-roofed village beyond. 'It goes without saying I don't mind all that, or we wouldn't be here together. You might be here alone ...'

'You don't take a honeymoon alone,' he interrupted.

'*You* might.' She laughed shortly.

He reached along the rail for her hand, but she pulled it away, saying, 'I'm still talking to you. I expect you to be crazy, and I expect to give in to you all along. I'm crazy too, I know. But I wish there were some way I could just once feel that my giving in meant anything to you. I wish you knew how to be gracious about it.'

'You think you humour me so much? I haven't noticed it.' His voice was sullen.

'I don't *humour* you at all. I'm just trying to live with you on an extended trip in a lot of cramped little cabins on an endless series of stinking boats.'

'What do you mean?' he cried excitedly. 'You've always said you loved the boats. Have you changed your mind, or just lost it completely?'

She turned and walked toward the prow. 'Don't talk to me,' she said. 'Go and buy your monkey.'

An expression of solicitousness on his face, he was following her. 'You know I won't buy it if it's going to make you miserable.'

'I'll be more miserable if you don't, so please go and buy it.' She stopped and turned. 'I'd love you to have it. I really would. I think it's sweet.'

'I don't get you at all.'

She smiled. 'I know. Does it bother you very much?'

After he had bought the monkey and tied it to the metal post of the bunk in the cabin, he took a walk to explore the port. It was a town made of corrugated tin and barbed wire. The sun's heat was painful, even with the sky's low-lying cover of fog. It was the middle of the day and few people were in the streets. He came to the edge of the town almost immediately. Here between him and the forest lay a narrow, slow-moving stream, its water the colour of black coffee. A few women were washing clothes; small children splashed. Gigantic grey crabs scuttled between the holes they had made in the mud along the bank. He sat down on some elaborately twisted roots at the foot of a tree and took out the notebook he always carried with him. The day before, in a bar at Pedernales, he had written: 'Recipe for dissolving the impression of hideousness made by a thing: Fix the attention upon the given object or situation so that the various elements, all familiar, will regroup themselves. Frightfulness is never more than an unfamiliar pattern.'

He lit a cigarette and watched the women's hopeless attempts to launder the ragged garments. Then he threw the burning stub at the nearest crab, and carefully wrote: 'More than anything else, woman requires strict ritualistic observance of the traditions of sexual behaviour. That is her definition of love.' He thought of the derision that would be called forth should he make such a statement to the girl back on the ship. After looking at his watch, he wrote hurriedly: 'Modern, that is, intellectual education, having been devised by males for males, inhibits and confuses her. She avenges …'

Two naked children, coming up from their play in the river, ran screaming past him, scattering drops of water over the paper. He called out to them, but they continued their chase without noticing him. He put his pencil and notebook into his pocket, smiling, and watched them patter after one another through the dust.

When he arrived back at the ship, the thunder was rolling down from the mountains around the harbour. The storm reached the height of its hysteria just as they got under way.

She was sitting on her bunk, looking through the open porthole. The shrill crashes of thunder echoed from one side of the bay to the other as they steamed toward the open sea. He lay doubled up on his bunk opposite, reading.

'Don't lean your head against that metal wall,' he advised. 'It's a perfect conductor.'

She jumped down to the floor and went to the washstand. 'Where are those two quarts of White Horse we got yesterday?'

He gestured. 'In the rack on your side. Are you going to drink?'

'I'm going to *have* a drink, yes.'

'In this heat? Why don't you wait until it clears, and have it on deck?'

'I want it now. When it clears I won't need it.'

She poured the whisky and added water from the carafe in the wall bracket over the washbowl.

'You realize what you're doing, of course.'

She glared at him. 'What am I doing?'

He shrugged his shoulders. 'Nothing, except just giving in to a passing emotional state. You could read, or lie down and doze.'

Holding her glass in one hand, she pulled open the door into the passageway with the other, and went out. The noise of the slamming door startled the monkey, perched on a suitcase. It hesitated a second and hurried under its master's bunk. He made a few kissing sounds to entice it out, and returned to his book. Soon he began to imagine her alone and unhappy on the deck, and the thought cut into the pleasure of his reading. He forced himself to lie still a few minutes, the open book face down across his chest. The boat was moving at full speed now, and the sound of the motors was louder than the storm in the sky.

Soon he rose and went on deck. The land behind was already hidden by the falling rain, and the air smelt of deep water. She was standing alone by the rail, looking down at the waves, with the empty glass in her hand. Pity seized him as he watched, but he could not walk across to her and put into consoling words the emotion he felt.

Back in the cabin he found the monkey on his bunk, slowly tearing the pages from the book he had been reading.

The next day was spent in leisurely preparation for disembarking and changing of boats: in Villalta they were to take a smaller vessel to the opposite side of the delta.

When she came in to pack after dinner, she stood a moment studying the cabin. 'He's messed it up, all right,' said her husband, 'but I found your necklace behind my big valise, and we'd read all the magazines anyway.'

'I suppose this represents man's innate urge to destroy,' she said, kicking a ball of crumpled paper across the floor. 'And the next time he tries to bite you, it'll be man's basic insecurity.'

'You don't know what a bore you are when you try to be caustic. If you want me to get rid of him, I will. It's easy enough.'

She bent to touch the animal, but it backed uneasily under the bunk. She stood up. 'I don't mind him. What I mind is you. *He* can't help being a little horror, but he keeps reminding me that you could if you wanted.'

Her husband's face assumed the impassivity that was characteristic of him when he was determined not to lose his temper. She knew he would wait to be angry until she was unprepared for his attack. He said nothing, tapping an insistent rhythm on the lid of a suitcase with his fingernails.

'Naturally I don't really mean you're a horror,' she continued.

'Why not mean it?' he said, smiling pleasantly. 'What's wrong with criticism? Probably I am, to you. I like monkeys because I see them as little model men. You think men are something else, something spiritual or God knows what. Whatever it is, I notice you're the one who's always being disillusioned and going around wondering how mankind can be so bestial. I think mankind is fine.'

'Please don't go on,' she said. 'I know your theories. You'll never convince yourself of them.'

When they had finished packing, they went to bed. As he snapped off the light behind his pillow, he said, 'Tell me honestly. Do you want me to give him to the steward?'

She kicked off her sheet in the dark. Through the porthole, near the horizon, she could see stars, and the calm sea slipped by just below her. Without thinking she said, 'Why don't you drop him overboard?'

In the silence that followed she realized she had spoken carelessly, but the tepid breeze moving with languor over her body was making it increasingly difficult for her to think or speak. As she fell asleep it seemed to her she heard her husband saying slowly, 'I believe you would. I believe you would.'

The next morning she slept late, and when she went up for breakfast her husband had already finished his and was leaning back, smoking.

'How are you?' he asked brightly. 'The cabin steward's delighted with the monkey.'

She felt a flush of pleasure. 'Oh,' she said, sitting down, 'did you give it to him? You didn't have to do that.' She glanced at the menu; it was the same as every other day. 'But I suppose really it's better. A monkey doesn't go with a honeymoon.'

'I think you're right,' he agreed.

Villalta was stifling and dusty. On the other boat they had grown accustomed to having very few passengers around, and it was an unpleasant surprise to find the new one swarming with people. Their new boat was a two-decked ferry painted white, with an enormous paddle wheel at the stern. On the lower deck, which rested not more than two feet above the surface of the river, passengers and freight stood ready to travel, packed together indiscriminately. The upper deck had a salon and a dozen or so narrow staterooms. In the salon the first-class passengers undid their bundles of pillows and opened their paper bags of food. The orange light of the setting sun flooded the room.

They looked into several of the staterooms.

'They all seem to be empty,' she said.

'I can see why. Still, the privacy would be a help.'

'This one's double. And it has a screen in the window. This is the best one.'

'I'll look for a steward or somebody. Go on in and take over.' He pushed the bags out of the passageway where the *cargador* had left them, and went off in search of an employee. In every corner of the boat the people seemed to be multiplying. There were twice as many as there had been a few moments before. The salon was completely full, its floor space occupied by groups of travellers with small children and elderly women, who were already stretched out on blankets and newspapers.

'It looks like Salvation Army headquarters the night after a major disaster,' he said as he came back into the stateroom. 'I can't find anybody. Anyway, we'd better stay in here. The other cubicles are beginning to fill up.'

'I'm not so sure I wouldn't rather be on deck,' she announced. 'There are hundreds of cockroaches.'

'And probably worse,' he added, looking at the bunks.

'The thing to do is take those filthy sheets off and just lie on the mattresses.' She peered out into the corridor. Sweat was trickling down her neck. 'Do you think it's safe?'

'What do you mean?'

'All those people. This old tub.'

He shrugged his shoulders.

'It's just one night. Tomorrow we'll be at Cienaga. And it's almost night now.'

She shut the door and leaned against it, smiling faintly.

'I think it's going to be fun,' she said.

'The boat's moving!' he cried. 'Let's go on deck. If we can get out there.'

Slowly the old boat pushed across the bay toward the dark east shore. People were singing and playing guitars. On the bottom deck a cow lowed continuously. And louder than all the sounds was the rush of water made by the huge paddles.

They sat on the deck in the middle of a vociferous crowd, leaning against the bars of the railing, and watched the moon rise above the mangrove swamps ahead. As they approached the opposite side of the bay, it looked as if the boat might plough straight into the shore, but a narrow waterway presently appeared, and the boat slipped cautiously in. The people immediately moved back from the railing, crowding against the opposite wall. Branches from the trees on the bank began to rub against the boat, scraping along the side walls of the cabins, and then whipping violently across the deck.

They pushed their way through the throng and walked across the salon to the deck on the other side of the boat; the same thing was happening there.

'It's crazy,' she declared. 'It's like a nightmare. Whoever heard of going through a channel no wider than the boat! It makes me nervous. I'm going in to read.'

Her husband let go of her arm. 'You can never enter into the spirit of a thing, can you?'

'You tell me what the spirit is, and I'll see about entering into it,' she said, turning away.

He followed her, 'Don't you want to go down on to the lower deck? They seem to be going strong down there. Listen.' He held up his hand. Repeated screams of laughter came up from below.

'I certainly don't!' she called, without looking around.

He went below. Groups of men were seated on bulging burlap sacks and wooden crates, matching coins. The women stood behind them, puffing on black cigarettes and shrieking with excitement. He watched them closely, reflecting that with fewer teeth missing they would be a handsome people. 'Mineral deficiency in the soil,' he commented to himself.

Standing on the other side of a circle of gamblers, facing him, was a muscular young native whose visored cap and faint air of aloofness suggested official position of some sort aboard the boat. With difficulty the traveller made his way over to him, and spoke to him in Spanish.

'Are you an employee here?'

'Yes, sir.'

'I am in cabin number eight. Can I pay the supplementary fare to you?'

'Yes, sir.'

'Good.'

He reached into his pocket for his wallet, at the same time remembering with annoyance that he had left it upstairs locked in a suitcase. The man looked expectant. His hand was out.

'My money is in my stateroom.' Then he added, 'My wife has it. But if you come up in half an hour I can pay you the fare.'

'Yes, sir.' The man lowered his hand and merely looked at him. Even though he gave an impression of purely animal force, his broad, somewhat simian face was handsome, the husband reflected. It was surprising when, a moment later, that face betrayed a boyish shyness as the man said, 'I am going to spray the cabin for your señora.'

'Thank you. Are there many mosquitoes?'

The man grunted and shook the fingers of one hand as if he had just burned them.

'Soon you will see how many.' He moved away.

At that moment the boat jolted violently, and there was great merriment among the passengers. He pushed his way to the prow and saw that the pilot had run into the bank. The tangle of branches and roots was a few feet from his face, its complex forms vaguely lighted by the boat's lanterns. The boat backed laboriously and the channel's agitated water rose to deck level and lapped the outer edge. Slowly they nosed along the bank until the prow once more pointed to midstream, and they continued. Then almost immediately the passage curved so sharply that the same thing happened again, throwing him sideways against a sack of something unpleasantly soft and wet. A bell clanged below deck in the interior of the boat; the passengers' laughter was louder.

Eventually they pushed ahead, but now the movement became painfully slow as the sharpness of the curves in the passage increased. Under the water the stumps groaned as the boat forced its sides against them. Branches cracked and broke, falling on to the forward and upper decks. The lantern at the prow was swept into the water.

'This isn't the regular channel,' muttered a gambler, glancing up.

Several travellers exclaimed 'What?' almost in unison.

'There's a pile of passages through here. We're picking up cargo at Corazón.'

The players retreated to a square inner arena which others were forming by shifting some of the crates. The husband followed them. Here they were comparatively safe from the intruding boughs. The deck was better lighted here, and this gave him the idea of making an entry in his notebook. Bending over a carton marked *Vermifugo Santa Rosalia*, he wrote: 'November 18th. We are moving through the bloodstream of a giant. A very dark night.' Here a fresh collision with the land knocked him over, knocked over everyone who was not propped between solid objects.

A few babies were crying, but most of them still slept. He slid down to the deck. Finding his position fairly comfortable, he fell into a dozing state which was broken irregularly by the shouting of the people and the jolting of the boat.

When he awoke later, the boat was quite stationary, the games had ceased, and the people were asleep, a few of the men continuing their conversation in small groups. He lay still, listening. The talk was all about places; they were comparing the unpleasant things to be found in various parts of the republic: insects, weather, reptiles, diseases, lack of food, high prices.

He looked at his watch. It was half-past one. With difficulty he got to his feet, and found his way to the stairs. Above, in the salon, the kerosene lamps illumined a vast disorder of prostrate figures. He went into the corridor and knocked on the door marked with an eight. Without waiting for her to answer, he opened the door. It was dark inside. He heard a muffled cough nearby, and decided that she was awake.

'How are the mosquitoes? Did my monkey man come and fix you up?' he asked.

She did not answer, so he lit a match. She was not in the bunk on the left. The match burned his thumb. With the second one, he looked at the right-hand bunk. A tin insecticide sprayer lay there on the mattress; its leak had made a large circle of oil on the bare ticking. The cough was repeated. It was someone in the next cabin.

'Now what?' he said aloud, uncomfortable at finding himself upset to this degree. A suspicion seized him. Without lighting the hanging lamp, he rushed to open her valises, and in the dark felt hurriedly through the flimsy pieces of clothing and the toilet articles. The whisky bottles were not there.

This was not the first time she had gone on a solitary drinking bout, and it would be easy to find her among the passengers. However, being angry, he decided not to look for her. He took off his shirt and trousers and lay down on the left-hand bunk. His hand touched a bottle standing on the floor by the head of the bunk. He raised himself enough to smell it; it was beer and the bottle was half full. It was hot in the cabin, and he drank the remaining warm, bitter liquid with relish and rolled the bottle across the room.

The boat was not moving, but voices shouted out here and there. An occasional bump could be felt as a sack of something heavy was heaved aboard. He looked through the little square window with the screen in it. In the foreground, dimly illuminated by the boat's lanterns, a few dark men, naked save for their ragged underdrawers, stood on a landing made in the mud and stared toward the boat. Through the endless intricacies of roots and trunks behind them he saw a bonfire blazing, but it was far back in the swamp. The air smelt of stagnant water and smoke.

Deciding to take advantage of the relative silence, he lay down and tried to sleep; he was not surprised, however, by the difficulty he found in relaxing. It was always hard to sleep when she was not there in the room. The comfort of her presence was lacking, and there was also the fear of being awakened by her return. When he allowed himself to, he would quickly begin to formulate ideas and translate them into sentences whose recording seemed the more urgent because he was lying comfortably in the dark. Sometimes he thought about her, but only as an unclear figure whose character lent flavour to a succession of backdrops. More often he reviewed the day just completed, seeking to convince himself that it had carried him a bit further away from his childhood. Often for months at a time the strangeness of his dreams persuaded him that at last he had turned the corner, that the dark place had finally been left behind, that he was out of hearing. Then, one evening as he fell asleep, before he had time to refuse, he would be staring closely at a long-forgotten object – a plate, a chair, a pincushion – and the accustomed feeling of infinite futility and sadness would recur.

The motor started up, and the great noise of the water in the paddle wheel recommenced. They pushed off from Corazón. He was pleased. Now I shan't hear her when she comes in and bangs around, he thought, and fell into a light sleep.

He was scratching his arms and legs. The long-continued, vague malaise eventually became full consciousness, and he sat up angrily. Above the sounds made by the boat he could hear another sound, one which came through the window: an incredibly high and tiny tone, tiny but constant in pitch and intensity. He jumped down from the berth and went to the window. The channel was wider here, and the overhanging vegetation no longer touched the sides of the boat. In the air, nearby, far away, everywhere, was the thin wail of mosquito wings. He was aghast, and completely delighted by the novelty of the phenomenon. For a moment he watched the tangled black wilderness slip past. Then with the itching he remembered the mosquitoes inside the cabin. The screen did not reach quite to the top of the window; there was ample space for them to crawl in. Even there in the dark as he moved his fingers along the frame to find the handle he could feel them; there were that many.

Now that he was fully awake, he lighted a match and went to her bunk. Of course she was not there. He lifted the Flit gun and shook it. It was empty, and as the match went out, he saw that the spot on the mattress had spread even farther.

'Son of a bitch!' he whispered, and going back to the window he tugged the screen vigorously upward to close the crack. As he let go of it, it fell out into the water, and almost immediately he was concious of the soft caress of tiny wings all about his head. In his undershirt and trousers he rushed out into the corridor. Nothing had changed in the salon. Almost everyone was asleep. There were screen doors giving on to the deck. He inspected them: they appeared to be more firmly installed. A few mosquitoes brushed against his face, but it was not the horde. He edged in between two women who were sleeping sitting with their backs against the wall, and stayed there in acute discomfort until again he dozed. It was not long before he opened his eyes to find the dim light of dawn in the air. His neck ached. He arose and went out on to the deck, to which most of the people from the salon had already crowded.

The boat was moving through a wide estuary dotted with clumps of plants and trees that rose out of the shallow water. Along the edges of the small islands stood herons, so white in the early grey light that their brightness seemed to come from inside them.

It was half-past five. At this moment the boat was due in Cienaga, where it was met on its weekly trip by the train that went into the interior. Already a thin spit of land ahead was being identified by eager watchers. Day was coming up swiftly; sky and water were the same colour. The deck reeked of the greasy smell of mangoes as people began to breakfast.

And now at last he began to feel pangs of anxiety as to where she might be. He determined to make an immediate and thorough search of the boat. She would be instantly recognizable in any group. First, he looked methodically through the salon, then he exhausted the possibilities on the upper decks. Then he went downstairs, where the gambling had already begun again. Toward the stern, roped to two flimsy iron posts, stood the cow, no longer bellowing. Nearby was an improvised lean-to, probably the crew's quarters. As he passed the small door, he peered through the low transom above it, and saw her lying beside a man on the floor. Automatically he walked on; then he turned and went back. The two were asleep, and half-clothed. In the warm air that came through the screened transom there was the smell of whisky that had been drunk and whisky that had been spilled.

He went upstairs, his heart beating violently. In the cabin, he closed her two valises, packed his own, set them all together by the door and laid the raincoats on top of them. He put on his shirt, combed his hair carefully, and went on deck. Cienaga was there ahead, in the mountains' morning shadow: the dock, a line of huts against the jungle behind, and the railway station to the right beyond the village.

As they docked, he signalled the two urchins who were waving for his attention, screaming, '*Equipajes!*' They fought a bit with one another until he made them see his two fingers held aloft. Then to make them certain, he pointed at each of them in turn, and they grinned. Still grinning, they stood beside him with the bags and coats, and he was among the first of the upper-deck passengers to get on land. They went down the street to the station with the parrots screaming at them from each thatched gable along the way.

On the crowded, waiting train, with the luggage finally in the rack, his heart beat harder than ever, and he kept his eyes painfully on the long dusty street that led back to the dock. At the far end as the whistle blew, he thought he saw a figure in white running among the dogs and children toward the station, but the train started up as he watched, and the street was lost to view. He took out his notebook, and sat with it on his lap, smiling at the shining green landscape that moved with increasing speed past the window.

A Change of Plan

Bruce Jay Friedman

AND SO FINALLY, after four years of drift, they had found all exits barricaded and gotten married in a sudden spurt, bombing their parents with the news. A Justice had been rounded up, also uncles in the area. After the ceremony, Cantrow's new father-in-law had taken him around and said, 'It's going to be great, isn't it.'

'How can you say that,' said a stray uncle, wandering by. 'Which one of us knows such things. Maybe it will. Then again, maybe it won't.' That night there was a need to get away, to sail as quickly as possible into the eye of the marriage, and off they went, south, driving in a frenzy, all that afternoon, all that night. Once, bleary-eyed, they had gone through a Southern town with two wheels up on a sidewalk. Later, moving through a misted patch of farmland, Cantrow spotted a monster turkey, his first live one, and gunned the motor, thinking it was a dreaded hawk. Only once had they stopped, for chocolate frosteds, Cantrow tipping his into her lap. With soaked shorts, she broke into laughter, then chuckled her way through five more towns. This is the kind of sense of humor she has, Cantrow thought. And I didn't even catch that.

Curling from side to side, as though the car itself were drunk, they were somehow blessed, missing head-on collisions; at the hotel, Cantrow told the clerk, 'We're not bums,' and got a room. Upstairs, zombielike, they made a feeble pass at sex, wanting to try it married, but collapsed instead into sleep. Two hours later, hardly fresh, Cantrow awoke and stared at his bride's slack form. So that's what I've got, he thought. Maybe for forty-seven years.

Down below, at poolside, the lifeguard winked and said, 'Ho, ho, ho,' a standard greeting to honeymooners. The pool water slapped Cantrow awake; so did a blond girl, sitting at the edge. She had a nice fleshiness, a good hundred thirty pounds to his bride's hundred four. He caught her scent, too, just like honey. He had never really smelled honey, but guessed it must be in that family.

'I didn't know they allowed big puppies in pools,' she said. And now there was her voice, crushed, feminine for a change. At a club, once, he had introduced his bride to a football-star friend of his. 'She's okay,' the friend had said privately, 'but I could never live with those pipes of hers.'

Cantrow fished himself out of the water and sat by the girl's side. She was eighteen, from Minnesota, vacationing between semesters. These were her folks, at the terrace bar, the heavyset man and the handsome woman in the white silk dress. Cantrow and the girl kidded around, wound up tickling each other. Then the shadow of the hotel seemed to fall on his back like a heavy beam. 'You probably know I'm married,' he said. 'Just since yesterday. Down here on my honeymoon.'

'And what else is new,' she said. Cheered on, Cantrow told her some jokes; they teased each other. But there was a whisper of difference. Before it became a roar, Cantrow suddenly panicked, took her arm and said, 'Look, this is crazy, but I've got to see you one more time and find out something. I really have to.' Their glances met, combined, turned soft together.

'We don't stay here,' she said. 'At the Regent.'

'I'll be there at six,' he said. 'I'll work it out. For cocktails.'

'Guess who I met at the pool,' he told his bride, later, in the room. 'Crazy guy from school, Blaum, always wore a tooth around his neck, called it the Sacred Tooth of Mickasee. Didn't care what you did to him, beat him up, anything, long as you didn't touch his tooth. 'Fool with my tooth and you're in trouble,' he'd say to you. Anyway, I told him I'd meet him later tonight for a drink. No girls, though. He's not himself when any are around and I want to see him carry on about that tooth again.' He hurried on. 'I'll just have a quick one with him and then I'll come back and we can really start.'

In the early evening, he dressed carefully, getting his hair just right, one loop down over the eye, with feigned carelessness, for extra appeal. At the Regent, she sat with her folks at a table, but joined him immediately at the bar. He liked the size of her in heels, the weight of her, the bounce of her hair, the honeyed look. A combo began to work in a deep beat; he gathered her in, made it once around the floor, then put his nose in her hair and said, 'That did it. Over to your folks we go.'

The parents were pushed back from the table, comfortable, expectant, as though waiting for a curtain to part. Cantrow stood before them and began to speak, then said, 'Hold it a second,' and unbuckled his belt for comfort. 'Okay, sir,' he said, 'I've just made one helluva mistake, about the biggest one a guy can make. But I met your daughter and I'm undoing it, no matter what it takes. You see, I got married yesterday and I'm down here on my honeymoon, but it was a bad idea from the beginning. There wasn't a damned thing in the world between us and I just got married because it seemed like the only way out. Anyway, I met your daughter and she's the one I want. I know it's crazy, but I could tell in a second. You should see the difference between them. There's no comparison. I just had to be with her a few minutes and I saw all the things I was really after. She's easier, more feminine, just real comfortable to be with. I don't know exactly what I expect from you. What I'd like, really, is for you to study the look in my eyes and know that I've never been more sincere in my life and that I'm not fooling around and that I'm the right guy for her. I'm getting out of the thing and then I'm coming after your daughter, but I just wanted to lay it out on the table and see how it struck you, whether you were with me or against me.'

The father yawned, drummed his fingers on the table and said, 'Not if they stripped me naked and dragged me four times around the world. Over the desert, through the jungle, under the seven seas.'

'Okay,' said Cantrow. 'Long as we're clear. But you don't know me, sir. You don't know what I can do. I'm coming after her anyway. Once I make up my mind on something, that's it.

'First thing I've got to do is get out of it,' he said, with a bow to the parents. 'You take it easy, honey,' he said, pecking her on the cheek.

'But I listen to my father,' she said, as he walked to the door.

'Another thing about you that turns me on.'

Pale and angular, Cantrow's bride slapped on pancake before a mirror. 'Hold it, hold it,' he said, tearing into the room. 'Whoa. We're not going out tonight. Any night, for that matter, unless we meet some day later on as platonic friends, and I'm not even really sure of that. There was no Blaum and no tooth. That is, there is a Blaum and the tooth part was no lie either, but I didn't just meet him. It's a new girl I ran into at the pool. I don't see any point in describing what went on, because that would be just like waving a red flag in your face. What's important is us and how flat it's always been when you take away those first few weeks, just one, if you really want to be strict about it. Look, I'm pulling out. I admit, I shouldn't have gone this far, but I didn't see it clearly until just before at the pool. There's a whole other way. With us, it would be one long downhill ride. Get yourself someone else. I admit, I'll be a little shaky on that issue if I stop and think about it, but I can stand it. Meanwhile, I'm on my way.'

'And I'm supposed to just listen to that.'

'Oh, we can kick it around if you like,' said Cantrow, packing, 'but how'd you like to lift this hotel on your back and move it across the street. That's roughly what you'd be up against trying to talk me out of this thing I've got in my head. Look, here's three hundred dollars for openers. I'm throwing in the car and just holler if you think that's not generous. The funny thing is, as we're making this break, I'm starting to like you more already.

'Maybe,' he said, slamming shut his suitcase, 'years later, when the sting is out of it for both of us, we really can meet for dinner.'

That night, Cantrow flew north and woke up Wenger, his attorney-cousin, at midnight. 'Cantrow with an emergency,' he said. 'Remember that marriage I told you about? I've got to get out of it now. We were just hitched for the shortest time you can imagine and then the whole thing blew up. Anyway, I'm actually out of it already since there isn't anything—tornadoes, nuclear war, you name it—that could get me back in. So you just take care of the legal part. I've got five grand from the service and believe me it wasn't easy to save. Cut down on everything, meals included, to get it together. Anyway, use the whole bundle if you need to and keep the change. Just get me out.'

'If we weren't cousins, you wouldn't call me at this hour.'

'I'll stick around one week, in case there are papers. Then I'm getting into something else.'

'Hi, Mom,' said Cantrow at his folks' apartment. 'The entire marriage is down the drain, but don't worry, I'm in good health and got out clean.'

'I saw the whole thing coming,' said Cantrow's mother. 'If you'd asked me, I could have recited the entire story before it happened. Okay, how about a trip to Europe, all expenses for a month. To clear your head.'

'No, Mom, I'm bunking in here for a week, then I've got to go out to the Midwest on something.'

'I knew it,' she said. 'Another little winner. One wasn't enough for my son. I can tell you the end of this story, too, if you want to sit and listen.'

With great crankiness, Wenger gave the go-ahead and Cantrow took a plane west, then tracked the girl down to a small teachers' college of Episcopal persuasion. Off-campus she lived with her folks and came home for meals. His first night in town, Cantrow announced his presence to her mother at the door. 'Hi, you probably remember me from the resort hotel. I don't expect you to let me see your daughter right off, but I thought I'd let you know I'm here and that wasn't a wild story I'd made up when I saw you at the bar.'

'My daughter's preparing for bed,' said the mother, easing the door shut. 'She studies very hard and needs her sleep.'

Later that night, Cantrow asked around and smoked out his one rival, a fair-skinned fellow of strange, shifting sexuality. Sliding in beside him at a bleakly lit campus hangout, Cantrow ordered the local special, beer and braunschweiger sandwiches, and said, 'Hi, I've just gotten down here and what I'm after is Sue Ellen Parker. Now look, we can do this like gentlemen, you just tapering off with another date or two to save face, or else we can go to muscle. You look pretty well set up, but the point is, if we fight, it doesn't matter how it goes. If you take me boxing, I'll bring in karate and if you know that I'll go to guns.'

'Would you really do all those things,' said the fellow with a wet stare, kaleidoscopically shifting sexes before Cantrow's very eyes.

The road partially clear, Cantrow called the girl herself. 'I'd be teasing if I pretended not to be flattered, but it's just so completely out of the question,' she said. 'I mean with Mother and Dad. And me, sort of.' Undismayed, driven, Cantrow hung on, peppered her with calls, nourished himself on her great phone voice. One night that honeyed blond fragrance seemed to trickle through the wire. She said she would sneak out and meet him on the corner. Cantrow hired a car, scooped her up and off they drove in silence to a wooded place she knew. Thin, towering Minnesota trees, crowded together, stripped and haunted. 'I won't sleep with you tonight,' she said, as they left the car, 'but let's take off our clothes and run through there, as far as we can go.'

'Suits me,' said Cantrow, knowing instantly he'd been right about her.

And so they began. All the things he had missed. Nude walks and swims. Hours of savoring honeyed flesh. Sudden love, almost anywhere, under stairwells, beneath a tree. Giving everything. Wonder of wonders. Getting back. 'I knew I wasn't crazy,' he told her one night, bewitched, at some lake's edge. 'It must have been a hell of a jolt to all concerned, but I knew I was on the right track.'

A month later she phoned, out of breath. 'Dad's calling a truce. From now on, it's the front door for us, darling.' Legitimate now, Cantrow arrived that night in a suit and tie. 'I never thought I'd see the day I'd be doing this,' said her father, 'But let's have us a handshake. You Eastern fellows sure are determined. Well, more power to you, son.'

Later that night, passion undiminished, they made love in the parlor. The next night in her very room. Pacing himself, Cantrow waited another week, then told her, 'Look, I haven't been fooling around.'

'I know, darling, I feel the same way. I've already said something and the folks' answer is, of course, anything we want.'

With blurred speed, the wedding plans were made. Cantrow's folks declined, but Wenger, the lawyer, came west with the final papers. Soon Cantrow, who had always dreamed of tails, stood erect in them and watched strange blond people with great Scandinavian profiles mill around him at the church. Mr. Parker came over, cuffed him in friendliness and said, 'Now this is one for the books, isn't it. The first time you came up to us and now here we are. I think it's great though, kind of thing you see in the movies.' He disappeared in a swirl of guests. Mrs. Parker took his place. Solid, tanned gold, an easeful ripened version of her daughter. She took his arm and said, 'I want you to know how warming I find all of this. And I have a confession to make. Even at the hotel I just knew. There was something so profound about the cast of your neck and shoulders.'

'And how about how I feel,' said Cantrow. 'I get sick when I think of how I could have let the whole thing slide and muffed the chance of a lifetime. Sue Ellen. Being here in Minnesota. The things that have happened. Mr. Parker. You. Even the way you just said that. That it was all so warming. And what was that word you used about my neck and shoulders. You know once in a while I'd check myself in mirrors and there really was something about them, although I guess I'd be the last one to say it about myself. But what was that you called them? Profound.

'Oh, Jesus, look,' he said covering her hand. 'I wonder if we could just talk for a second, I'll talk and you don't say a word till I'm finished.'

Envoi

When the writer Dorothy Parker went on honeymoon, Robert Ross, editor of the *New Yorker*, chased her for some late copy. Her telegraph in reply read:

> *Too busy fucking, and vice versa.*

> *The state of marriage hath in it the labour of love and the delicacies of friendship, the blessing of society and the union of hands and hearts; it hath in it less of beauty but more of safety than the single life; it hath more of care, but less danger; it is more merry and more sad, is fuller of sorrows and fuller of joys; it lies under more burdens, but is supported by all the strengths of love and charity, and those burdens are delightful.*
>
> Jeremy Taylor

When the biographer Elizabeth Longford was asked whether, in her long married life with Lord (Frank) Longford, she had ever contemplated divorce, she replied, 'Murder often, divorce never.'

Bibliography

I Bliss

Ketton-Cremer, R. W., *Felbrigg: The Story of a House*, Hart-Davis, 1962

Cooper, William, *Scenes from Married Life*, Macmillan, 1961

West, Rebecca, *Cousin Rosamund*, Virago, 1988

Lawrence, D. H.,*The Rainbow*, Penguin, 2007

Larkin, Philip, *Whitsun Weddings*, Faber & Faber, 1964

II Getting to Know You

Donne, John, *Complete Poetry and Selected Prose*, Nonsuch Press, 1929

de Maupassant, Guy, *Bel-Ami*, trans. Eric Sutton, Hamish Hamilton, 1948

Ottoline at Garsington: Memoirs of Lady Ottoline Morrell, 1915-18, ed. Robert Gathorne Hardy, Faber & Faber, 1974

Sayers, Dorothy L., *Busman's Honeymoon*, Victor Gollancz, 1937

Woolsey, Gamel, *One Way of Love*, Virago 1987

The Mendelssohns on Honeymoon, ed. Peter Ward Jones, Clarendon Press, 1997

Byron, Lord, *Byron's Letters and Journals*, vol. 4, ed. Leslie A. Marchand, John Murray, 1975

Cressy, David, *Birth Marriage and Death*, OUP, 1997

Herrick, Robert, *Selected Poems*, Penguin, 1961

Tolstoy, Lev, *Anna Karenina*, Dent, 1933

Barrett Browning, Elizabeth, *In Her Letters*, ed. Percy Lubbock, Smith, Elder, 1906

Cecilia: Life & Letters of Cecilia Ridley, ed. Ursula Ridley,
   Spredden Press, 1990
Shields, Carol, *Larry's Party*, 4th Estate, 1997
Homecoming, from *Caroline Clive*, ed. Mary Clive, Bodley
   Head, 1949
de Balzac, Honoré, *The Physiology of Marriage*, George Barrie
   and Sons, 1899

III Confessions
Wilson, A.N., *Tolstoy: A Biography*, Hamish Hamilton, 1988
Hardy, Thomas, *Tess of the D'Urbervilles*, Penguin Classics, 2003
Shields, Carol, *The Stone Diaries*, 4th Estate, 1993

IV Unusual Arrangements
Chitty, Susan, *The Beast and The Monk: A life of Charles
   Kingsley*, Hodder and Stoughton, 1974
Levy, Andrea, *Small Island*, Headline Review, 2004
Chaudhuri, Nirad, *Thy Hand Great Anarch!*, Chatto & Windus,
   1987
Wordsworth, Dorothy, *Grasmere Journal*, ed. Pamela Woolf,
   OUP 1991
Hudson, Derek, *Munby: Man of Two Worlds*, John Murray,
   1972
Mereweather, Rev. J. D., *Diary of a Working Clergyman in
   Australia and Tasmania, kept during the years 1850-1853*,
   Hatchard, 1859

V Royal Weddings
Oxford Book of Marriage, ed. Helge Rubinstein, OUP, 1990
Greville, Charles C. F., *The Greville Memoirs*, Longmans, Green
   and Co, 1885
Hibbert, Christopher, *George IV*, vol. 1, Longman 1972
Original Letters Illustrative of English History, 1st series, 3 vols,
   ed. Sir Henry Ellis, 1825
de La Tour du Pin, Mme., *Memoirs*, Harvill, 1999
Norwich, John Julius, *Still More Christmas Crackers*, Penguin,
   2001

Nelson and Emma, ed Roger Hudson, The Folio Society, 1994

VI Honeymoon Journeys

Fremantle, Betsey, *The Wynne Diaries*, Oxford, 1935
The Letters of Samuel Palmer, ed. Raymond Lister, OUP, 1975
The Journals of Honoria Lawrence: India Observed 1837-54, ed.
  John Lawrence & Audrey Woodiwiss, Hodder and
  Stoughton, 1980
Life and Letters of Stopford Brooke, ed. L. P. Jacks, John Murray,
  1917
*A Victorian Diarist: extracts from the journals of Mary, Lady
  Monkswell*, ed. E. C. F. Collier, John Murray, 1946
Birchall, Emily, *Wedding-Tour: January-June 1873*, ed. David
  Verey, Sutton, 1985
Cooper, Diana, *The Rainbow Comes and Goes*, Century,
  London, 1984
Gellhorn, Martha, *Travels with Myself and Another*, Eland, 2002
Hughes, Ted, *Birthday Letters*, Faber & Faber, 1998
Bayley, John, *Iris*, Duckworth, 1998
Kinsella, Sophie, *Shopaholic and Sister*, Black Swan, 2004

VII A Sense of Foreboding

Huang, Lynn, *Quarterly Literary Review Singapore*, Vol.5, No.3,
  Apr 2006
Colette, *Earthly Paradise*, ed. Robert Phelps, Penguin, 1974
Flaubert, Gustave, *Madame Bovary*, trans. J. L. May, Bodley
  Head, 1928
Blakiston, Noel, *The Collected Stories of Noel Blakiston*,
  Constable, 1975
Parker, Dorothy, *The Collected Dorothy Parker*, Penguin, 2001
Rhys, Jean, *Wide Sargasso Sea*, Penguin, 2001
Eliot, George, *Middlemarch*, Penguin Classics, 1994
Hemingway, Ernest, *The Snows of Kilimanjaro*, Vintage, 2007
Greene, Graham, *May We Borrow Your Husband? and Other
  Comedies of Sexual Life*, Vintage Classics, 2000
Dinesen, Isak, *Winter's Tales*, Penguin Classics, 2001

VIII Marrying for Money or Convenience

Trollope, Anthony, *The Small House at Allington*, Penguin Classics, 2005

Thackeray, W. M., *Vanity Fair*, Penguin Classics, 2003

Chekhov, Anton, 'Anna on the Neck', Walter J. Black, 1929

Trollope, Anthony, *Is He Popenjoy?*, Oxford Paperbacks, 1986

Dickens, Charles, *Our Mutual Friend*, Penguin Classics, 2004

de Maupassant, Guy, *The Complete Short Stories*, Blue Ribbon Books, 1934

IX Honeymoon Disasters

Shelley, Mary, *Frankenstein*, Penguin Classics, 2004

Lutyens, Mary, *Millais and the Ruskins* and *The Ruskins and the Grays*, John Murray, 1967 & 1972 respectively

de Maupassant, Guy, *The Complete Short Stories*, Blue Ribbon Books, 1934

Tolstoy, Leo, *Kreutzer Sonata*, Charles Scribners Sons, 1913

Szerb, Antal, *Journey by Moonlight*, Pushkin Press, 2005

Shields, Carol, *The Stone Diaries*, 4th Estate, London, 1993

Coward, Noel, *Private Lives*, Methuen, 2000

Bowles, Paul, *Call at Corazón*, Peter Owen, 1988

Friedman, Bruce J., *The Collected Short Fiction of Bruce Jay Friedman*, Grove/Altantic, 1997

ELAND

61 Exmouth Market, London EC1R 4QL
Email: info@travelbooks.co.uk

Eland was started in 1982 to revive great travel books
which had fallen out of print. Although the list has diversified
into biography and fiction, it is united by a quest to define the
spirit of place. These are books for travellers, and for those who are
content to travel in their own minds. Eland books open out our
understanding of other cultures, interpret the unknown and reveal
different environments as well as celebrating the humour and
occasional horrors of travel. We take immense trouble to select
only the most readable books and many readers
collect the entire series.

All our books are printed on fine, pliable, cream-coloured paper.
Most are still gathered in sections by our printer and sewn as well as
glued, almost unheard of for a paperback book these days.
This gives larger margins in the gutter, as well as
making the books stronger.

Extracts from each and every one of our books can be read
on our website, at www.travelbooks.co.uk. If you would like a free
copy of our catalogue, please contact us by email or in writing.